A Study Companion to
Introduction to the History of Christianity

A Study Companion to
Introduction to the History of Christianity

BETH WRIGHT

Readings selected by Will Bergkamp

Fortress Press

Minneapolis

A STUDY COMPANION TO INTRODUCTION TO THE HISTORY OF CHRISTIANITY

Cover image: Abraham with the angels (mosaic), Byzantine School, (6th century) / San Vitale, Ravenna, Italy / The Bridgeman Art Library; The Holy Family (Barcelona, Spain) ©iStockphoto / stan tiberiu lore-dan; Christ Pantocrator, 1607 (oil on panel), Bulgarian School, (17th century) / National Art Gallery, Sofia, Bulgaria / Giraudon / The Bridgeman Art Library
Cover design: Laurie Ingram
Book design: PerfecType, Nashville, TN

Library of Congress Cataloging-in-Publication Data
Print ISBN: 978-1-4514-6467-2
eBook ISBN: 978-1-4514-6514-3

The paper used in this publication meets the minimum requirements of American National Standard for Information Sciences — Permanence of Paper for Printed Library Materials, ANSI Z329.48-1984.

Manufactured in the U.S.A.

CONTENTS

FOR THE STUDENT:
HOW TO USE THIS GUIDE

This study guide is intended to help you get the most out of *Introduction to the History of Christianity*—to further your understanding of the history of Christianity and to spark your critical thinking about the church's structures, values, leading figures, and relationships with other social forces. Each section of the guide corresponds to a part in the book and includes key terms, key figures, primary sources, a summary of each chapter, additional readings with questions for discussion and reflection, and selected online resources.

Before you begin reading the text, or after reading a chapter to ensure you understood the main ideas, read the *Chapter Summaries*. These offer a basic overview of each chapter's major themes and issues.

Also before you read each part, it might be useful to note the *Key Terms* and *Key Personalities* listed in the corresponding section of this guide. These are the headings for a selected list of terms (concepts particular to a period of Christian history, names of important institutions or movements, etc.) and one of significant individuals (church leaders, theologians, etc.). You will want to be at least familiar with these by the time you have finished reading the section. Many of the key terms are listed in the glossary; for those that are not, the Key Terms list provides the page numbers where they are first defined in the text. For the Key Personalities, year of birth and death are given, as well as brief information on their significance. These are followed by related publications, which typically include at least one primary source and a biographical treatment.

Excerpts from primary sources are included as often as possible. No reader, however lengthy, can do justice to the scope and breadth of Christian history. And no selection of readings can truly represent the complexity of any one writer's thought. These challenges become all the more apparent when faced with the constraints of a study guide. And yet encountering great Christian thinkers through their own words is valuable and rewarding. Thus, the primary source readings in this study companion were selected with the goal of introducing you to the human in the historical. They were selected with the hope that through them you will get at least a brief glimpse of the personalities, the passions, and the perspectives of each writer. Please consider them an invitation to go further in your explorations of Christian history.

When reading primary sources, whether in the main text or in this guide, you'll want to consult "Reading Historical Documents," beginning on page 171 of this guide. There you'll find suggested questions to keep in mind when reviewing a historical document and further resources for the study of historical texts. In this guide, a brief primary source is presented with questions and answers, providing you with a model of how to pursue an inquiry into a historical document.

To deepen your understanding of the events, people, and themes discussed in the book, review the *Additional Readings*. Each section of the guide offers three excerpts that are related chronologically and thematically to the corresponding section in the book. The additional readings are accompanied by *Questions for Discussion and Reflection*, which can help you make connections between the selection and the main text and further your understanding of the relevant themes. Readings include scholarly discussion of historical questions, theological treatises, church documents, and a range of additional sources.

Each section of the guide ends with *Selected Online Resources*. The websites included in this guide are simply a sample of Internet resources related to church history, Christianity, and major Christian figures and movements. Online museum exhibits, academic research sites, biographies of important figures, and historical data are all available on the web. Use the sites offered here as a jumping-off point. When your interest is caught by a particular topic or individual mentioned in a chapter, you can do online research to learn more before heading to the library shelves. Here are a few resources for doing academic research online:

▶ "Internet Research": http://www.aacc.edu/library/InternetResearch.cfm
▶ "Boolean Searching on the Internet": http://www.internettutorials.net/boolean.asp
▶ "Use Google Scholar Effectively for Research": http://www.library.illinois.edu/ugl/howdoi/use_google _scholar.html

The chapter entitled "Supplemental Readings" offers excerpts from five additional books in the history of Christianity and questions for discussion. These readings may help spur you in researching a topic of interest for an essay or other class assignment.

Following "Reading Historical Documents" is a guide to writing research papers on topics in the history of Christianity. In this last chapter you will find bibliographies of reference works (both print and online). Also included are suggested research methods and tips on writing effective papers, as well as footnote and bibliographic citation formats.

Guide to Part 1: Beginnings

Key Terms

The number in parentheses refers to the page where the term is explained. Those terms marked with asterisks also appear in the Glossary.

agape (93)* Greek word for "love" that has come to express the Christian understanding of God's love, which does not depend on any worthiness or attractiveness of the object of his love. Christians are taught to demonstrate this love to each other in Christian fellowship and to others.

apologists (90)* Early Christian writers who used reason to defend and explain the faith to nonbelievers.

canon (26)* Authoritative collection of Christian scripture comprising the accepted books of the Old and New Testaments.

Dead Sea Scrolls (28)* Sacred writings of a breakaway Jewish sect discovered in 1947 at Qumran, on the western shore of the Dead Sea. The several scrolls and fragments include much of the Hebrew Bible, as well as hymns, treatises, and rules for the life of the sect. Many scholars identify the sect with the Essenes.

Gnosticism (68)* Movement of esoteric teachings rivaling, borrowing from, and contradicting early Christianity. Gnostic sects were based on myths that described the creation of the world by a deluded demiurge and taught a way of salvation through *gnosis*, or knowledge of one's true divine self. Gnostics contrasted their knowledge with faith, which they considered inferior.

heresy (77–78)* The denial of a defined, orthodox doctrine of the Christian faith. The word means "chosen thing" and refers to the heretic's preference for an individual option over the consensus of the church.

kingdom of God (31)* The rule of God on earth. Jesus of Nazareth proclaimed the arrival of the kingdom in himself.

Logos* (76) Greek for "word" or "principle." In Stoicism it identified the principle of reason, immanent in nature. Speculations about the logos were developed by the Jewish philosopher Philo of Alexandria. The Prologue to the Gospel of John identifies Christ with the preexistent logos of God.

martyr (54)* Title, meaning "witness," originally applied to Christians who died, rather than renounce their faith, during times of persecution. Now applied to anyone who dies for a religious belief.

messiah (24)* A Hebrew word meaning "anointed one" and referring to the person chosen by God to be king. (1) After the end of the Israelite monarchy it came to refer to a figure who would restore Israel, gathering the tribes together and ushering in the Kingdom of God. Modern Jews are divided as to whether the messiah is a symbolic or a representative figure, and whether the founding of the Jewish state is a prelude to his coming. (2) In the Christian New Testament, Jesus of Nazareth is described by messianic titles, e.g. messiah, Christ, "the King," "the One who Comes." The account of Jesus' entry into Jerusalem is deliberately phrased in messianic terms. Jesus himself was cautious about claiming to be the messiah.

Septuagint (27)* Greek version of the Hebrew scriptures produced by Jews in Alexandria, completed in 132 BCE. Often abbreviated as LXX.

Key Personalities

Numbers in parentheses refer to the pages where the text provides the individual's biographical details and historical significance.

Eusebius (75)

(c. 263–c. 339) Considered the father of church history: his work *Church History* was the first attempt to write Christian history on a comprehensive scale. His political ideas influenced the empire of Byzantium.

PRIMARY SOURCES

1. From Eusebius, *The Church History, Book 1:1,* Translated by G. A. Williamson (Minneapolis: Augsburg Books, 1975), 31–33.

The chief matters to be dealt with in this work are the following:

a. The lines of succession from the holy apostles, and the periods that have elapsed from our Saviour's time to our own; the many important events recorded in the story of the Church; the outstanding leaders and heroes of that story in the most famous Christian communities; the men of each generation who by preaching or writing were ambassadors of the divine word.

b. The names and dates of those who through a passion for innovation have wandered as far as possible from the truth, proclaiming themselves as founts of Knowledge falsely so called while mercilessly, like savage wolves, making havoc of Christ's flock.

c. The calamities that immediately after their conspiracy against our Saviour overwhelmed the entire Jewish race.

d. The widespread, bitter, and recurrent campaigns launched by unbelievers against the divine message, and the heroism with which when occasion demanded men faced torture and death to maintain the fight in its defence.

e. The martyrdoms of later days down to my own time, and at the end of it all the kind and gracious deliverance accorded by our Saviour.

Could I do better than start from the beginning of the dispensation of our Saviour and Lord, Jesus the Christ of God?

I trust that kindly disposed readers will pardon the deficiencies of the work, for I confess that my powers are inadequate to do full justice to so ambitious an undertaking. I am the first to venture on such a project and to set out on what is indeed a lonely and untrodden path; but I pray that I may have God to guide me and the power of the Lord to assist me. . . It is, I think, most necessary that I should devote myself to this project, for as far as I am aware no previous Church historian has been interested in records of this kind; records which those who are eager to learn the lessons of history will, I am confident, find most valuable. It is true that in the *Chronological Tables* that I compiled some years ago I provided a summary of this material; but in this new work I am anxious to deal with it in the fullest detail. As I said before, my book will start with a conception too sublime and overwhelming for man to grasp—the dispensation and divinity of our Saviour Christ. Any man who intends to commit to writing the record of the Church's history is bound to go right back to Christ Himself, whose name we are privileged to share, and to start with the beginning of a dispensation more divine than the world realizes.

Reading Questions

What can you surmise about the intended audience of this text? Based on this opening passage, what might the overall thesis of the text be?

RELATED WORKS

Eusebius. *The Church History*. Trans. and commentary by Paul L. Maier. Grand Rapids, MI: Kregel, 2007.

Johnson, Aaron, and Jeremy Schott, eds. *Eusebius of Caesarea: Tradition and Innovations*. Hellenic Studies Series. Washington, DC: Center for Hellenic Studies, 2013.

Ignatius (79)

(died c. 98–117). The bishop of the church at Antioch in the early second century. Known for his seven letters written on his way to Rome to be executed. Addressed to churches around the empire and to Bishop Polycarp, his letters argued for each congregation to be led by one bishop. He believed he possessed the Holy Spirit's gift of prophecy.

PRIMARY SOURCES

From *The Early Christian Fathers,* edited and translated by Henry Bettenson (New York, Oxford University Press, 1956), 42–43, 48–49.

To the Magnesians

I advise you, be eager to act always in godly accord; with the bishop presiding as the counterpart of God, the presbyters as the counterpart of the council of apostles, and the deacons (most dear to me) who have been entrusted with the service (diaconate) under Jesus Christ, who was with the father before all the ages and appeared at the end of time. Therefore do all of you attain conformity with God, and reverence each other; and let none take up a merely natural attitude towards his neighbor, but love each other continually in Jesus Christ. Let there be nothing among you which will have power to divide you, but be united with the bishop and with those who preside, for an example and instruction in incorruptibility.

Thus, as the Lord did nothing without the Father (being united with him), either by himself or by means of his apostles, so you must do nothing without the bishop and the presbyters. And do not try to think that anything is praiseworthy which you do on your own account: but unite in one prayer, one supplication, one mind, one hope; with love and blameless joy. For this is Jesus Christ, and there is nothing better than he. Let all therefore hasten as to one shrine, that is, God, as to one sanctuary, Jesus Christ, who came forth from the one Father, was always with one Father, and has returned to the one Father. *To the Magnesians,* vi-vii

To the Smyrnaeans

I perceived that you are settled in unshakable faith, nailed, as it were, to the cross of our Lord Jesus Christ, in flesh and spirit, and with firm foundations in love in the blood of Christ, with full conviction with respect to our Lord that he is genuinely of David's line according to the flesh, son of God according to the divine will and power, really born of a virgin and baptized by John that 'all righteousness might be fulfilled' by him, really nailed up in the flesh

for us in the time of Pontius Pilate and the tetrarchy of Herod—from this fruit of the tree, that is from his God-blessed passion, we are derived—that he might 'raise up a standard' for all ages through his resurrection, for his saints and faithful people, whether among Jews or Gentiles, in one body of his church. For he suffered all this on our account, that we might be saved. And he really suffered, as he really raised himself. Some unbelievers say that he suffered in appearance only. Not so—they themselves are mere apparitions. Their fate will be like their opinions, for they are unsubstantial and phantom-like. *To the Smyrnaeans,* i-ii

Reading Question

Paul (Saul) of Tarsus, another key figure from Part 1, is also known for the letters he wrote—some of which are found in scripture. How do Paul's letters to the Corinthians (1 and 2 Corinthians) from the New Testament compare to these letters from Ignatius?

Related Works

Howell, Kenneth J. *Ignatius of Antioch & Polycarp of Smyrna.* Early Christian Fathers. Rev. and exp. ed. Zanesville, OH: CH Resources, 2009.

Staniforth, Maxwell, trans. *Early Christian Writings: The Apostolic Fathers.* Penguin Classics. London: Penguin, 1987.

Irenaeus (80)

(c. 115–c. 202) The most important of the anti-Gnostic authors. His writing helped develop Christian theology by promoting the canon and establishing the role of the Eucharist while basing his arguments on Scripture.

PRIMARY SOURCES

From *Theological Anthropology*, edited and translated by J. Patout Burns (Philadelphia: Fortress Press, 1981), 26–28 and *Understandings of the Church*, edited and translated by E. Glenn Hinson (Philadelphia, Fortress Press, 1987), 44-45.

Human beings acquired the knowledge of good and evil. Good is to obey God, to believe in him, to keep his command; this means life for human beings. On the other hand, not to obey God is evil; this is death for human beings. God has exercised patience, and human beings have come to know both the good of obedience and the evil of disobedience. Thus by experiencing them both the mind's eye would choose the better things with discernment and never become sluggish or negligent of God's command. By learning through experience the evil of not obeying God, which would deprive them of life, human beings would never try it. Rather knowing the good of obeying God, which preserves their life, they would diligently maintain it. Human beings have this twofold power of perceptions which gives the knowledge of good and evil so that they might choose the better things intelligently. How can someone be intelligent about good when he does not know what is contrary to it? Certain understanding of the issue to be decided is more solid than a conjecture based on guessing. The tongue experiences sweet and sour by tasting; the eye distinguishes black from white by seeing; the ear perceives the difference between sounds by hearing. In this same way, by experiencing good and evil, the mind comes to understand good and is strengthened to preserve it by obeying God. First by repentance it rejects disobedience because it is bitter and evil. By grasping the nature of what is opposed to the sweet and good, it will never again try to taste disobedience to God. If a person avoids the twofold power of perception and the knowledge of both of these, therefore, he implicitly destroys his humanity.

How will one who has not yet become human be God? How can one just created be perfect? How can one who has not obeyed his Maker in a mortal nature be immortal? You should first follow the order of human existence and only then share in God's glory. You do not make God; God makes you. If you are God's artifact, then wait for the hand of the Master which makes everything at the proper time, at the proper time for you who are being created. Offer him a soft and malleable heart; then keep the shape in which the master molds you. Retain your moisture, so that you do not harden and lose the imprint of his fingers. By preserving your structure you will rise to perfection. God's artistry will conceal what is clay in you. His hand fashioned a foundation in you; he will cover you inside and out with pure gold and silver. He will so adorn you that the King himself will desire your beauty. If, however, you immediately harden yourself and reject his artistry, if you rebel against god and are ungrateful because he made you human, then you have lost not only his artistry but life itself at the same time. To create belongs to God's goodness; to be created belongs to human nature. If, therefore, you commit to him the submission and trust in him which are yours, then you hold on to his artistry and will be God's perfect work. *Against Heresies* (IV:39,1-2)

Reading Questions

In one sentence, how would you summarize Irenaeus's argument about the "twofold power of perceptions" which humans have? Do you find his argument about human potential to choose "the better things" to be consistent with your experience?

True knowledge consists of the teaching of the apostles and the ancient constitution of the church throughout the world, and the stamp of the body of Christ according to the successions of bishops to whom [the apostles] handed on that church which exists in every place, which has come down to us. In the church is found the most complete handling of truth conserved without any fabrication of Scriptures. She receives truth without adding to it or subtracting from it. There is reading without falsification, and legitimate and careful explanation in line with the Scriptures, both without danger and without blasphemy. [True knowledge consists] especially of the gift of love, which is more precious than knowledge, more glorious than prophecy, excelling all the other spiritual gifts. Accordingly, the church everywhere sends forth a multitude of martyrs all the time because of the love which she has toward God. But all the others not only do not have those who demonstrate this thing among themselves, but they even say that such witness is not necessary, for their true witness is what they think. The only exception is that one or two now and then in the whole period since the Lord appeared have borne reproach for the name at the same time with our martyrs (as

if that person also obtained mercy) and was led with them like some kind of retinue given to them. For the church alone purely sustains the reproach of those who suffer persecution for righteousness' sake and endure all the punishments and are put to death because of their love for God and confession of His Son. Often she is weakened and yet immediately increases her members and gets well, just like her type, Lot's wife, who became a pillar of salt. She is also like the ancient prophets who endured persecution, as the Lord says, "For so did they persecute the prophets who were before you", for she suffers persecution anew certainly at the hands of those who do not receive the Word of God while the same Spirit rests upon her. Now the prophets indeed prophesied along with the other things which they were prophesying that whomever the Spirit of God rested upon and were obedient to the Word of the Father and served him as they could would suffer persecution and be stoned and be killed. For in themselves the prophets were prefiguring al these things because of their love of God and because of his Word. *Against Heresies* (IV:53-54)

Reading Questions

How would you define the *goals* of Irenaeus in writing this text? Is the text primarily informative and descriptive? Persuasive? How is your understanding of this text changed when you read the story of Lot's wife in the biblical book of Genesis, chapter 19?

RELATED WORKS

Foster, Paul, and Sara Parvis, eds. *Irenaeus: Life, Scripture, Legacy*. Minneapolis: Fortress Press, 2012.

Irenaeus of Lyons. *Against the Heresies*. 3 vols. Trans. Dominic J. Unger. Ancient Christian Writers. New York: Paulist, 1992–2012.

Jesus of Nazareth (30–32)

(c. 6 BCE–c. 30 CE) Teacher, prophet, and worker of miracles in first-century Palestine; founder of Christianity. He taught the coming of the Kingdom of God with forgiveness and new life for all who believed. His claims to be the promised Messiah (or Christ) roused opposition from the religious authorities, and he was put to death by crucifixion. After his death, his followers claimed he was risen from the dead and seen alive by many. Christians, members of his church, believe him to be fully divine and fully human, and await his promised second coming, which will bring the fulfillment of the Kingdom of God.

RELATED WORKS

Allison, Dale C., Jr. *Jesus of Nazareth: Millenarian Prophet*. Minneapolis: Fortress Press, 1998.

Destro, Adriana, and Mauro Pesce. *Encounters with Jesus: The Man in His Place and Time*. Minneapolis: Fortress Press, 2011.

Theissen, Gerd. *The Shadow of the Galilean: The Quest of the Historical Jesus in Narrative Form*. 20th anniversary ed. Minneapolis: Fortress Press, 2007.

Justin Martyr (77)

(c. 100–c. 165) One of the greatest Christian apologists of the second century. His writings aimed to clarify Christian beliefs and defend Christians against charges of atheism and immorality.

PRIMARY SOURCES

From "The First Apology" *Early Christian Fathers*, Translated by Edward R. Hardy, Library of Christian Classics, Volume 1 (Philadelphia: Westminster Press, 1953), 46ff.

To the Emperor Titus Aelius Hadrianus Antonius Pius Augustus Caesar, and to Verissimus his son, the Philosopher, and to Lucius the Philosopher , son of Caesar by nature and of Augustus by adoption, a lover of culture, and to the Sacred Senate and the whole Roman people—on behalf of men of every nation who are unjustly hated and reviled, I, Justin, son of Priscus and grandson of Bacchius, of Flavia Neapolis in Syria Palestina, being myself one of them, have drawn up this plea and petition.

Reason requires that those who are truly pious and philosophers should honor and cherish the truth alone, scorning merely to follow the opinions of the ancients, if they are worthless. Nor does sound reason only require that one should not follow those who do or teach what is unjust; the lover of truth ought to choose in every way, even at the cost of his own life to speak and do what is right, though death should take him away. So do you, since you are called pious and philosophers and guardians of justice and lovers of culture, at least give us a hearing—and it will appear if you are really such. . .

Certainly we do not honor with many sacrifices and floral garlands the objects that men have fashioned up in temple and called gods. We know that they are lifeless and dead and do not represent the form of God—for we do not think of God as having the kind of form which some claim that they imitated to be honored—but rather exhibit the names and shapes of the evil demons who have manifested themselves. You know well enough without our mentioning it how the craftsmen prepare their material, scraping, and cutting and molding and beating. And often they make what they call gods out of vessels used for vile purposes, changing and transforming by art merely their appearance. We consider it not only irrational but an insult to God whose glory and form are ineffable, to give his name to corruptible things which themselves need care. . .

When you hear that we look for a kingdom, you rashly suppose that we mean something merely human. But we speak of a Kingdom with God, as is clear from our confessing Christ when you bring us to trial, though we know that death is the penalty for this confession. . .

We are in fact of all men your best helpers and allies in securing good order, convinced as we are that no wicked man, no covetous man or conspirator, or virtuous man either, can be nidden from God, and that everyone goes to eternal punishment or salvation in accordance with the character of his actions. . .

What sound-minded man will not admit that we are not godless, since we worship the Fashioner of the Universe, declaring him, as we have been taught, to have no need of blood and libations and incense, but praising him by the word of prayer and thanksgiving. . .

Reading Questions

What can you surmise about the "occasion" of this text—the context that prompted its writing? Can you develop a definition of piety based on this document?

RELATED WORKS

Foster, Paul, and Sara Parvis, eds. *Justin Martyr and His Worlds.* Minneapolis: Fortress Press, 2007.

Minns, Denis, and Paul Parvis, trans. and eds. *Justin, Philosopher and Martyr: Apologies.* Oxford Early Christian Texts. Oxford: Oxford University Press, 2009.

Origen (53)

(c. 184–c. 254) Theologian who tried to present biblical Christianity using the ideas of Hellenism. He believed that all creatures would eventually be saved, a view condemned as heretical in 553.

PRIMARY SOURCES

From *Biblical Interpretation in the Early Church,* edited and translated by Karlfried Froehlich (Philadelphia, Fortress Press, 1984) 48-49 and *Understandings of the Church,* edited and translated by E. Glenn Hinson (Philadelphia, Fortress Press, 1987), 63-66.

In our investigation of such weighty matters we are not content with common notions and the evidence of things one can see. Rather, from Scriptures that we believe to be divine, the so-called Old as well as the New Testament, we adduce testimonies as witnesses to that which we consider a convincing proof of our statements. Since we also attempt to confirm our faith by reason and since we have not yet discussed the divinity of the Scriptures, let us comment briefly on this topic, spelling out for this purpose the reasons which move us to speak of those writings as divine. First of all, even before we use the text and the content of these writings themselves, we must treat of Moses, the lawgiver of the Hebrews, and of Jesus Christ, the originator of the saving teachings of Christianity.

Despite the fact that there have been many legislators among Greeks and barbarians, and that numerous teachers have advocated doctrines laying claim to the truth, we have not come across any lawgiver who has been able to inspire zeal for the acceptance of his words among other nations. And while those who profess to be concerned with truth in their philosophy have introduced a whole arsenal of arguments as part of their alleged rational demonstration, none of them has been able to excite different nations, or even significant portions of a single nation, for that which he considers to be the truth. Yet, had this been possible, the legislators would gladly have extended to the entire human race the validity of the laws they regarded as good. The teachers, for their part, would have loved to disseminate all over the world what they imagined to be the truth. But since they could not persuade people speaking other languages and belonging to so many other nations to observe their laws and accept their teachings, they did not even dare to make a start in this direction; they concluded, not unreasonably, that it would be impossible for them to succeed in any such endeavor. Yet the entire inhabited world of Greek and barbarian nations is teeming with thousands of people who are eager to follow us, who abandon their traditional laws and their presumed deities for the observance of the law of Moses and for the instruction offered in the words of Jesus Christ. This is happening despite the fact that the followers of the law of Moses encounter the hatred of idol worshipers, and those who accept the word of Jesus Christ even risk the sentence of death in addition to that hatred.

We must keep before our eyes what is happening: in spite of constant anti-Christian machinations which cause some confessors of Christianity to lose their lives and others to lose their possessions, it has been possible for the word to be preached throughout the inhabited world even in the absence of an abundant supply of teachers, and Greeks and barbarians, wise and unwise, have adopted the religion proclaimed by Jesus. When we consider this situation we will not hesitate to call the achievement superhuman. *On First Principles* (I, 1-2)

. . . But the God who sent Jesus destroyed the whole conspiracy of demons and made the gospel of Jesus to take hold everywhere in the world for the conversion and rectification of humankind and caused churches to be set up everywhere in opposition to the assemblies of the superstitious and undisciplined and unrighteous. For such is the character of most of the citizens in the assemblies of the cities. But the churches of God which have been taught by Christ are "like lights in the world" when compared to the assemblies of the people among whom they live. For who would not agree that even the worst persons from the church and those least worthy in comparison with the better members are far better than people in the popular assemblies.

For the church of God, for instance, at Athens, is a meek and stable one which wants to please God, who is over everything, but the Athenian assembly is rebellious and not at all comparable to the church of God there. And you could say the same thing about the church of God which is in Corinth and the popular assembly in Corinth, and to give another example, about the church of God which is in Alexandria and the popular assembly in Alexandria. Now if the person who hears this is open-minded and investigates matters with a love for truth, that person will marvel at the one who both planned and was able to bring into existence and to sustain the churches of God everywhere, sojourning in the assemblies of the people in each city. So too would you find a council of the church of God when compared with the council in each city. Some councilors of the church are worthy to hold public office in a city of God, if there is any in the whole world. But not all public councilors everywhere have the moral character worthy of the legal superiority which they seem to exercise over the citizens. So too must we compare the ruler of the church in each city with the public ruler in the city, so that you may grasp that even among the councilors and rulers of the church of God who fail miserably and who live indifferent lives by comparison with those who are more energetic, we find, generally speaking, a more rapid progress toward the virtues than is characteristic of councilors and rulers in the cities. *Against Celsus* (III, 29-30)

Reading Questions

What assumptions does Origen have about the purpose of the law? Do you agree with these assumptions? How might you critique his argument?

RELATED WORKS

Martens, Peter W. *Origen and Scripture: The Contours of the Exegetical Life.* Oxford Early Christian Studies. Oxford: Oxford University Press, 2012.

Roberts, Alexander, and James Donaldson, eds. *Ante-Nicene Fathers: The Writings of the Fathers Down to A.D. 325.* Vol. 4: Tertullian, Part Fourth; Minucius Felix; Commodian; Origen, Parts First and Second. Peabody, MA: Hendrickson, 1994.

Paul (Saul) of Tarsus (39–40)

(died 64) Apostle of Christianity who established new churches throughout Asia Minor and Macedonia. Originally a Pharisee, he was converted by a vision of Christ on the road to Damascus. He met Peter in Jerusalem and was active in Christian work despite threats against his life. His letters to churches from Corinth to Ephesus became part of the New Testament canon.

RELATED WORKS

Elliott, Neil, and Mark Reasoner, eds. *Documents and Images for the Study of Paul.* Minneapolis: Fortress Press, 2010.

Johnson, Luke Timothy. *The Writings of the New Testament.* 3rd ed. Minneapolis: Fortress Press, 2010.

Taylor, Walter F., Jr. *Paul: Apostle to the Nations—An Introduction.* Minneapolis: Fortress Press, 2012.

Tertullian (51)

(c. 160–c. 225) He was the first major Christian author to write in Latin. His main concerns were Christianity's relationship with the Roman state, the defense of orthodoxy, and the moral behavior of Christians.

PRIMARY SOURCES

From *The Early Christian Fathers,* edited and translated by Henry Bettenson (New York, Oxford University Press, 1956), 154 and *Understandings of the Church,* edited and translated by E. Glenn Hinson (Philadelphia, Fortress Press, 1987), 52-55.

Therefore that sect (the Christians), seeing that it commits none of these crimes which are generally found in the case of illicit factions, should not merely receive milder treatment but should be granted the status of a tolerated faction. For, if I am not mistaken, the motive for the prohibition of factions is based on a careful regard for public order, that the community may not be split into parties, a state of things which might easily result in disturbances in elections, meetings, councils, assemblies, and public entertainments, by the contention of rival interests, especially at a time when men have begun to make money by offering their services for acts of violence. But with us all ardour for glory or position has grown cold and we have no compulsion to form associations for this end; nor is anything more alien to us than political activity. We acknowledge only one universal commonwealth, the whole world. *Apology,* 38.

I will proceed then to explain the features of this Christian sect not so much to refute the evil as to show the good, and perhaps also to disclose the truth.

We are a body united by a common religious commitment and unity of teaching and hope. We meet together and form congregations so that we may wrestle with God in prayers as if in hand-to-hand combat. This violence pleases God. We pray also for the emperors, for their ministers and those in authority, for the situation of the world, for peace, for delay of the end. We meet to recall the divine Scriptures if anything in the present time necessitates some sort of forewarning or acknowledgment. With holy words certainly we feed our faith, stimulate our hope, firm up our trust, and deepen our instruction no less by the inculcations of divine precepts. In this gathering also we deliver exhortations, rebukes, and divine censures. For we carry out our judgment with great seriousness as among persons who are being watched by God, and it is viewed as the highest prejudgment of the judgment to come if anyone should err so badly that that person would be removed from communion in prayer and assembly and every other holy transaction.

Older men who have proven themselves preside over us, having attained this honor not by money but by witness to their character, for God's business has nothing to do with money. And even though there is a kind of collection box, money is not collected from some kind of high fees as if this was a commercial religion. One day a month, or whenever one wishes and if one wishes and can, each person puts in a small donation. For nobody is forced to give but does so voluntarily. These donations are, as it were, "deposits of piety." The money is not spent, you can be sure, on sumptuous foods or drinking bouts or fancy restaurants, but to bury poor people and to meet the needs of boys and girls and destitute parents, and also old people now forced into idleness at home, and likewise those who have suffered shipwreck, and if any in the mines and on the islands and in prisons become wards of their confessions insofar as it is for the sake of the church. *Apology* 39

Reading Questions

This text from Tertullian is called an "apology." Based on this text, what can you determine about the goals of an apologetic writing (Hint: "Apologists" is a glossary term)? Can you use this document to create a Tertullianesque list of the positive characteristics of Christians during this time period? Would you agree with the assertions on this list? What might you add or remove?

Related Works

Dunn, Geoffrey D. *Tertullian*. The Early Church Fathers. London: Routledge, 2004.

Tertullian. *Tertullian's Treatise on the Resurrection*. Trans. and ed. Ernest Evans. London: SPCK, 1960.

Chapter Summaries

1. Jesus

Many historical sources, including opponents of the early Jewish Christian community, provide evidence for the existence of Jesus of Nazareth. Additional documents, including the Dead Sea Scrolls, provide insights into Jesus's world and what life would have been like for Jews in Israel-Palestine under the Roman Empire. The New Testament consists of writings dating to within a century after his death, including the Gospels and the letters of Paul. The Gospels are biographies that focus on Jesus' miracles and his message about the kingdom of God. The letters from Paul were directed to various early Christian communities that struggled to stay true to Jesus' message and to spread the good news.

2. The Church Begins

The early church owed its successful survival and expansion to the efforts of the apostles, the most well-known being Paul (formerly Saul) of Tarsus and Peter, one of Jesus' disciples and the one of whom popes are considered the direct spiritual descendants.

Our knowledge of Paul's life and achievements comes from the book of Acts and his surviving letters. He took it upon himself to lead the mission to the Gentiles, although he himself was a Jew who had converted after apparently having a vision of the risen Christ. He traveled all over the Roman Empire and founded churches, to which he addressed several of the letters found in the New Testament.

The early Christian church had its roots in the Jewish synagogue, and its forms of worship were strongly influenced by Jewish traditions.

3. Establishing Christianity

As the early Christians began to distinguish themselves from Judaism, they faced persecution. Those who would not perform the required sacrifices and refused to renounce their faith were put to death, sometimes in large numbers under emperors such as Decius (249–251).

Certain early leaders and thinkers had great influence on the development of the church and orthodox Christianity. Origen's major work systematically presented fundamental Christian doctrines. Tertullian defended against heresy and developed the doctrine of the Trinity.

4. Spreading the Good News

The good news of Jesus Christ in the first few centuries after the crucifixion was spread most effectively through open-air preaching. Christianity also spread through personal witness, often from friend to friend, and the example of the lives and deaths of martyrs. When public preaching was too dangerous, private instruction was used to develop the faith of new converts and prepare them for baptism.

5. Archaeology and Earliest Christianity

Archaeological study of papyri, stone inscriptions, and the development of church architecture all contribute to our understanding of ancient Christianity. Major discoveries like that of the Dead Sea Scrolls have shed light on the contemporary Jewish world, providing context for Christian origins.

6. What the First Christians Believed

Since the earliest Christians were Jews, the first influences on the church were from Judaism, and all early Christian theology was Jewish. There was conflict between the Christians and the Jews, who opposed the Christians' use of the Old Testament.

Various early Christian movements had influence on the development of the faith, among them Gnosticism and Montanism. The Gnostics believed that people could be saved through a secret knowledge (*gnosis*).

Writers like Origen and apologists like Justin Martyr established basic doctrines and argued against heresy. The canon was created by early church leaders who chose those texts that had the most authority in church life and practice. Standard faith practices such as baptism and recitation of a religious creed were developing and spreading during this time.

7. How the First Christians Worshipped

Paul provides the earliest description of worship in the Christian church in his first letter to the Corinthians. He was concerned about a breakdown of fellowship during the *agape* meal shared by believers. He referred to hymns, creeds, and prayers, fragments of which survive in his letters. Ancient documents from other writers attest to the use of creeds during baptism as well as the form of the Lord's Supper, or Eucharist.

Additional Readings

1. From *Junia: The First Woman Apostle* (Fortress Press, 2005)

In his book Eldon Jay Epp explains how the original reference in Romans 16:7 to Junia, a woman who was an apostle, was changed in later versions of the New Testament. He carefully documents the evidence for reading the Greek name typically translated as Junias to be instead the feminine Junia, going back to the early Christian writer Chrysostom (32):

> In his commentary on Romans, Joseph A. Fitzmyer listed some sixteen Greek and Latin commentators of the first Christian millennium who understood [the Greek word *Iounian*] in Rom 16:7 as "Junia," feminine. . . . By far the most influential of these, and among the earliest, was Chrysostom, whose statement is pointed and unambiguous:
>
> > "Greet Andronicus and Junia . . . who are outstanding among the apostles": To be an apostle is something great. But to be outstanding among the apostles—just think what a wonderful song of praise that is! They were outstanding on the basis of their works and virtuous actions. Indeed, how great the wisdom of this woman must have been that she was even deemed worthy of the title of apostle.

Epp explains in his conclusion the significance of this change made to the biblical text (79–80):

> Chrysostom . . . appears early in the apparently unanimous list of writers from the church's first millennium who understood [the Greek word *Iounian*] as feminine, a view adopted by virtually all printed Greek New Testaments until the twenty-seventh Nestle edition appeared in 1927—with perhaps a single exception. Certainly "Junia" was also understood by all the English versions of Rom 16:7 up to the 1830s. . . . If this perfectly natural reading of [the Greek word *Iounian*] in Rom 16:7 as feminine, followed by all early church writers who treated the passage, had continued in late medieval to modern times, lengthy and tedious studies like the present one would be unnecessary, as would the manipulations and machinations of countless male scholars (presumably otherwise enlightened) over the past two centuries. But far more significant and regrettable is the unnecessary alienation of women that has taken place and continues in many quarters of the church, though that situation has roots earlier and broader than the Junia issue, by which the latter also was most certainly influenced.

QUESTION FOR DISCUSSION AND REFLECTION

Reading the section in Part 1 "How the New Testament Came Down to Us" (98–100) in light of Epp's discussion, what questions might now arise about the process of compiling the canonical biblical text? Consider issues such as language and translation challenges, theological perspectives, and social and cultural norms.

2. From *The Dead Sea Scrolls and the New Testament* (Fortress Press, 2005)

George J. Brooke discusses in chapter 12, "The Wisdom of Matthew's Beatitudes," how scholarship on the Dead Sea Scrolls has further illuminated the beatitudes in the Gospel of Matthew. The Dead Sea Scrolls are comprised of a series of manuscripts, the remains of which were discovered in a group of caves in Qumran. "The 11 caves at and near Qumran," writes Brooke in the introduction, "have produced the remains of between 850 and 900 manuscripts" (xv). Brooke writes of one fragment, labeled 4QBeatitudes, "We are probable dealing with a manuscript that comes from some time between 50 B.C.E. and 50 C.E. . . . The following revised translation into English is based on [an] edition of the Hebrew text in which several manuscript pieces are put together" (218).

[Blessed is the man who speaks the truth (?)] (1) with a pure heart,
    and does not slander with his tongue. (space)
Blessed are those who hold fast to her statutes,
    and do not take hold of (2) the ways of iniquity. (space)
Blessed are those who rejoice in her,
    and do not utter in the ways of foolishness. (space)
Blessed are those who seek her (3) with pure hands,
    and do not search for her with a deceitful heart. (space)
Blessed is the man who has attained Wisdom. (space)
    He walks (4) in the Law of the Most High,
    and prepares his heart for her ways. (space)
And he controls himself by her instructions,
    and always takes pleasure in her corrections,
    (5) and does not forsake her in the afflictions of tes[ting.] (space)
And in the time of oppression he does not abandon her,
    and does not forget her [in the days of] dread,
    (6) and in the submission of his soul does not reject [her. (space?)]

You can directly compare the fragment text to a biblical translation (Matthew 5:3-12 NRSV):

Blessed are the poor in spirit, for theirs is the kingdom of heaven.
Blessed are those who mourn, for they will be comforted.
Blessed are the meek, for they will inherit the earth.
Blessed are those who hunger and thirst for righteousness, for they will be filled.
Blessed are the merciful, for they will receive mercy.
Blessed are the pure in heart, for they will see God.
Blessed are the peacemakers, for they will be called children of God.
Blessed are those who are persecuted for righteousness' sake, for theirs is the kingdom of heaven.
Blessed are you when people revile you and persecute you and utter all kinds of evil against you falsely
    on my account.

Here are some of Brooke's observations about these two texts (222–33):

> In both Matthew and 4QBeatitudes the first and the eighth beatitude have common ingredients. In Matthew the first and eighth end with the same clause, 'For theirs is the kingdom of heaven' (Matt. 5.3, 10). In 4QBeatitudes the heart is mentioned in both. . . . The metaphor of hunger and thirst implies earnest desire for righteousness. So in Sirach 24.19–21 those who 'desire' Wisdom will 'hunger' and 'thirst' for more. The hunger and thirst of Matthew 5.6 can thus be matched in the search for Wisdom of the seventh beatitude of 4QBeatitudes. Since 'for righteousness' sake' in Matthew 5.10 is substituted with 'for my sake' in the ninth beatitude, we may also assume that the righteousness of Matthew 5.6 can be personified: while those inspired by 4QBeatitudes will search for Wisdom, those struck by the Matthaean Beatitudes will seek for Jesus. . . .
>
> Because of the appearance of Wisdom in the ninth element of 4QBeatitudes, it is appropriate to make some remarks here on the Matthaean concern to identify Jesus with Wisdom. With reference to the sayings that follow immediately after the beatitudes, [some scholars note] that in rabbinic metaphorical use 'salt' chiefly denotes Wisdom; light is a common metaphor for the Law. . . . Perhaps such a tradition explains the position of the salt and light sayings in the Sermon on the Mount: the disciples are to be true to the wisdom and law disclosed by Jesus in his summary teaching, and perhaps even in his person. . . .
>
> It might be that 4QBeatitudes give us some further evidence that Matthew's Beatitudes are to be read in light of the initiation performed when new members joined the community.

QUESTIONS FOR DISCUSSION AND REFLECTION

From your understanding of the origins and significance of the Dead Sea Scrolls (review Part 1, page 28), what would you theorize about the fragment's writer, his beliefs, his message, and his audience? What additional observations can you make in comparing 4QBeatitudes with Matt. 5:3-11?

See also "Reading Historical Documents" (page 171 in this volume) for other questions to consider.

3. From *A Woman's Place: House Churches in Earliest Christianity* (Fortress Press, 2006)

Carolyn Osiek and Margaret Y. MacDonald write in chapter 7, "Women Leaders of Households and Christian Assemblies," about Christian women who host house churches (157–59):

> The mother of John Mark in Jerusalem has a household in which a good number (*hikanoi*) of the believing community are gathered in nocturnal prayer, expecting to hear in the morning that the imprisoned Peter had been executed. Instead, as the story goes, Peter is miraculously freed from prison and in the middle of the night goes straight to Mary's house, where the slave Rhoda leaves him standing at the door in her confusion (Acts 12:12-17). The narrative indicates that Mary's house is the recognized center of activity for the community and the natural place where they would assemble in times of crisis. . . .

Lydia the purple merchant of Philippi has her own household (*ho oikos autēs*), all of whose members receive baptism together. This kind of communal solidarity in conversion occurs rarely in the Pauline letters . . . but is narrated elsewhere in Acts (10:44-48, of the household of Cornelius in Caesarea; 16:33, of the anonymous jailer's household in Philippi). The complete loyalty of the household to its head, even to the extent of accepting a new religious allegiance, is perhaps Luke's ideal, and it conforms to the classic ideology of the subordinate household fully obedient to its head. . . . Paul and Silas accept hospitality at Lydia's insistence for an indefinite period, so that her house becomes the center of evangelization and instruction as well as ritual celebration. . . .

Other possibilities for women running their own households include the independently traveling Phoebe (Rom. 16:1-2), who is also *diakonos*, some kind of recognized local ministry, and *prostatis*, a term of authority at least in the patronage system. It is not out of the question that she also had a husband at home, though this does not seem likely. . . . If Euodia and Syntyche are significant leaders of the church in Philippi, as seems likely, they may also each be leaders and hostesses of a house church (Phil. 4:2-3).

QUESTION FOR DISCUSSION AND REFLECTION

The text above cites New Testament passages that refer to women who were leaders in Christian house churches. What insights do Osiek and MacDonald provide about topics discussed in Part 1? For example, how does their discussion of women church leaders add to an understanding of the historical and philosophical context of early Christianity?

Selected Online Resources

▶ The Tertullian Project—a collection of material about Tertullian that provides both the text of original documents and historical context for them
http://tertullian.org/

▶ "Women in Ancient Christianity" by Karen L. King—essay by a biblical scholar on the important role of women in the early church
http://www.pbs.org/wgbh/pages/frontline/shows/religion/first/women.html

▶ "Elaine Pagels on the Book of Revelation"—a short video (7:16) from PBS's *Religion & Ethics NewsWeekly* program featuring the biblical scholar Elaine Pagels (author of *The Gnostic Gospels*) discussing the last book of the New Testament, including its historical and political contexts
http://video.pbs.org/video/2201446478/

▶ "The Christian Catacombs"—a brief photo essay describing the structure and art of the Roman catacombs
http://www.vatican.va/roman_curia/pontifical_commissions/archeo/inglese/documents/rc_com_archeo
_doc_20011010_cataccrist_en.html

▶ "Early Christian Art"—photo essay discussing themes of early Christian art http://smarthistory.khanacademy.org/early-christian-art-in-the-2nd-and-3rd-centuries.html

▸ "Development of the Biblical Canon"—two timelines of events in the development of the Bible, one for the Old Testament and one for the New Testament
http://www.columbia.edu/cu/augustine/a/canon.html

▸ "The Quest for the Historical Paul"—the scholar James Tabor writes about the biblical and other sources for our knowledge of Paul
http://www.biblicalarchaeology.org/daily/people-cultures-in-the-bible/people-in-the-bible/the-quest
-for-the-historical-paul

▸ "Jesus Seminar Forum"—the home page of the online forum for the Jesus Seminar, a group of scholars studying the historical Jesus
http://virtualreligion.net/forum

Guide to Part 2: Acceptance and Conquest

Key Terms

The number in parentheses refers to the page where the term is explained. Those terms marked with asterisks also appear in the Glossary.

Apostles' Creed (143)* A statement of faith used by Western Christian churches and often repeated in services. Introduced during the reign of Charlemagne (c. 742–814).

asceticism (169)* Austere practices designed to lead to the control of the body and the senses. These may include fasting and meditation, the renunciation of possessions, and the pursuit of solitude.

Christology (117)* Teaching about the nature of the person of Christ.

Council of Constantinople (130) Assembly of Christian bishops summoned to Constantinople in 381 by Emperor Theodosius. The second ecumenical council confirmed the Nicene Creed and marked the effective end of Arianism within the empire.

Council of Nicaea (119) Assembly of Christian bishops summoned to Nicaea, present day İznik, Turkey, in 325 by Emperor Constantine. It was the first ecumenical council and the first attempt to attain theological consensus throughout Christendom, though only some 220 bishops attended and very few from the West.

***filioque* (196)** Latin for "and the son." Late addition to the Nicene Creed expressing the "double procession" of the Spirit: "the Holy Spirit who proceeds from the Father *and the Son.*" It remains today one of the significant points of disagreement between Eastern and Western churches.

homoousios* (127) Greek for "of one substance." Term used in the Nicene Creed to describe the orthodox Christological relationship between the Father and the Son, holding that Jesus Christ was of the same substance as God.

homoiousios* (127) Greek for "of like substance." Term used, for example, at the Councils of Ariminum and Seleucia (359), to define the Son as "of like being" with the Father, a view associated by

Athanasius and his followers with Arius and Arianism.

martyrion (142)* Church that contains the relics of martyrs or marks the site of the grave of a martyr.

monophysitism (135)* Fifth-century doctrine that asserts Christ had one divine nature and rejects the orthodox teaching about the incarnation of Christ agreed at the Ecumenical Council of Chalcedon.

Nicene Creed (117)* The fullest version of the orthodox Christian creed, compiled to counter Christological heresies in the fourth century.

Key Personalities

Numbers in parentheses refer to the pages where the text provides the individual's biographical details and historical significance.

Athanasius (121)

(296–373) Bishop of Alexandria who strongly resisted the teachings of Arianism, and developed the Christian doctrines of the incarnation and the Trinity.

PRIMARY SOURCES

From *The Trinitarian Controversy,* edited and translated by William G. Rusch (Philadelphia, Fortress Press, 1980), 63-64 and *The Christological Controversy,* edited and translated by Richard A. Norris, Jr. (Philadelphia, Fortress Press, 1980), 87-88.

Heresies—as many are divorced from the truth—are conspicuous, even to themselves, by their insane contrivance. Their impiety has been obvious to all long ago.

It is clear that those who invent heretical thoughts have departed from us, as the blessed John wrote that thought of such individuals never, nor now is, with us. Therefore, as the Savior said, "they not gathering with us, scatter", with the devil, watching those who sleep, so that sowing their own poison of destruction they may have companions in death. But there is one final heresy, the Arian, which has gone forth as the forerunner of the Antichrist. Wily and villainous, seeing that her older sisters have plainly been identified as heresies, the Arian heresy employs the speech of the Scripture, as did her father the devil. She uses force to enter into the paradise of the church. She attempts to pass herself off as Christian, so that by the plausibility of false thinking (she possesses no reason!) she might beguile certain individuals to think ill of Christ. She has already led astray some foolish individuals, so that they have not only been corrupted in hearing, but receiving they ate just as Eve. Thus, being ignorant, they think that "the bitter is sweet" and declare the abominable heresy beautiful. Persuaded by you, I believed it necessary to tear apart the breastplate of this foul heresy and to point out the foul smell of her folly, so that those who are distant from her might flee her, and those deceived by her might repent, and with the eyes of their heart opened might discern that, just as darkness is not light, falsehood is not truth, the Arian heresy is not good. Those who consider the Arian Christians are in great error; they have not read the Scriptures, and they do not know

Christianity and the faith in it. *Orations against the Arians 1:1*

What is the basic meaning and purport of Holy Scripture? It contains, as we have often said, a double account of the Savior. It says that he has always been God and is the Son, because he is the Logos and radiance and Wisdom of the Father. Furthermore, it says that in the end he became a human being, he took flesh for our sakes from the Virgin Mary, the God-bearer.

One can find this teaching indicated throughout Holy Scripture, as the Lord himself has said, "Search the Scriptures, for it is they which bear witness concerning me." Lest I write too much, however, by pulling together all the relevant texts, let me content myself with mention of John as representative. He says, "In the beginning was the Logos and the Logos was with God and the Logos was God. He was in the beginning with God. All things came to be through him, and apart from him not one thing came to be." He goes on, "And the Logos become flesh and dwelt among us, and we saw his glory—glory as of one uniquely born from the Father." Then there are Paul's words: "Who, being in the form of God, did not judge equality with God a thing to be clutched, but emptied himself, taking the form of a slave, coming to be in the likeness of human beings; and being found in the shape of a human being, he humbled himself and become obedient to the point of death, even death on a cross."

Anyone who makes his way through the whole of Scripture with the meaning of these texts in mind will, on the basis of

what they say, see how it is that the Father said to the Son in the beginning, "Let there be light" and "Let there be a firmament" and "Let us make humanity." But at the consummation of the ages the Father sent the Son into the cosmos, "not in order to judge the cosmos, but in order that through him the cosmos might be saved." And it stands written: "Behold a virgin shall conceive, and shall bear a son; and they shall call his name Emmanuel, which in translation means 'God with us'".

So if someone wants to study Holy Scripture, let him learn from the ancient writers what it says, but from the Gospels let him perceive the Lord made a human being. For "the Word," John says, "was made flesh and dwelt among us." *Orations against the Arians, 3:29-30.*

Reading Questions

Review the discussion of the Arian Controversy in your textbook (pages 108-109). How do the details of this particular controversy affect your reading of this text from Athanasius? Can you identify any of the scripture passages quoted here? How would you describe the way in which Athanasius uses scripture in his argument?

RELATED WORKS

Athanasius. *The Life of Antony and the Letter to Marcellinus.* Trans. Robert C. Gregg. Classics of Western Spirituality, vol. 16. New York: Paulist, 1980.

Drake H. A. *Constantine and the Bishops: The Politics of Intolerance.* Baltimore: Johns Hopkins University Press, 2002.

Augustine of Hippo (156–57)

(354–430) Bishop of Hippo in North Africa who was converted to Christianity from the teaching of the Manichaeans. He stressed the absolute grace of God in men and women's salvation and the depravity of human beings through original sin.

PRIMARY SOURCES

From *Morality and Ethics in Early Christianity*, edited and translated by Jan L. Womer (Philadelphia, Fortress Press, 1987), 108-111 and *City of God, Book XI:1 (From Nicene and Post-Nicene Fathers series*—public domain*)*

> I had already written a reply to your letter, but before I was able to send it to you, I heard that my dear son Faustus would stop here on his way to visit you. After he was given the letter that I wanted him to bring to you, he informed me that you had requested that I send some personal advice to help you as you seek eternals salvation in your hope through our Lord Jesus Christ. Even though I am quite busy right now, he insisted that I take time because of his deep concern and love for you. I have given in to him and written a rather hasty response in order not to disappoint you, my distinguished and honorable son.
>
> In brief, my response is summed up in the words: "Love the Lord your God with all your heart, and with all your soul, and with all your strength; and love your neighbor as yourself." These are the words our Lord used on earth when he summed up the faith in the gospel: "On these two commandments hang all the law and the prophets." You should grow each day in this love both by prayer and by good works, so

that he may help and guide you in this gift he gives you, and bring it to perfection in your life. This is the love, the apostle says, that is "placed in our hearts by the Holy Spirit which is given to us"; it is this love that is the "fulfilling of the law"; and it is the same love that makes faith work, for he says, "Neither circumcision nor uncircumcision avails anything, but faith, which works by love."

It is in this love that all our holy ancestors, patriarchs, prophets, and apostles pleased God. In this love all true martyrs came up against the devil and gave their lives, and because it did not grow cold or weaken in them, they were victorious. In this love all true believers make daily progress, not toward an earthly kingdom but toward the heavenly kingdom, not to a temporal but to an eternal inheritance, not gaining gold and silver but gaining the incorruptible riches of the angels, not seeking the possessions of the good life of this world—which bring insecurity and cannot be taken with us when we die—but seeking the vision of God. This vision brings grace and a peace that transcends the beauty of creatures on earth and even in heaven; it is greater than the loveliness of even the greatest saints; it exceeds the glory of the angels and heavenly powers; it excels what language can express or the mind can comprehend. We do not need to give up hope as we seek this wonderful promise, but rather we need to have faith that we will achieve it because he who promised it is exceedingly great. The apostle John said, "We are the children of God and we do not yet know what we shall be, but we do know that when he appears, we shall be like him, for we will see him as he is." *Letter 189: To Boniface*

Reading Question

How would you characterize Augustine of Hippo as a pastoral leader based on this letter?

The city of God we speak of is the same to which testimony is borne by that Scripture, which excels all the writings of all nations by its divine authority, and has brought under its influence all kinds of minds, and this not by a casual intellectual movement, but obviously by an express providential arrangement. For there it is written, "Glorious things are spoken of thee, O city of God."446 And in another psalm we read, "Great is the Lord, and greatly to be praised in the city of our God, in the mountain of His holiness, increasing the joy of the whole earth."447 And, a little after, in the same psalm, "As we have heard, so have we seen in the city of the Lord of hosts, in the city of our God. God has established it for ever." And in another, "There is a river the streams whereof shall make glad the city of our God, the holy place of the tabernacles of the Most High. God is in the midst of her, she shall not be moved."448 From these and similar testimonies, all of which it were tedious to cite, we have learned that there is a city of God, and its Founder has inspired us with a love which makes us covet its citizenship. To this Founder of the holy city the citizens of the earthly city prefer their own gods, not knowing that He is the God of gods, not of false, i.e., of impious and proud gods, who, being deprived of His unchangeable and freely communicated light, and so reduced to a kind of poverty-stricken power, eagerly grasp at their own private privileges, and seek divine honors from their deluded subjects; but of the pious and holy gods,

who are better pleased to submit themselves to one, than to subject many to themselves, and who would rather worship God than be worshipped as God. But to the enemies of this city we have replied in the ten preceding books, according to our ability and the help afforded by our Lord and King. Now, recognizing what is expected of me, and not unmindful of my promise, and relying, too, on the same succor, I will endeavor to treat of the origin, and progress, and deserved destinies of the two cities (the earthly and the heavenly, to wit), which, as we said, are in this present world commingled, and as it were entangled together. And, first, I will explain how the foundations of these two cities were originally laid, in the difference that arose among the angels. *City of God, Book XI, Chapter 1*

Reading Questions

What clues can you find in the text that might help you to determine Augustine's audience? From this opening description, can you imagine or create a scheme or drawing to depict the two cities?

RELATED WORKS

Augustine, Saint. *Augustine: Political Writings*. Ed. and trans. E. M. Atkins and R. J. Dodaro. Cambridge Texts in the History of Political Thought. Cambridge, UK: Cambridge University Press, 2001.

Augustine, Saint. *Confessions*. Trans. F. J. Sheed. Indianapolis: Hackett, 2006.

Wynn, Phillip. *Augustine on War and Military Service*. Minneapolis: Fortress Press, 2013.

Basil the Great (129)

(c. 300–379). Bishop of Caesarea and one of the three Cappadocian Fathers, along with Gregory of Nyssa and Gregory of Nazianzus. His writings on monasticism were influential in Eastern Christianity. He also wrote an important treatise on the Trinity that paved the way for the Council of Constantinople.

PRIMARY SOURCES

From *Nicene and Post-Nicene Fathers series 2, Volume 8, pages 2-3*—public domain

> Your desire for information, my right well-beloved and most deeply respected brother Amphilochius, I highly commend, and not less your industrious energy. I have been exceedingly delighted at the care and watchfulness shewn in the expression of your opinion that of all the terms concerning God in every mode of speech, not one ought to be left without exact investigation. You have turned to good account your reading of the exhortation of the Lord, "Every one that asketh receiveth, and he that seeketh findeth," and by your diligence in asking might, I ween, stir even the most reluctant to give you a share of what they possess. And this in you yet further moves my admiration, that you do not, according to the manners of the most part of the men of our time, propose your questions by way of mere test, but with the honest desire to arrive at the actual truth. There is no lack in these days of captious listeners and questioners; but to find a character desirous of information, and seeking the truth as a remedy for ignorance, is very difficult. Just as in the hunter's snare, or in the soldier's ambush, the trick is generally ingeniously concealed, so it is with the inquiries of the majority of the questioners who advance arguments, not so much with the view of getting any good out of them, as in order that, in the event of their failing to elicit answers which chime in with their own desires, they may seem to have fair ground for controversy.

> . . . To count the terms used in theology as of primary importance, and to endeavour to trace out the hidden meaning in every phrase and in every syllable, is a characteristic wanting in those who are idle in the pursuit of true religion, but distinguishing all who get knowledge of "the mark" "of our calling;" for what is set before us is, so far as is possible with human nature, to be made like unto God. Now without knowledge there can be no making like; and knowledge is not got without lessons. The beginning of teaching is speech, and syllables and words are parts of speech. It follows then that to investigate syllables is not to shoot wide of the mark, nor, because the questions raised are what might seem to some insignificant, are they on that account to be held unworthy of heed. Truth is always a quarry hard to hunt, and therefore we must look everywhere for its tracks. The acquisition of true religion is just like that of crafts; both grow bit by bit; apprentices must despise nothing. If a man despise the first elements as small and insignificant, he will never reach the perfection of wisdom.

> Yea and Nay are but two syllables, yet there is often involved in these little words at once the best of all good things, Truth, and that beyond which wickedness cannot go, a Lie. But why mention Yea and Nay? Before now, a martyr bearing witness for Christ has been judged to have paid in full

the claim of true religion by merely nodding his head. If, then, this be so, what term in theology is so small but that the effect of its weight in the scales according as it be rightly or wrongly used is not great? Of the law we are told "not one jot nor one tittle shall pass away;" how then could it be safe for us to leave even the least unnoticed? The very points which you yourself have sought to have thoroughly sifted by us are at the same time both small and great. Their use is the matter of a moment, and peradventure they are therefore made of small account; but, when we reckon the force of their meaning, they are great. They may be likened to the mustard plant which, though it be the least of shrub-seeds, yet when properly cultivated and the forces latent in its germs unfolded, rises to its own sufficient height.

. . . While, then, I am aware that the controversy contained in little words is a very great one, in hope of the prize I do not shrink from toil, with the conviction that the discussion will both prove profitable to myself, and that my hearers will be rewarded with no small benefit. Wherefore now with the help, if I may so say, of the Holy Spirit Himself, I will approach the exposition of the subject, and, if you will, that I may be put in the way of the discussion, I will for a moment revert to the origin of the question before us.

Lately when praying with the people, and using the full doxology to God the Father in both forms, at one time "with the Son together with the Holy Ghost," and at another "through the Son in the Holy Ghost," I was attacked by some of those present on the ground that I was introducing novel and at the same time mutually contradictory terms. You, however, chiefly with the view of benefiting them, or, if they are wholly incurable, for the security of such as may fall in with them, have expressed the opinion that some clear instruction ought to be published concerning the force underlying the syllables employed. I will therefore write as concisely as possible, in the endeavour to lay down some admitted principle for the discussion. *On the Holy Spirit, Chapter 1.*

Reading Questions

What argument does this text make about the relationship between truth and religious doctrine? Do you agree with Basil's thesis?

RELATED WORKS

Barrois, Georges, trans. and ed. *The Fathers Speak: St. Basil the Great, St. Gregory of Nazianzus, St. Gregory of Nyssa.* Crestwood, NY: St. Vladimir's Seminary Press, 1986.

Basil, Saint. *On the Holy Spirit.* Trans. David Anderson. Crestwood, NY: St. Vladimir's Seminary Press, 1997.

Boethius (168)

(c. 480–524) An important influence on medieval education and thought. He wrote five *Tractates* defending orthodox theology. His best-known work is *The Consolation of Philosophy.*

PRIMARY SOURCES

From *Theological Tractates,* translated by E.K. Rand & Hugh Fraser Stewart (New York: G.P. Putnam's Sons, 1918), 71.

This Catholic church, then, spread throughout the world, is known by three particular marks: whatever is believed and taught in it has the authority of the Scriptures, or of universal tradition, or at least of its own and proper usage. And this authority is binding on the whole Church as is also the universal tradition of the Fathers, while each separate church exists and is governed by its private constitution and its proper rites according to difference of locality and the good judgment of each.

Reading Question

Boethius presents here three marks of the church; can you describe them in more detail? Do you agree or disagree with his argument about what gives the church authority?

RELATED WORKS

Boethius. *The Consolation of Philosophy*. Ed. and trans. Victor Watts. Rev. ed. Penguin Classics. London: Penguin, 2000.

Cassiodorus (174)

(died c. 583). His writing promoted secular learning as a complement to biblical study. He also supervised the translation of many important Greek Christian works into Latin.

RELATED WORKS

Cassiodorus, Senator. *An Introduction to Divine and Human Readings*. Trans. Leslie Webber Jones. New York: Columbia University Press, 1946.

Cassiodorus, Senator. *Explanation of the Psalms*. Trans. P. G. Walsh. 3 vols. New York: Paulist, 1990–91.

Columba (177)

(521–97) An abbot and missionary born in Ireland who traveled to the island of Iona, where he established a monastery. He famously preached to people under the sway of Druid opponents to Christianity.

PRIMARY SOURCES

From *Life of Saint Columba, Founder of Hy*, Written by Adamnan, Ninth Abbot of that Monastery, ed. William Reeves, (Edinburgh: Edmonston and Douglas, 1874), http://www.fordham.edu/halsall/basis/columba-e.asp

> On another occasion also, when the blessed man was living for some days in the province of the Picts, he was obliged to cross the river Nesa (the Ness); and when he reached the bank of the river, he saw some of the inhabitants burying an unfortunate man, who, according to the account of those who were burying him, was a short time before seized, as he was swimming, and bitten most severely by a monster that lived in the water; his wretched body was, though too late, taken out with a hook, by those who came to his assistance in a boat. The blessed man, on hearing this, was so far from being dismayed, that he directed one of his companions to swim over and row across the coble that was moored at the farther bank. And Lugne Mocumin hearing the command of the excellent man, obeyed without the least delay, taking off all his clothes, except his tunic, and leaping into the water. But the monster, which, so far from being satiated, was only roused for more prey, was lying at the bottom of the stream, and when it

felt the water disturbed above by the man swimming, suddenly rushed out, and, giving an awful roar, darted after him, with its mouth wide open, as the man swam in the middle of the stream. Then the blessed man observing this, raised his holy hand, while all the rest, brethren as well as strangers, were stupefied with terror, and, invoking the name of God, formed the saving sign of the cross in the air, and commanded the ferocious monster, saying, "Thou shalt go no further, nor touch the man; go back with all speed." Then at the voice of the saint, the monster was terrified, and fled more quickly than if it had been pulled back with ropes, though it had just got so near to Lugne, as he swam, that there was not more than the length of a spear-staff between the man and the beast. Then the brethren seeing that the monster had gone back, and that their comrade Lugne returned to them in the boat safe and sound, were struck with admiration, and gave glory to God in the blessed man. And even the barbarous heathens, who were present, were forced by the greatness of this miracle, which they themselves had seen, to magnify the God of the Christians. *The Life of Columba, Chapter XXVIII*

Reading Question

What does this text indicate about the spirituality of Columba and those living in his time? This text may be one of the first references to the Loch Ness Monster; how does its inclusion here pique your interest in primary text research?

RELATED WORKS

Adomnan, Saint. *Life of St. Columba: Adomnán of Iona.* Trans. Richard Sharpe. Penguin Classics. London: Penguin, 1995.

O'Loughlin, Thomas. *Celtic Theology: Humanity, World and God in Early Irish Writings.* London: Continuum, 2000.

Constantine (104–6)

(272–337) The emperor of Rome who converted to Christianity in 312, apparently because he believed that the Christian God had answered his prayer for help in defeating Maxentius in battle. He recognized Christianity as a "legitimate" religion of the Roman state in 313.

PRIMARY SOURCES

From *The Early Church and the State,* edited and translated by Agnes Cunningham, SSCM (Philadelphia, Fortress Press, 1982), 41-43.

> For a long time now, recognizing that freedom of religion must not be denied but that each person must be assured the possibility of access to divine things according to his reason, his choice, and his preference, we have invited Christians to adhere to the faith of their sect and their religious belief. However, since many different conditions seem, clearly, to have been included in the edict in which this permission was granted to these very Christians, perhaps it has happened that some of them have been, subsequently, ostracized and hindered from practicing their religion.
>
> When I, Constantine Augustus, and I, Licinius Augustus, met under happy auspices in Milan, in order to discuss all the

problems regarding security, the public welfare, and those matters which seemed to us to assure the good of the greater number, we believed it necessary to address, first of all, those matters which promote respect of the divine Being. In other words, we thought to grant to Christians, as to all people, the freedom and the possibility of following the religion of their choice. Thus, all that is divine in the heavenly above might look with benevolence and kindness on us and on all who are subject to our authority. That is why, with salutary and just intention, we believed it necessary to decide never to refuse anyone the possibility of belonging to the Christian religion or to another which seemed better for that one. May the supreme divine Being, to whom we render free and enthusiastic homage, manifest his usual favor and goodness to us, in all things. Thus, it is right that Your Excellency know that we have decided to abolish the stipulations which seem to us entirely inopportune and foreign to our mercy. We suppress completely the restrictions concerning Christians, contained in documents sent to you previously. Henceforth, we grant to all those who are determined to follow the Christian religion the right to do so freely and without reservation. They are not to be harassed or molested.

We have thought it necessary to bring these decisions in their fullness to Your Concern, in order that you may well know that we have granted to these Christians open and entire permissions to practice their religion.

Realizing fully that we grant them this right, Your Devotedness knows that the same possibility of practicing religion and cult openly and freely is assured to all other citizens, as is appropriate to our era of peace, so that every individual might have the liberty of participating in the worship of his choice. Our decision has been motivated by the desire to avoid even the appearance of having placed the least restriction on any cult or on any religion.

Furthermore, this is what we have deemed it necessary to decide, concerning the community of Christians: the places treated under particular instructions in the letters sent previously to you—places where Christians formerly customarily assembled—are to be restored to them without cost or any other required indemnity. All trickery or ambiguous behavior in this matter is out of the question, on the part of those who are supposed to have purchased these properties earlier, either through our treasure or through any other agent. In the same manner, those who have acquired these places gratuitously must also return them to the Christians as soon as possible. Furthermore, if those who have acquired these possessions through purchase or donation claim any compensation from our kindness, they are to present themselves to our representative so that, through our indulgence, their concerns also may be addressed.

All these places are to be returned to the community of the Christians through your representative, immediately and without delay. It is a fact that the Christians possessed not only the places where they ordinarily assembled, but other property as well. These properties belonged by right to their communities—that is, to churches and not to individuals. You are to restore to these Christians—that is, to their community and to their church—all such property, on the conditions mentioned above, without any question or dispute whatever. The one exception, already referred to, is that those who restore any property received gratuitously can expect to be reimbursed through our graciousness. In all of this, you are to give your most efficacious support to the community of Christians to which we have referred, so that our mandate might be fulfilled as soon as possible and, also, that, in this way, our concern for public tranquility might be fostered. It is only thus, as we have noted above, that the divine favor which we have experienced in the most serious situations in the past will continue to assure the success of our undertakings, for such is the pledge of public prosperity.

Moreover, so that the application of our generous prescription may be brought to the knowledge of all, it is fitting that these decisions be promulgated by you in proclamation, in notices posted everywhere and you bring this news to the attention of all the people. In this way, no one can remain ignorant of the decision made by us in a spirit of benevolence. *The Edict of Milan*

Reading Questions

Based on what you read in the opening chapters of the textbook about early Christian persecution, what can you say about the significance of this text for Christians living in the time of Constantine? How does this text compare to the discussions of religious freedom in North America?

Related Works

Constantine I. *Constantine and Christendom: The Oration to the Saints; The Greek and Latin Accounts of the Discovery of the Cross; The Edict of Constantine to Pope Silvester.* Trans. Mark Edwards. Translated Texts for Historians, vol. 39. Liverpool: Liverpool University Press, 2003.

Potter, David. *Constantine the Emperor.* New York: Oxford University Press, 2012.

Cyril of Alexandria (135)

(died 444) Elected patriarch in 412, he convened the Council of Alexandria in 430. He fought against Nestorian dualism, arguing for Christ's "one nature."

Primary Sources

From *The Christological Controversy*, edited and translated by Richard A Norris Jr. (Philadelphia, Fortress Press, 1980) 131-135.

> . . . I shall even now remind you, as my brother in Christ, to make the balance of your teaching and your thinking about the faith as safe as possible for the laity, and also to keep in mind that to cause even one of these little ones who believe in Christ to stumble wins implacable wrath.
>
> If, though, there should be a great number of people who are distressed, surely we stand in need of all our skill, at once for the sake of removing the scandal in a sensible fashion, and for the same of opening up the healthful teaching of the faith for those who seek the truth. This, moreover, will be done most rightly if, as we encounter the

teachings of the holy fathers, we are eager to make much of them, and if, "testing ourselves," as it is written, "to see if we are in the faith", we form our own ideas in accordance with their correct and unexceptionable opinions

Now the great and holy synod stated that the unique Son himself—naturally begotten out of God the Father, true God out of true God, light out of light, through whom the Father made everything that exists—descended, was enfleshed, became human, rose on the third day, and ascended into the heavens.

It is incumbent on us to be true to these statements and teachings and to comprehend what is meant by saying that the Logos from God took flesh and became human. We do not say that the Logos became flesh by having his nature changed, nor for that matter that he was transformed into a complete human being composed out of soul and body. On the contrary, we say that in an unspeakable and incomprehensible way, the Logos united to himself, in his hypostasis, flesh enlivened by a rational soul, and in this way became a human being and has been designated 'Son of man." He did not become a human being simply by an act of will or "good pleasure," any more than he did so by merely taking on a person.

Furthermore, we say that while the natures which were brought together into a true unity were different, there is nevertheless, because of the unspeakable and unutterable convergence into unity, one Christ and one Son out of the two. This is the sense in which it is said that, although he existed and was born from the Father before the ages, he was also born of a woman in his flesh. The idea is not that he found the beginning of his existence inside the holy Virgin, nor is it that he necessarily stood in need of a second birth through her in addition to his birth from the Father, for it is at once stupid and pointless to assert that one who exists prior to every age, coeternal with the Father, is in need of a second way of coming into being. Since, however, the Logos was born of a woman after he had, "for us and for our salvation," united human reality hypostatically to himself, he is said on this ground to have had a fleshly birth. It is not the case that first of all an ordinary human being was born of the holy Virgin and that the Logos descended upon him subsequently. On the contrary, since the union took place in the very womb, he is said to have undergone a fleshly birth by making his own the birth of the flesh which belonged to him.

We assert that this is the way in which he suffered and rose from the dead. It is not that the Logos of God suffered in his own nature, being overcome by stripes or nailpiercing or any of the other injuries; for the divine, since it is incorporeal, is impassible. Since, however, the body that had become his own underwent suffering, he is—once again—said to have suffered these things for our sakes, for the impassible One was within the suffering body. Moreover, we reason in exactly the same way in the case of his dying. God's Logos is by nature immortal and incorruptible and Life and

Lifegiver, but since, as Paul says, "by the grace of God" his very own body "tasted death on behalf of every person," he himself is said to have suffered this death which came about on our account. It is not that he actually experience death as far as anything which touches his [divine] nature is concerned; to think that would be insanity. Rather it is that, as I said earlier, his flesh tasted death.

So also, when his flesh was raised, the resurrection is also said to be his, not as if he fell into corruption (which God forbid!) but because, again, his body was raised.

This is the sense in which we confess one Christ and Lord. We do not worship a human being in conjunction with the Logos, lest the appearance of a division creep in by reason of that phrase "in conjunction with." No, we worship one and the same, because the body of the Logos is not alien to him but accompanies him even as he is enthroned with the Father. Again, it is not that there are two Sons enthroned together but rather that there is one, on account of the [Logos's] union with the flesh. If, however, we set aside this union in the order of the hypostasis as if it were pointless or unseemly, we fall into the assertion of two Sons, for it becomes necessary to divide the integral whole and to say that on the one hand there is a proper human being who is dignified with the title of "Son," while on the other hand there is the proper Logos of God, who possesses by nature both the name and the exercise of sonship.

Therefore, the one Lord Jesus Christ must not be divided into two Sons. . . He did not depart from his divine status or cease to be born of the Father; he continued to be what he was, even taking on flesh. This is what the teaching of the correct faith everywhere proclaims. And this is how we shall find the holy fathers conceived things. Accordingly, they boldly called the holy Virgin "God's mother" [theotokos], not because the nature of the Logos or the deity took the start of its existence in the holy Virgin but because the holy body which was born of her, possessed as it was of a rational soul, and to which the Logos was hypostatically united, is said to have had a fleshly birth.

These things I write you now out of the love which is in Christ, and I exhort you as a brother and "charge you before the Christ and the elect angels" to think and teach these things in company with us, so that the peace of the churches may be preserved and that the bond of like-mindedness and love may continue unbroken for God's priests. *Cyril of Alexandria's Second Letter to Nestorius.*

Reading Questions

Based on this text, what is at stake in the debate over the divinity and humanity of Jesus Christ? What doctrines and teaching of the church are mentioned here, and how are they affected by the Christological controversy?

RELATED WORKS

McGuckin, John. *Saint Cyril of Alexandria and the Christological Controversy.* Reprint, Crestwood, NY: St. Vladimir's Seminary Press, 2010.

Yarnold, E. J., trans. and ed. *Cyril of Jerusalem*. The Early Church Fathers. London: Routledge, 2000.

Gregory the Great (151–52)

(540–604). Also known as Pope Gregory I; the first pope who was a former monk. He successfully defended Rome against the Lombard and concluded peace negotiations. He wrote a textbook for training clergy and helped popularize allegorical interpretations of Scripture.

Primary Sources

From *Nicene and PostNicene Fathers series 2 volume 12*—public domain

The conduct of a prelate ought so far to transcend the conduct of the people as the life of a shepherd is wont to exalt him above the flock. For one whose estimation is such that the people are called his flock is bound anxiously to consider what great necessity is laid upon him to maintain rectitude. It is necessary, then, that in thought he should be pure, in action chief; discreet in keeping silence, profitable in speech; a near neighbour to every one in sympathy, exalted above all in contemplation; a familiar friend of good livers through humility, unbending against the vices of evil-doers through zeal for righteousness; not relaxing in his care for what is inward from being occupied in outward things, nor neglecting to provide for outward things in his solicitude for what is inward. But the things which we have thus briefly touched on let us now unfold and discuss more at length.

Of the Life of the Pastor, Part II, Chapter 1

Gregory to Maurilius and Vitalianus, magistris militum.

We have entreated your Glory through our son Vitalianus both by word and letter, charging you to communicate with him. But on the eleventh day of the month of January Ariulph sent us this letter which we forward to you. Wherefore, when you have read it, see if the people of Suana have stood fast in the fidelity they promised to the republic, and take adequate hostages from them, such as you can rely on; and moreover bind them anew by oaths, restoring to them what you took from them in the way of a pledge, and bringing them to a right mind by your discourses. But, should you quite distinctly ascertain that they have treated with Ariulph about their surrender to him, or at any rate have given him hostages, as the letter of Ariulph which we have forwarded to you leads us to suspect, then (after wholesome deliberation, lest your souls or mine be burdened with respect to our oaths), do ye whatever ye may judge to be of advantage to the republic. But let your Glory so act that neither anything be done for which we could be blamed by our adversaries, nor (which may the Lord avert) anything neglected which the advantage of the republic requires. Furthermore, my glorious sons, take anxious heed, since the enemy, so far as I have ascertained, has an army collected, and is said to be stationed at Narina; and if, God being angry with him, he should resolve to bend his course hitherward, do you plunder his positions so far as the Lord may aid you, or certainly let those whom you send carefully require night-watches, lest news of any sad event should reach us. *Book II, Ep. XXX*

Gregory to John, Bishop of Ravenna.

That I have not replied to the many letters of your Blessedness attribute not to sluggishness on my part, but to weakness, seeing that, on account of my sins, when Ariulph, coming to the Roman city, killed some and mutilated others, I was affected with such great sadness as to fall into a colic sickness. But I wondered much why it was that that well-known care of your Holiness for me was of no advantage to this city and to my needs. When, however, your letters reached me, I became aware that you are indeed taking pains to act, but yet have no one on whom you can bring your action to bear. I therefore attribute it to my sins that this man with whom we are now concerned both evades fighting against our enemies and also forbids our making peace; though indeed at present, even if he wished us to make it, we are utterly unable, since Ariulph, having the army of Authar and Nordulf, desires their subsidies to be given him ere he will deign to speak to us at all about peace. . .

If, however, there is any opportunity of prevailing with him, let your Fraternity work upon him, so that we may make peace with Ariulph, if to some small extent we may, since the soldiery have been removed from the city of Rome, as he himself knows. But the Theodosiacs, who have remained here, not having received their pay, are with difficulty induced to guard the walls; and how shall the city subsist, left destitute as it is by all, if it has not peace?

. . . With regard to the city of Naples, in view of the urgent insistence of the most excellent Exarch, we give you to understand that Arigis, as we have ascertained, has associated himself with Ariulph, and is breaking his faith to the republic, and plotting much against this same city; to which unless a duke be speedily sent, it may already be reckoned among the lost.

Reading Questions

What do these texts suggest to you about the role of clergy and expectations for their behavior? What do they suggest about the role of church officials in warfare? How does this compare to the role of clergy today?

RELATED WORKS

Markus, R. A. *Gregory the Great and His World.* Cambridge, UK: Cambridge University Press, 1997.

Moorhead, John, trans. and ed. *Gregory the Great.* The Early Church Fathers. London: Routledge, 2005.

Jerome (162–63)

(c. 342–420) Translator of the Bible into Latin (the 'Vulgate' version) who also wrote many commentaries on the text.

PRIMARY SOURCES

From *Nicene and PostNicene Fathers series 2 volume 6, 487*—public domain

Addressed to Paula and Eustochium, Bethlehem, a.d. 388.

I remember that, about five years ago, when I was still living at Rome, I read Ecclesiastes to the saintly Blesilla, so that I might provoke her to the contempt of this earthly scene, and to count as nothing all that she saw in the world; and that she asked me to throw my remarks upon all the more obscure passages into the form of a short commentary, so that, when I was absent, she might still understand what she read. She was withdrawn from us by her sudden death, while girding herself for our work; we were not counted worthy to have such an one as the partner of our life; and, therefore, Paula and Eustochium, I kept silence under the stroke of such a wound. But now, living as I do in the smaller community of Bethlehem, I pay what I owe to her memory and to you. I would only point out this, that I have followed no one's authority. I have translated direct from the Hebrew, adapting my words as much as possible to the form of the Septuagint, but only in those places in which they did not diverge far from the Hebrew. I have occasionally referred also to the versions of Aquila, Symmachus, and Theodotion, but so as not to alarm the zealous student by too many novelties, nor yet to let my commentary follow the side streams of opinion, turning aside, against my conscientious conviction, from the fountainhead of truth. *Preface to the Commentary on Ecclesiastes*

Reading Questions

What does this text reveal to you about the nature of biblical translation? What priorities does Jerome seem to have as he adapts the biblical text into a new language and comments on it? What would your translation priorities be?

RELATED WORKS

Clark, Elizabeth A. *Jerome, Chrysostom, and Friends: Essays and Translations*. Studies in Women and Religion, vol. 2. New York: Edwin Mellen Press, 1979.

Jerome, Saint. *The Homilies of Saint Jerome*. 2 vols. Trans. Marie Liguori Ewald. Washington, DC: Catholic University of America Press, 1964–66.

Nestorius (134)

(c. 381–c.451) Bishop of Constantinople beginning in 428. He opposed Arian heretics and defended Anastasius. He distinguished the two natures of Christ and defended his view when accused of heresy with a pseudonymous apologetics.

PRIMARY SOURCES

From *The Christological Controversy*, edited and translated by Richard A Norris Jr. (Philadelphia: Fortress Press, 1980), 135-140.

The rebukes which your astonishing letter brings against us I forgive. What it deserves is a healing generosity of spirit and the reply which comes to it at the proper time by way of actual deeds. This, though, does not permit silence, for if silence be kept, great danger is involved. On this account, standing against your prolixity as far as may be possible, I will attempt to make my exposition brief and maintain my distaste for obscure and indigestible haranguing.

I shall begin from Your Charity's all wise utterances, having first quoted them expressly. Here, then, are some statements from the astonishing teaching of your letter.

"The great and holy synod stated that the unique Son himself—naturally begotten out of God the Father, true God out of true God, light out of light, through whom the Father made everything that exists— descended, was enfleshed, became human, suffered, rose." These are Your Piety's words, and you doubly acknowledge them as yours.

Now hear our brotherly exhortation on behalf of true religion, in accordance with the testimony which that great one, Paul gave to Timothy his friend. "Give heed to reading, to exhortation, to teaching . . . for by doing this you will save both yourself and your hearers."

What does this phrase "give heed" mean to me? That in reading the doctrine of those holy men superficially, you did not recognize the excusable want of perception in your judgment that they assert the possibility of the Logos who is coeternal with God. So if it seems right, examine what was said more closely, and you will discover that the divine chorus of the Fathers did not say that the coessential Godhead is passible or that the Godhead which is coeternal with the Father has only just been born, or that he who has raised up the temple which was destroyed has [himself] risen. And if you will give me your attention for the sake of brotherly correction, I will explain to you the utterances of those holy men and deliver you from calumnies

against them and, through them, against the Holy Scriptures.

"We also believe," they said, "in our Lord Jesus Christ, his only-begotten Son." Observe how they first of all establish, as foundations, the titles which are common to the deity and the humanity—"Lord" and "Jesus" and "Christ" and "Only Begotten" and "Son"—and then build on them the teaching about his becoming human and his passion and resurrection, in order that, since the titles which signify and are common to both natures are set in the foreground, the things which pertain to the sonship and lordship are not divided and the things peculiar to the natures within the unitary sonship do not get endangered by the suggestion of a confusion. . .

I could say many things about this— first that those holy fathers spoke not of birth when they were thinking of God's saving dispensation but of coming to be in a human being—but I realize that my opening promise of brevity constrains my speech and turns me to your Charity's second head. . . To me it seemed right to center interest on the primary issues, for I do not see how he reintroduced as passible and newly created on who had first been proclaimed as impassible and incapable of a second birth—as if the qualities which attach naturally to God the Logos are corrupted by his conjunction with his temple; or as if people consider it a small thing that the sinless temple, which is also inseparable from the divine nature, underwent birth and death on behalf of sinners; or as if the Lord's saying, cried out to the Jews, is not worthy of belief: "Destroy this temple and in three days I will raise it." He did not say, "Destroy my divinity and in three days I will raise it."

Wishing again to expand on this theme too, I am brought to a halt by the recollection of my promise. Nevertheless, I must speak, while using brevity.

Everywhere in Holy Scripture, whenever mention is made of the saving dispensation of the Lord, what is conveyed to us is the birth and suffering not of the deity but of the humanity of Christ, so that by a more exact manner of speech the holy Virgin is called Mother of Christ, not Mother of God. . .

. . . The body therefore is the temple of the Son's deity, and a temple united to it by a complete and divine conjunction, so that the nature of the deity associates itself with the things belonging to the body, and the body is acknowledged to be noble and worthy of the wonders related in the Gospels.

To attribute also to him, in the name of this association the characteristics of the flesh that has been conjoined with him—I mean birth and suffering and death—is, my brother, either the work of a mind which truly errs in the fashion of the Greeks or that of a mind diseased with the insane heresy of Arius and Appolinaris and the others. Those who are thus carried away with the idea of this association are bound, because of it, to make the divine Logos have a part in being fed with milk and participate to some degree in growth and stand in need of angelic assistance because of his fearfulness at the time of the passion. I say nothing about circumcision and sacrifice and tears and hunger, which, being joined with

him, belong properly to the flesh as things which happened for our sake. These things are taken falsely when they are put off on the deity, and they become the occasion of just condemnation for us who perpetrate the falsehood. . .

It is right for you, since you are withstood, to give thought to those who are scandalized. And thanks be to your soul, mindful as it is of divine things, giving thought to people here as well. Know, however, that you have been misled by the clergy of your own persuasion, by those deposed here by the holy synod because they thought like Manichaeans. The affairs of the church make progress in every quarter, and the laity are increasing at such a rate, through the grace of God, that those who see the multitudes cry out the words of the prophet, "The earth shall be filled with the knowledge of the Lord as a great water covers the sea." Also the affairs of the emperors are in a state of overflowing joy because the teaching has been illumined. And—in order that I may bring my letter to an end—may people discover that amongst us, where all heresies hateful to God and the correct teaching of the church are concerned, this word has been fulfilled: "The house of Saul went on and became weaker and the house of David went on and became stronger."

This is our counsel, given as from brother to brother. . . I and all who are with me send many greetings to the whole brotherhood of your company. May you continue in good health and praying for us, O most entirely honored and beloved of God! *Nestorius's Second Letter to Cyril.*

Reading Questions

Compare this text to the text from Cyril above. How would you compare their writings in terms of argument, tone, content? How does each text affect your reading of the other? Does your comparison of the two texts enliven or deepen your understanding of the Christological controversy?

RELATED WORKS

Nestorius, Patriarch of Constantinople. *The Bazaar of Heracleides*. Trans. and ed. G. R. Driver and Leonard Hodgson. New York: AMS, 1978.

Chapter Summaries

8. Constantine and the Christian Empire

Constantine interpreted his defeat of Maxentius in 312 as a sign that the Christian God responded to his prayers for assistance, and he therefore proclaimed himself a Christian and his empire as well. Paganism was not immediately destroyed, however. Its influence on the church could be seen in the cult of saints and martyrs, which expanded in the fourth century. After Constantine, who proclaimed toleration of religion in his Edict of Milan, Christian emperors varied in their opposition to paganism, from bare tolerance to outright ban.

9. Councils and Creeds

The controversy over Arianism forever marked the church's doctrine of the Trinity. Because of the conflict, Constantine called the Council of Nicaea in 325 to attempt to reconcile the various factions. The Creed of Nicaea was the significant result; later modified at the Council of Chalcedon in 451, it is known today as the Nicene Creed. Other Councils followed the one at Nicaea, all attempting to find agreement on doctrine and authority within the church.

10. Buildings and Belief

With Constantine's proclamation of freedom of religion came the growth of the church and the need for buildings to accommodate increasing numbers of worshippers. The role of the clergy became more distinct as the liturgy evolved.

Churches were often sited at the location of important events in Christian tradition, such as the apostles' martyrdom or burial. The altar in both Eastern and Western churches was typically separated from ordinary worshippers.

11. Worship and the Christian Year

Constantine also left his stamp on the calendar, ordering Sunday to be honored as a public holiday. Easter and Christmas were both preceded by preparation of candidates for baptism. Eventually infant baptism replaced adult believer baptism as the norm.

Latin replaced Greek as the language of worship by the mid-fourth century. Sacramentaries, lectionaries, and homiliaries were compiled for clergy's use in leading worship.

12. Clergy, Bishops, and Pope

In this period bishops were responsible for all churches in a city, aided by presbyters and other minor clergy. They received the most income of all the church leaders. Churches were primarily found only in urban areas until the fourth century, when villages began to establish their own congregations and landowners created churches to which they appointed the clergy.

The Bishop of Rome became more significant and more powerful during this time of growth. Latin was the language used to unify the Christian world, and its literary heritage influenced the development of Christian literature.

13. The Church in North Africa

The Donatists, a protest movement focused on purity of discipline and committed to opposition to the Catholic Church, dominated the fourth-century church in North Africa after the reign of Emperor Julian.

Manicheism was successful in Africa despite being banned. Its austerity and radicalism appealed to many.

Augustine is one of the most important figures in church history from this region. He was first a follower of Manicheism but later influenced by Ambrose of Milan. His writings have had a major impact on Christian theology throughout the ages.

14. The Fall of the Roman Empire

While scholars continue to debate the causes of the fall of the Roman Empire, Christianity is acknowledged by most as at least a factor. The church also took advantage of the invasions of foreign peoples to convert many of the "barbarians," including the Visigoths, who became Arian Christians.

During the Roman Empire the church was both part of the established government authority and an advocate for the poor. Food distribution and hospital care were some of the activities organized by church leaders.

15. Ascetics and Monks

The Christian monastic tradition began in the late third century. From desert hermits to Benedictine monks, Christian ascetics led prayerful lives of simplicity, marked by celibacy and poverty.

The first monks lived in the Egyptian and Syrian deserts. Pachomius was the founder of communal monasticism, around 320. The monastic movement reached the Celts around the early sixth century. Benedict's Rule defined Western monastic life beginning in the late sixth century.

Additional Readings

1. From *Her Story: Women in Christian Tradition* (Fortress Press, 2006)

Barbara J. MacHaffie writes about Egeria, an early-fifth-century pilgrim to the Holy Land (30):

> The only information we have about Egeria must be inferred from her manuscript itself. In it there is
> evidence that she was a wealthy woman: she was on the pilgrimage for several years, she traveled with
> an extensive entourage, and she was given preferential treatment in many places by those in authority.
> The Bishop of Edessa greets her as one who has come from the remote end of the earth, possibly a ref-
> erence to her home in Gaul or Spain. While she is not as learned in the classics and Latin as aristocratic
> women, she reveals herself to be well read in the Scriptures. She frequently discussed the Bible with
> her hosts and often tried to interpret her travels in light of biblical stories. She bombards the Bishop of
> Carrae . . . with a whole series of questions about the geographic movements of Abraham's family. . . .
> It is probable that Egeria belonged to a group of virgin women who were bound together by strong
> ties of affection, who studied the Bible together, and who had some liturgical responsibilities. She fre-
> quently refers to her readers as "ladies," "my venerable sisters," and "my light." They were not members
> of a religious or monastic order, and there is no hint in Egeria's account that she lived a life of poverty.
>
> . . . Egeria's work is not simply a catalogue of places but provides insights into local practices, peo-
> ple, and traditions, which are often missing in most travel diaries. Her work is of great value because
> of the information it provides on early Christian worship and architecture in the age of Constantinian
> church building, as well as the condition of the biblical sites in the fifth century. But her diaries had
> theological significance as well. Believing that she was called by God to her travels, Egeria enlivens and
> confirms the truth of the Bible for herself and her community.

QUESTIONS FOR DISCUSSION AND REFLECTION

See Part 2, chapter 11, page 144, for an excerpt from Egeria's pilgrimage diary. From the excerpt and MacHaffie's
description, what might you conclude about why a woman like Egeria would have chosen to go on a long,
dangerous journey to the Holy Land? What insights does her travelogue provide about Christian beliefs and
practices during the early fifth century?

2. From "Lay Piety in the Sermons of John Chrysostom," chapter 1 of *A People's History of Christianity, vol. 3, Byzantine Christianity* (Fortress Press, 2006)

Jaclyn Maxwell writes about how Chrysostom's sermons attempted to "convince his listeners to integrate Christianity into the entirety of their lives" (20). He believed that "if people could develop Christian habits, then a
virtuous life would come naturally, without much effort or thought" (21). Moreover, Chrysostom urged laypeople to emulate monks in their daily worship practices (25):

> I praise and admire the monks that have occupied the desert places. . . . For they, after having made
> their dinners—or rather after supper (for dinner they know not at any time, because they know that

the present time is one of mourning and fasting)—after supper then, they sing certain hymns of thanksgiving to God. . . . So that you too may say them continually, I will rehearse to you the whole of that sacred song. The words of it then stand as follows: "Blessed God, who feeds me from my youth up, who gives food to all flesh; fill our hearts with joy and gladness, that always having all sufficiency we may abound unto every good work in Christ Jesus our Lord; with whom be unto You glory, honor and might, with the Holy Spirit, forever. Amen. Glory to You, O Lord, glory to You, O Holy One, glory to You, O King, that You have given us meat to make us glad. Fill us with the Holy Ghost, that we may be found well-pleasing before You, not being ashamed, when You render to every man according to his works."

Maxwell comments that "because of the proximity of monastic communities laypeople could visit monks to observe their pious way of life and receive prayers and instruction" (26) and that Chrysostom in fact told his audience that the monks lived near the town in order to instruct the people on how to live. As she explains, "accounts of Syrian monks in Late Antiquity indicate that most of them were indeed amenable to visitors who sought blessings, cures, and advice or who visited out of curiosity" (26).

Questions for Discussion and Reflection

What view of monastic life do you find in Chrysostom? Compare his portrayal of monastic life and the role of monks in relation to the laity with the description of life under the Rule of Benedict in Part 2, pages 178–79. What kind of authority would members of monastic communities appear to have over laity in the late Roman Empire? Why might someone of that era in particular find monastic life appealing?

3. From *On the Trinity* (Cambridge University Press, 2002)

Augustine writes in his Preface (3–4):

In this Trinity, as we have said elsewhere, those names, which are predicated relatively, the one of the other, are properly spoken of as belonging to each person in particular, as Father and Son, and the Gift of both, the Holy Spirit; for the Father is not the Trinity, nor the Son the Trinity, nor the Gift the Trinity. But when they are spoken of singly with respect to themselves, then they are not spoken of as three in the plural number but as one, the Trinity itself. Thus the Father is God, the Son is God, the Holy Spirit is God; the Father is good, the Son is good, the Holy Spirit is good; and the Father is omnipotent, the Son is omnipotent, and the Holy Spirit is omnipotent; but yet here are not three gods, nor three goods, nor three omnipotents, but one God, one good, and one omnipotent, the Trinity itself. And the same applies to everything else that may be said of them, not in relation of one to the other, but individually in respect to themselves.

   . . . Therefore, they are called three persons or three substances, not that any diversity of essence is to be understood, but so that we may be able to answer by some one word when anyone asks three what or what three things. So great is the equality in this Trinity, that not only is the Father not greater than the Son in that which pertains to the divinity, but neither are the Father and the Son anything greater than the Holy Spirit, nor is each person singly, whichever of the three it may be, anything less than the Trinity itself.

. . . Meanwhile let us hold fast to this rule, that what has not yet become clear to our intellect may still be preserved by the firmness of our faith.

QUESTIONS FOR DISCUSSION AND REFLECTION

Review the biography and discussion of Augustine's beliefs in Part 2, pages 156–57. In this text what influences do you see in his thinking? What principles is he relying on? Compare his view of the Trinity as it is presented here to other views discussed in Part 2; see, for example, "The Arian Controversy" (pages 108–9), "The Creed of Nicaea" (pages 119–20), and "The Cappadocians' Theology" (pages 128–29). What similarities and differences between Augustine and the other views of God, Christ, and the Holy Spirit can you identify?

See also "Reading Historical Documents" (page 171 in this volume) for other questions to consider.

Selected Online Resources

▶ "Emperor Constantine"—biographical essay
http://www.roman-empire.net/decline/constantine-index.html

▶ "Basilica of Santa Maria Maggiore, Rome, 5th Century A.D."—a brief (4:38) video featuring two art historians discussing the history and architecture of an early basilica, including close-ups of artwork within the church
http://www.noodle.org/learn/details/197997/basilica-of-santa-maria-maggiore-rome-5th-century-ad

▶ "Helena, Egeria, Paula, Birgitta and Margery: The Bible and Women Pilgrims"—essay, with accompanying map, on Julia Bolton Holloway's journeys to retrace pilgrimage routes taken by women in the fourth to fifteenth centuries
http://www.umilta.net/egeria.html

▶ "Augustine of Hippo"—an extensive site including links to some of Augustine's works online, images, and bibliographies
http://www9.georgetown.edu/faculty/jod/augustine/

▶ "Early Christian History"—articles on a range of topics, including heretical movements and important figures
http://www.earlychristianhistory.info/index.html

▶ "Coptic Art"—brief essay and several photographs
http://www.digitalegypt.ucl.ac.uk/art/coptic.html

Guide to Part 3: A Christian Society

Key Terms

The number in parentheses refers to the page where the term is explained. Those terms marked with asterisks also appear in the Glossary.

Crusades (228)* The military expeditions undertaken by Christian armies from Europe from the eleventh to the fourteenth centuries, intended to liberate the Holy Land from Islam.

icon (193)* A likeness of a divine figure or saint, painted on wood or inlaid in mosaic and used in public or private devotion.

Iconoclastic controversy (193) A dispute over the use of icons (images of Christ, the Virgin Mary, or a saint) spurred by the banning of icons by Emperor Leo III in 726. The supporters of icons eventually prevailed after more than a century of bitter dispute.

Inquisition (233)* Papal office for identifying heretics, founded by Pope Gregory IX and staffed by the Franciscan and Dominican religious orders.

Torture became an approved aid to interrogation in 1252.

mysticism (290)* The search for direct personal experience of the divine, leading to union with God's love and will.

patriarch (226)* (1) in Judaism and Christianity, refers to the founders of the faith, such as Abraham, Isaac, and Jacob. (2) Head of one of the Eastern Orthodox churches. The Ecumenical Patriarch of Constantinople is a figurehead for Orthodox Christians.

sacrament (236)* "An outward and visible sign of an inward and spiritual grace" (*Book of Common Prayer*). Reformed Churches count only baptism and the Eucharist as sacraments, both being instituted by Christ. Roman Catholic and Orthodox Churches add confirmation, marriage, ordination, penance, and extreme unction (the anointing of the sick).

schism (227)* A deliberate division or split between Christians that disrupts the unity of the church.

Key Personalities

Numbers in parentheses refer to the pages where the text provides the individual's biographical details and historical significance.

Peter Abelard (245)

(1079–1142) A major Christian thinker and writer famous for his discussion of faith and reason within Christian theology. He promoted the consistency and reasonableness of Christianity and was a pioneer of scholasticism. He is famous for his doomed relationship with the abbess Héloise, with whom he shared a lively correspondence for many years as they led their separate monastic lives.

PRIMARY SOURCES

From Peter Abelard: *Historia Calamitatum*: The Story of My Misfortunes, trans. Henry Adams Bellows (1922; Internet Medieval Sourcebook, 2013), http://www.fordham.edu/Halsall/basis/abelard-histcal.asp

> NOW there dwelt in that same city of Paris a certain young girl named Heloise, the niece of a canon who was called Fulbert. Her uncle's love for her was equaled only by his desire that she should have the best education which he could possibly procure for her. Of no mean beauty, she stood out above all by reason of her abundant knowledge of letters. Now this virtue is rare among women, and for that very reason it doubly graced the maiden, and made her the most worthy of renown in the entire kingdom. It was this young girl whom I, after carefully considering all those qualities which are wont to attract lovers, determined to unite with myself in the bonds of love, and indeed the thing seemed to me very easy to be done. So distinguished was my name, and I possessed such advantages of youth and comeliness, that no matter what woman I might favour with my love, I dreaded rejection of none. Then, too, I believed that I could win the maiden's consent all the more easily by reason of her knowledge of letters and her zeal therefor; so, even if we were parted, we might yet be together in thought with the aid of written messages. Perchance, too, we might be able to write more boldly than we could speak, and thus at all times could we live in joyous intimacy.

> Thus, utterly aflame with my passion for this maiden, I sought to discover means whereby I might have daily and familiar speech with her, thereby the more easily to win her consent. For this purpose I persuaded the girl's uncle, with the aid of some of his friends to take me into his household—for he dwelt hard by my school—in return for the payment of a small sum. My pretext for this was that the care of my own household was a serious handicap to my studies, and likewise burdened me with an expense far greater than I could afford. Now he was a man keen in avarice and likewise he was most desirous for his niece that her study of letters should ever go forward, so, for these two reasons I easily won his consent to the fulfillment of my wish, for he was fairly agape for my money, and at the same time believed that his niece would vastly benefit by my teaching. More even than this, by his own earnest entreaties he fell in with

my desires beyond anything I had dared to hope, opening the way for my love; for he entrusted her wholly to my guidance, begging me to give her instruction whensoever I might be free from the duties of my school, no matter whether by day or by night, and to punish her sternly if ever I should find her negligent of her tasks. In all this the man's simplicity was nothing short of astounding to me; I should not have been more smitten with wonder if he had entrusted a tender lamb to the care of a ravenous wolf. When he had thus given her into my charge, not alone to be taught but even to be disciplined, what had he done save to give free scope to my desires, and to offer me every opportunity, even if I had not sought it, to bend her to my will with threats and blows if I failed to do so with caresses? There were, however, two things which particularly served to allay any foul suspicion: his own love for his niece, and my former reputation for continence.

Why should I say more? We were united first in the dwelling that sheltered our love, and then in the hearts that burned with it. Under the pretext of study we spent our hours in the happiness of love, and learning held out to us the secret opportunities that our passion craved. Our speech was more of love than of the books which lay open before us; our kisses far outnumbered our reasoned words. Our hands sought less the book than each other's bosoms—love drew our eyes together far more than the lesson drew them to the pages of our text. In order that there might be no suspicion, there were, indeed, sometimes blows, but love

gave them, not anger; they were the marks, not of wrath, but of a tenderness surpassing the most fragrant balm in sweetness. What followed? No degree in love's progress was left untried by our passion, and if love itself could imagine any wonder as yet unknown, we discovered it. And our inexperience of such delights made us all the more ardent in our pursuit of them, so that our thirst for one another was still unquenched.

In measure as this passionate rapture absorbed me more and more, I devoted ever less time to philosophy and to the work of the school. Indeed it became loathsome to me to go to the school or to linger there; the labour, moreover, was very burdensome, since my nights were vigils of love and my days of study. My lecturing became utterly careless and lukewarm; I did nothing because of inspiration, but everything merely as a matter of habit. I had become nothing more than a reciter of my former discoveries, and though I still wrote poems, they dealt with love, not with the secrets of philosophy. Of these songs you yourself well know how some have become widely known and have been sung in many lands, chiefly, methinks, by those who delighted in the things of this world. As for the sorrow, the groans, the lamentations of my students when they perceived the preoccupation, nay, rather the chaos, of my mind, it is hard even to imagine them. . .

Reading Question

How would you characterize this text: biography? history? romance? What does this text reveal about the patriarchal structure of eleventh-century Europe?

RELATED WORKS

Abelard, Peter. *Commentary on the Epistle to the Romans*. Trans. Steven R. Cartwright. Fathers of the Church: Mediaeval Continuation, vol. 12. (Washington, DC: Catholic University of America Press, 2011).

Clanchy, M. T. *Abelard: A Medieval Life* (Oxford: Blackwell, 1997).

Anselm (244)

(1033–1109) Archbishop of Canterbury, philosopher, and early scholastic theologian. He taught that faith must lead to the right use of reason. His greatest work, *Cur Deus Homo* (*Why God Became Human*), proposed that Christ's death had satisfied the sins humanity had incurred against God.

PRIMARY SOURCES

From St. Anselm: *Proslogium; Monologium: An Appendix In Behalf Of The Fool By Gaunilo; And Cur Deus Homo*, trans. Sidney Norton Deane, (Chicago: The Open Court Publishing Company, 1903, reprinted 1926) http://www.fordham.edu/Halsall/basis/anselm-intro.asp

> I HAVE been often and most earnestly requested by many, both personally and by letter, that I would hand down in writing the proofs of a certain doctrine of our faith, which I am accustomed to give to inquirers; for they say that these proofs gratify them, and are considered sufficient. This they ask, not for the sake of attaining to faith by means of reason, but that they may be gladdened by understanding and meditating on those things which they believe; and that, as far as possible, they may be always ready to convince any one who demands of them a reason of that hope which is in us.

> And this question, both infidels are accustomed to bring up against us, ridiculing Christian simplicity as absurd; and many believers ponder it in their hearts; for what cause or necessity, in sooth, God became man, and by his own death, as we believe and affirm, restored life to the world; when he might have done this, by means of some other being, angelic or human, or merely by his will. Not only the learned, but also many unlearned persons interest themselves in this inquiry and seek for its solution. Therefore, since many desire to consider this subject, and, though it seem very difficult in the investigation, it is yet plain to all in the solution, and attractive for the value and beauty of the reasoning; although what ought to be sufficient has been said by the holy fathers and their successors, yet I will take pains to disclose to inquirers what God has seen fit to lay open to me. And since investigations, which are carried on by question and answer, are thus made more plain to many, and especially to less quick minds, and on that account are more gratifying, I will take to argue with me one of those persons who agitate this subject; one, who among the rest impels me more earnestly to it, so that in this way Boso may question and Anselm reply. *Cur Deus Homo? Chapter 1*

Reading Question

Anselm uses the character, Boso, as his questioner in *Cur Deus Homo?* How might this kind of dialectic style serve a writer like Anselm?

> Truly there is a God, although the fool has said in his heart, There is no God.

AND so, Lord, do you, who do give understanding to faith, give me, so far as you knowest it to be profitable, to understand that you are as we believe; and that you are that which we believe. And indeed, we believe that you are a being than which nothing greater can be conceived. Or is there no such nature, since the fool has said in his heart, there is no God? (Psalms xiv. 1). But, at any rate, this very fool, when he hears of this being of which I speak—a being than which nothing greater can be conceived—understands what be hears, and what he understands is in his understanding; although he does not understand it to exist.

For, it is one thing for an object to be in the understanding, and another to understand that the object exists. When a painter first conceives of what he will afterwards perform, he has it in his understanding, but be does not yet understand it to be, because he has not yet performed it. But after he has made the painting, he both has it in his understanding, and he understands that it exists, because he has made it.

Hence, even the fool is convinced that something exists in the understanding, at least, than which nothing greater can be conceived. For, when he hears of this, he understands it. And whatever is understood, exists in the understanding. And assuredly that, than which nothing greater can be conceived, cannot exist in the understanding alone. For, suppose it exists in the understanding alone: then it can be conceived to exist in reality; which is greater.

Therefore, if that, than which nothing greater can be conceived, exists in the understanding alone, the very being, than which nothing greater can be conceived, is one, than which a greater can be conceived. But obviously this is impossible. Hence, there is doubt that there exists a being, than which nothing greater can be conceived, and it exists both in the understanding and in reality.

God cannot be conceived not to exist.—God is that, than which nothing greater can be conceived.—That which can be conceived not to exist is not God.

AND it assuredly exists so truly, that it cannot be conceived not to exist. For, it is possible to conceive of a being which cannot be conceived not to exist; and this is greater than one which can be conceived not to exist. Hence, if that, than which nothing greater can be conceived, can be conceived not to exist, it is not that, than which nothing greater can be conceived. But this is an irreconcilable contradiction. There is, then, so truly a being than which nothing greater can be conceived to exist, that it cannot even be conceived not to exist;. and this being you are, O Lord, our God.

So truly, therefore, do you exist, O Lord, my God, that you can not be conceived not to exist; and rightly. For, if a mind could conceive of a being better than you, the creature would rise above the Creator; and this is most absurd. And, indeed, whatever else there is, except you alone, can be conceived not to exist. To you alone, therefore, it belongs to exist more truly than all other beings, and hence in a higher degree than all others. For, whatever else exists does not exist so truly, and hence in a less degree it belongs to it to exist. Why, then, has the fool said in his heart, there is no God (Psalms xiv. 1), since it is so evident, to a rational mind, that you do exist in the highest degree of all? Why, except that he is dull and a fool? *Prosologion Chapters 2-3*

Reading Questions

How would you summarize Anselm's argument here in favor of the existence of God? What sources of evidence does he draw upon? Do you find his argument satisfying?

RELATED WORKS

Anselm, Saint. *The Major Works.* Ed. and trans. Brian Davies and G. R. Evans. Oxford: Oxford University Press, 1998.

Vaughn, Sally N. *Archbishop Anselm 1093–1109: Bec Missionary, Canterbury Primate, Patriarch of Another World.* Surrey, UK: Ashgate, 2012.

Thomas Aquinas (250)

(1225–74) Dominican theologian and philosopher whose teachings form the basis of official Roman Catholic theology. He was a brilliant public speaker and a prolific writer. He attempted to follow Aristotle's principles while distinguishing what was acceptable to Christianity within the new knowledge he encountered. He taught a fundamental distinction between faith and reason, asserting that God's existence can be proved, but that the doctrines of the Trinity and the incarnation are revealed and must be accepted on faith.

PRIMARY SOURCES

From *The Summa Theologica of St. Thomas Aquinas,* Second and Revised Edition, 1920
Literally translated by Fathers of the English Dominican Province
Online Edition Copyright © 2008 by Kevin Knight
http://www.newadvent.org/summa

Question 1, Article 1. Whether, besides philosophy, any further doctrine is required?

Objection 1. It seems that, besides philosophical science, we have no need of any further knowledge. For man should not seek to know what is above reason: "Seek not the things that are too high for thee" (Sirach 3:22). But whatever is not above reason is fully treated of in philosophical science. Therefore any other knowledge besides philosophical science is superfluous.

Objection 2. Further, knowledge can be concerned only with being, for nothing can be known, save what is true; and all that is, is true. But everything that is, is treated of in philosophical science—even God Himself; so that there is a part of philosophy called theology, or the divine science, as Aristotle has proved (Metaph. vi). Therefore, besides philosophical science, there is no need of any further knowledge.

On the contrary, It is written (2 Timothy 3:16): "All Scripture, inspired of God is profitable to teach, to reprove, to correct, to instruct in justice." Now Scripture, inspired of God, is no part of philosophical science, which has been built up by human reason. Therefore it is useful that besides philosophical science, there should be other knowledge, i.e. inspired of God.

I answer that, It was necessary for man's salvation that there should be a knowledge revealed by God besides philosophical science built up by human reason. Firstly, indeed, because man is directed to God, as to an end that surpasses the grasp of his reason: "The eye hath not seen, O God, besides Thee, what things Thou hast prepared for them that wait for Thee" (Isaiah 64:4). But the end must first be known by men who are to direct their thoughts and actions to the end. Hence it was necessary for the salvation of man that certain truths which exceed human reason should be made known to him by divine revelation. Even as regards those truths about God which human reason could have discovered, it was necessary that man should be taught by a divine revelation; because the truth about God such as reason could discover, would only be known by a few, and that after a long time, and with the admixture of many errors. Whereas man's whole salvation, which is in God, depends upon the knowledge of this truth. Therefore, in order that the salvation of men might be brought about more fitly and more surely, it was necessary that they should be taught divine truths by divine revelation. It was therefore necessary that besides philosophical science built up by reason, there should be a sacred science learned through revelation.

Reply to Objection 1. Although those things which are beyond man's knowledge may not be sought for by man through his reason, nevertheless, once they are revealed by God, they must be accepted by faith.

Hence the sacred text continues, "For many things are shown to thee above the understanding of man" (Sirach 3:25). And in this, the sacred science consists.

Reply to Objection 2. Sciences are differentiated according to the various means through which knowledge is obtained. For the astronomer and the physicist both may prove the same conclusion: that the earth, for instance, is round: the astronomer by means of mathematics (i.e. abstracting from matter), but the physicist by means of matter itself. Hence there is no reason why those things which may be learned from philosophical science, so far as they can be known by natural reason, may not also be taught us by another science so far as they fall within revelation. Hence theology included in sacred doctrine differs in kind from that theology which is part of philosophy.

Question 2, Article 3. Whether God exists?

Objection 1. It seems that God does not exist; because if one of two contraries be infinite, the other would be altogether destroyed. But the word "God" means that He is infinite goodness. If, therefore, God existed, there would be no evil discoverable; but there is evil in the world. Therefore God does not exist.

Objection 2. Further, it is superfluous to suppose that what can be accounted for by a few principles has been produced by many. But it seems that everything we see in the world can be accounted for by other principles, supposing God did not exist. For all natural things can be reduced to one principle which is nature; and all voluntary things can be reduced to one principle which is human reason, or will. Therefore there is no need to suppose God's existence.

On the contrary, It is said in the person of God: "I am Who am." (Exodus 3:14)

I answer that, The existence of God can be proved in five ways.

The first and more manifest way is the argument from motion. It is certain, and evident to our senses, that in the world some things are in motion. Now whatever is in motion is put in motion by another, for nothing can be in motion except it is in potentiality to that towards which it is in motion; whereas a thing moves inasmuch as it is in act. For motion is nothing else than the reduction of something from potentiality to actuality. But nothing can be reduced from potentiality to actuality, except by something in a state of actuality. Thus that which is actually hot, as fire, makes wood, which is potentially hot, to be actually hot, and thereby moves and changes it. Now it is not possible that the same thing should be at once in actuality and potentiality in the same respect, but only in different respects. For what is actually hot cannot simultaneously be potentially hot; but it is simultaneously potentially cold. It is therefore impossible that in the same respect and in the same way a thing should be both mover and moved, i.e. that it should move itself. Therefore, whatever is in motion must be put in motion by another. If that by which it is put in motion be itself put in motion, then this also must needs be put in motion by another, and that by another again. But this cannot go on to infinity, because then

there would be no first mover, and, consequently, no other mover; seeing that subsequent movers move only inasmuch as they are put in motion by the first mover; as the staff moves only because it is put in motion by the hand. Therefore it is necessary to arrive at a first mover, put in motion by no other; and this everyone understands to be God.

The second way is from the nature of the efficient cause. In the world of sense we find there is an order of efficient causes. There is no case known (neither is it, indeed, possible) in which a thing is found to be the efficient cause of itself; for so it would be prior to itself, which is impossible. Now in efficient causes it is not possible to go on to infinity, because in all efficient causes following in order, the first is the cause of the intermediate cause, and the intermediate is the cause of the ultimate cause, whether the intermediate cause be several, or only one. Now to take away the cause is to take away the effect. Therefore, if there be no first cause among efficient causes, there will be no ultimate, nor any intermediate cause. But if in efficient causes it is possible to go on to infinity, there will be no first efficient cause, neither will there be an ultimate effect, nor any intermediate efficient causes; all of which is plainly false. Therefore it is necessary to admit a first efficient cause, to which everyone gives the name of God.

The third way is taken from possibility and necessity, and runs thus. We find in nature things that are possible to be and not to be, since they are found to be generated, and to corrupt, and consequently, they are possible to be and not to be. But it is impossible for these always to exist, for that which is possible not to be at some time is not. Therefore, if everything is possible not to be, then at one time there could have been nothing in existence. Now if this were true, even now there would be nothing in existence, because that which does not exist only begins to exist by something already existing. Therefore, if at one time nothing was in existence, it would have been impossible for anything to have begun to exist; and thus even now nothing would be in existence—which is absurd. Therefore, not all beings are merely possible, but there must exist something the existence of which is necessary. But every necessary thing either has its necessity caused by another, or not. Now it is impossible to go on to infinity in necessary things which have their necessity caused by another, as has been already proved in regard to efficient causes. Therefore we cannot but postulate the existence of some being having of itself its own necessity, and not receiving it from another, but rather causing in others their necessity. This all men speak of as God.

The fourth way is taken from the gradation to be found in things. Among beings there are some more and some less good, true, noble and the like. But "more" and "less" are predicated of different things, according as they resemble in their different ways something which is the maximum, as a thing is said to be hotter according as it more nearly resembles that which is hottest; so that there is something which is truest, something best, something noblest and, consequently, something which is uttermost being; for those things that are greatest in truth are greatest in being, as it is written in Metaph. ii. Now the maximum in any genus is the cause of all in that genus; as fire, which is the maximum heat, is the cause of all hot things. Therefore there must also be something which is to all beings the cause of their being, goodness, and every other perfection; and this we call God.

The fifth way is taken from the governance of the world. We see that things which lack intelligence, such as natural bodies, act for an end, and this is evident from their acting always, or nearly always, in the same way, so as to obtain the best result. Hence it is plain that not fortuitously, but designedly, do they achieve their end. Now whatever lacks intelligence cannot move towards an end, unless it be directed by some being endowed with knowledge and intelligence; as the arrow is shot to its mark by the archer. Therefore some intelligent being exists by whom all natural things are directed to their end; and this being we call God.

Reply to Objection 1. As Augustine says (Enchiridion xi): "Since God is the highest good, He would not allow any evil to exist in His works, unless His omnipotence and goodness were such as to bring good even out of evil." This is part of the infinite goodness of God, that He should allow evil to exist, and out of it produce good.

Reply to Objection 2. Since nature works for a determinate end under the direction of a higher agent, whatever is done by nature must needs be traced back to God, as to its first cause. So also whatever is done voluntarily must also be traced back to some higher cause other than human reason or will, since these can change or fail; for all things that are changeable and capable of defect must be traced back to an immovable and self-necessary first principle, as was shown in the body of the Article.

Reading Questions

How does the format of this text, with its numbered objections, shape your reading? What does it tell you about the goals and purpose of the text? How would you summarize Aquinas's five main arguments in favor of the existence of God?

RELATED WORKS

Aquinas, Thomas, Saint. *Aquinas's Shorter Summa: St. Thomas Aquinas's Own Concise Version of His Summa Theologica.* (Manchester, NH: Sophia Institute Press, 2002).

Turner, Denys. *Thomas Aquinas: A Portrait.* (New Haven, CT: Yale University Press, 2013).

Bernard of Clairvaux (222)

(1090–1153) Founder of more than sixty-five monasteries and the most influential Christian of his age. In his writing he emphasized God's love and how physical love could be transformed into a spiritual passion for Christ. He was also a strong critic of the powerful. He described Christian life as an experience of progress in love.

PRIMARY SOURCES

From *On Loving God* (c.1128; Christian Classics Ethereal Library, 2013), 15-18, http://www.ccel.org /ccel/bernard/loving_god.pdf

And now let us consider what profit we shall have from loving God. . .

It is natural for a man to desire what he reckons better than that which he has already, and be satisfied with nothing which lacks that special quality which he misses. Thus, if it is for her beauty that he loves his wife, he will cast longing eyes after a fairer woman. If he is clad in a rich garment, he will covet a costlier one; and no matter how rich he may be he will envy a man richer than himself. Do we not see people every day, endowed with vast estates, who keep on joining field to field, dreaming of wider boundaries for their lands? Those who dwell in palaces are ever adding house to house, continually building up and tearing down, remodeling and changing. Men in high places are driven by insatiable ambition to clutch at still greater prizes. And nowhere is there any final satisfaction, because nothing there can be defined as absolutely the best or highest. But it is natural that nothing should content a man's desires but the very best, as he reckons it. Is it not, then, mad folly always to be craving for things which can never quiet our longings, much less satisfy them? No matter how many such things one has, he is always lusting after what he has not; never at peace, he sighs for new possessions. Discontented, he spends himself in fruitless toil, and finds only weariness in the evanescent and unreal pleasures of the world. In his greediness, he counts all that he has clutched as nothing in comparison with what is beyond his grasp, and loses all pleasure in his actual possessions by longing after what he has not, yet covets. No man can ever hope to own all things. Even the little one does possess is got only with toil and is held in fear; since each is certain to lose what he hath when God's day, appointed though unrevealed, shall come. But the perverted will struggles towards the ultimate good by devious ways, yearning after satisfaction, yet led astray by vanity and deceived by wickedness. Ah, if you wish to attain to the consummation of all desire, so that nothing unfulfilled will be left, why weary yourself with fruitless efforts, running hither and thither, only to die long before the goal is reached?

It is so that these impious ones wander in a circle, longing after something to gratify their yearnings, yet madly rejecting that which alone can bring them to their desired end, not by exhaustion but by attainment. They wear themselves out in vain travail, without reaching their blessed consummation, because they delight in creatures, not in the Creator. They want to traverse creation, trying all things one by one, rather than think of coming to Him who is Lord of all. And if their utmost longing were realized, so that they should have all the world for their own, yet without possessing Him who is the Author of all being, then the same law of their desires would make them contemn what they had and restlessly seek Him whom they still lacked, that is, God Himself. Rest is in Him alone.

Man knows no peace in the world; but he has no disturbance when he is with God.

. . . I have said already that the motive for loving God is God Himself. And I spoke truly, for He is as well the efficient cause as the final object of our love. He gives the occasion for love, He creates the affection, He brings the desire to good effect. He is such that love to Him is a natural due; and so hope in Him is natural, since our present love would be vain did we not hope to love Him perfectly some day. Our love is prepared and rewarded by His. He loves us first, out of His great tenderness; then we are bound to repay Him with love; and we are permitted to cherish exultant hopes in Him. *On Loving God, Chapter VII.*

Reading Question

This text makes a strong division between those who are impious and those who are pious. By what criteria does Bernard of Clairvaux make this division?

Related Works

Bernard, of Clairvaux. *Bernard of Clairvaux: Parables and The Sentences.* Ed. Maureen M. O'Brien. Cistercian Fathers series, no. 55. Kalamazoo, MI: Cistercian Publications, 2000.

Evans, G. R. *Bernard of Clairvaux.* Great Medieval Thinkers. New York: Oxford University Press, 2000.

John Chrysostom (206)

(c. 350–407) Known as the greatest of early Christian preachers; chosen as bishop of Constantinople against his will. He devoted himself to ascetic practices for several years, including living in a mountain cave. Famous for his piety and bravery in the face of fierce opposition, he applied his knowledge of the Greek Bible to practical life concerns affecting his lay audience.

Primary Sources

From *Homily on the Paralytic Let Down Through the Roof*, trans. Rev. W.R.W. Stephens (Christian Classics Ethereal Library, 2013), 304-305, http://www.ccel.org/ccel/schaff/npnf109.pdf

> . . . Let this speech be our utterance also over each event which befalls us; whether it be loss of property, or infirmity of body, or insult, or false accusation or any other form of evil incident to mankind, let us say these words "The Lord gave, the Lord hath taken away; as it seemed good to the Lord so has it come to pass; blessed be the name of the Lord for ever." If we practice this spiritual wisdom, we shall never experience any evil, even if we undergo countless sufferings, but the gain will be greater than the loss, the good will exceed the evil: by these words thou wilt cause God to be merciful unto thee, and wilt defend thyself against the tyranny of Satan. For as soon as thy tongue has uttered these words forthwith the Devil hastens from thee: and when he has hastened away, the cloud of dejection also is dispelled and the thoughts which afflict us take to flight, hurrying off in company with him, and in addition to all this thou wilt win all manner of blessings both here and in Heaven. And you have a convincing example in the case of Job, and of the Apostle, who having for God's sake despised the troubles of this world, obtained the everlasting blessings. Let us then be trustful and in all things which befall us let us rejoice and give thanks to the merciful God, that we may pass through this present life with serenity, and obtain the blessings to come, by the grace and lovingkindness of our Lord Jesus Christ to whom be glory, honour and might always, now and ever, world without end. Amen.

Reading Question

Chrysostom is known for his eloquence—in fact the Greek work Chrysostom can be translated as "golden mouth"; do you find this sample of his preaching to live up to that name? The homily mentions the biblical character Job. How might reading the book of Job in the Old Testament shape your understanding of this text?

Related Works

John Chrysostom, Saint. *Apologist: Saint John Chrysostom*. Trans. Margaret A. Schatkin and Paul W. Harkins. Washington, DC: Catholic University Press, 1985.

Kelly, J. N. D. *Golden Mouth: The Story of John Chrysostom—Ascetic, Preacher, Bishop*. Ithaca, NY: Cornell University Press, 1998.

Francis of Assisi (223)

(1182–1226) Founder of the Franciscan monastic order who lived by a simple rule of life, rejecting possessions, ministering to the sick, and having a special concern for nature. He obtained approval from Pope Innocent III in 1210 to lead his Friars Minor (Lesser Brothers) in preaching and caring for the poor and sick. He gave up his leadership role when Pope Honorius III confirmed a new rule creating a more elaborate system within Francis's order.

PRIMARY SOURCES

From *The Writings of St. Francis of Assisi,* trans. Paschal Robinson, (1905; Internet Sacred Text Archive), 152, http://www.sacred-texts.com/chr/wosf/wosf22.htm

> Most high, omnipotent, good Lord,
> Praise, glory and honor and benediction all, are Thine.
> To Thee alone do they belong, most High,
> And there is no man fit to mention Thee.
>
> Praise be to Thee, my Lord, with all Thy creatures,
> Especially to my worshipful brother sun,
> The which lights up the day, and through him dost Thou brightness give;
> And beautiful is he and radiant with splendor great;
> Of Thee, most High, signification gives.
>
> Praised be my Lord, for sister moon and for the stars,
> In heaven Thou hast formed them clear and precious and fair.
>
> Praised be my Lord for brother wind
> And for the air and clouds and fair and every kind of weather,
> By the which Thou givest to Thy creatures nourishment.
> Praised be my Lord for sister water,
> The which is greatly helpful and humble and precious and pure.
>
> Praised be my Lord for brother fire,
> By the which Thou lightest up the dark.
> And fair is he and gay and mighty and strong.
>
> Praised be my Lord for our sister, mother earth,
> The which sustains and keeps us
> And brings forth diverse fruits with grass and flowers bright.
>
> Praised be my Lord for those who for Thy love forgive
> And weakness bear and tribulation.
> Blessed those who shall in peace endure,
> For by Thee, most High, shall they be crowned.
> Praised be my Lord for our sister, the bodily death,
> From the which no living man can flee.
> Woe to them who die in mortal sin;
> Blessed those who shall find themselves in Thy most holy will,
> For the second death shall do them no ill.
>
> Praise ye and bless ye my Lord, and give Him thanks,
> And be subject unto Him with great humility.
> *Canticle of the Sun*

Reading Questions

How does the language in this song strike you? What image of God does it evoke? Can you research any more recent adaptations of the song in art and music?

RELATED WORKS

Francis, of Assisi. *The Writings of Francis of Assisi: Letters and Prayers.* Ed. Michael W. Blastic, Jay M. Hammon, J. A. Wayne Hellmann. Studies in Early Franciscan Sources, vol. 1. St. Bonaventure, NY: Franciscan Institute Publications, 2011.

House, Adrian. *Francis of Assisi: A Revolutionary Life.* New York: Paulist, 2003.

Jan Hus (281)

(c. 1369–1415) A martyr to the causes of church reform and Czech nationalism. He emphasized personal piety and purity of life, and he condemned corruption in the clergy. He believed that church authorities could not establish doctrine contrary to Scripture. His heroic death aroused nationalistic feelings among many Czech people, who established the Hussite Church in Bohemia.

Primary Sources

From Jan Huss, *The Church* trans. David S. Schaff (New York: Scribner & Sons, 1915), 111ff.

> Because many priests abandon the imitation of Christ, the high priest, and boast of the power committed to the church, without doing works that correspond, therefore up to this time we have been speaking of the power of this kind. For they extract out of Matt. 18:16, "Whatsoever thou shalt bind on earth shall be bound in heaven," that whatsoever they do, every man ought altogether to approve. And from the words of Matt. 23:2, "The scribes and Pharisees sit on Moses' seat, therefore all things whatsoever they bid you, these do," they extract that every inferior is to obey them in all things. And so these priests clamorously apply to themselves at their own pleasure whatsoever appeals to them out of Christ's Gospel, and without any ministry of love on their own part to correspond. But what plainly calls for toil and worldly self-abnegation and the imitation of Christ, that they spurn away as something in applicable to themselves, or make believe they hold it when they do not.

> . . . the true worshippers of Christ. . . ought to resist every assumed power which seeks to remove them from the imitation of Christ by force or craft, for, in thus resisting such power we do not resist the ordinance of God but the abuse of power. And such abuse, in respect to the power of the keys, the simoniacs exercise who allege that they can either damn the deserving or loose those who are bound. . .

> This abuse of power they exercise who sell and buy the sacred orders, episcopates, canonries, and parishes—*plebanias*. They secure and sell simoniacally who make spoil out of the sacraments, living in pleasure, avarice, and luxury or who, by any other kind of criminality, defile the power of the priesthood. *The Church—Chapter XI.*

Reading Questions

What definitions for the verbs "bind" and "loose" are suggested by this text? Do you agree with Huss's admonitions about how clergy ought to use this authority?

Related Works

Fudge, Thomas A. *Jan Hus: Religious Reform and Social Revolution in Bohemia.* International Library of Historical Studies. London: Tauris, 2010.

Hus, Jan. *The Letters of John Hus.* Trans. Matthew Spinka. Totowa, NJ: Rowman and Littlefield, 1972.

Pope Innocent III (219)

(c. 1160–1216) Known for great diplomatic skills as pope. He had a great knowledge of canon as well as civil law. He believed he had unique authority as

Vicar of Christ and nullified a German kingship. In 1215 he called the Fourth Lateran Council, which confirmed the subordinate status of Jews in society by identifying them with badges and restricting them to life in ghettos.

Primary Sources

From *The Canons of the Fourth Lateran Council* (1215; Internet Medieval Sourcebook, 2013), http://www.fordham.edu/halsall/basis/lateran4.asp

Dissolute prelates—It is a matter for regret that there are some minor clerics and even prelates who spend half of the night in banqueting and in unlawful gossip, not to mention other abuses, and in giving the remainder to sleep. They are scarcely awakened by the diurnal concerts of the birds. Then they hasten through matins in a hurried and careless manner. There are others who say mass scarcely four times a year and, what is worse, do not even attend mass, and when they are present they are engaged outside in conversation with lay people to escape the silence of the choir; so that, while they readily lend their ears to unbecoming talk, they regard with utter indifference things that are divine. These and all similar things, therefore, we absolutely forbid under penalty of suspension, and strictly command in virtue of obedience that they celebrate diligently and devoutly the diurnal and nocturnal offices so far as God gives them strength

On Simony and Avarice in Clerics—It has frequently come to the ears of the Apostolic See that some clerics demand and extort money for burials, nuptial blessings, and similar things, and, if perchance their cupidity is not given satisfaction, they fraudulently interpose fictitious impediments. On the other hand, some laymen, under the pretext of piety but really on heretical grounds, strive to suppress a laudable custom introduced by the pious devotion of the faithful in behalf of the church (that is, of giving freely something for ecclesiastical services rendered). Wherefore, we forbid that such evil exactions be made in these matters, and on the other hand command that pious customs be observed, decreeing that the sacraments of the Church be administered freely and that those who endeavor maliciously to change a laudable custom be restrained by the bishops of the locality when once the truth is known.

Jews appearing in public—In some provinces a difference in dress distinguishes the Jews or Saracens from the Christians, but in certain others such a confusion has grown up that they cannot be distinguished by any difference. Thus it happens at times that through error Christians have relations with the women of Jews or Saracens, and Jews and Saracens with Christian women. Therefore, that they may not, under pretext of error of this sort, excuse themselves in the future for the excesses of such prohibited intercourse, we decree that such Jews and Saracens of both sexes in every Christian province and at all times shall be marked off in the eyes of the public from other peoples through the character of their dress. Particularly, since it may be read in the writings of Moses [Numbers

15:37-41], that this very law has been enjoined upon them.

Moreover, during the last three days before Easter and especially on Good Friday, they shall not go forth in public at all, for the reason that some of them on these very days, as we hear, do not blush to go forth better dressed and are not afraid to mock the Christians who maintain the memory of the most holy Passion by wearing signs of mourning.

This, however, we forbid most severely, that any one should presume at all to break forth in insult to the Redeemer. And since we ought not to ignore any insult to Him who blotted out our disgraceful deeds, we command that such impudent fellows be checked by the secular princes by imposing them proper punishment so that they shall not at all presume to blaspheme Him who was crucified for us.

Reading Questions

What can you discover about the behavior of clergy from these canons? What does the text reveal about the relationship between Christians and Jews in thirteenth century Europe? What sorts of underlying assumptions can you detect in this text? How do you respond to these assumptions?

RELATED WORKS

Innocent III, Pope. *Selected Letters of Pope Innocent III Concerning England (1198–1216).* Ed. C. R. Cheney and W. H. Semple. London: T. Nelson, 1953.

Moore, John C. *Pope Innocent III (1160/61–1216): To Root Up and to Plant.* Notre Dame, IN: University of Notre Dame Press, 2009.

Savonarola (284)

(1452–98) A preacher of reform who was executed for his activities. His sermons warned of judgment on the city of Florence to be followed by a golden age. He also denounced the papal court of Alexander VI.

PRIMARY SOURCES

From *A Guide to Righteous Living and Other Works* trans. Konrad Eisenbichler (Centre for Reformation and Renaissance Studies, 2003), 17.

> The reason why I entered into a religious order is this: first, the great misery of the world, the wickedness of men, the rapes, the adulteries, the thefts, the pride, the idolatry, the vile curses, for the world has come to such a state that one can no longer find anyone who does good; so much so that many times every day I would sing this verse with tears in my eyes: Alas, flee from cruel lands, flee from the shores of the greedy. I did this because I could not stand the great wickedness of the blind people of Italy, especially when I saw that virtue had been completely cast down and vice raised up.—*Letter to his father (25 April 1475)*

Reading Question

What does this letter from Savonarola reveal about his level of conviction and passion? How does this text affect your understanding of his biography—including his decision to stand against the power of the papacy?

RELATED WORKS

Savonarola, Girolamo. *Prison Meditations on Psalms 51 and 31.* Trans. and ed. John Patrick Donnelly. Milwaukee: Marquette University Press, 1994.

Weinstein, Donald. *Savonarola: The Rise and Fall of a Renaissance Prophet*. New Haven, CT: Yale University Press, 2011.

Thomas Becket (217)

(c. 1118–70) Archbishop of Canterbury. He struggled with King Henry II over the church's right to autonomy from the crown. When he was murdered after excommunicating bishops who supported the king, a cult developed around him.

PRIMARY SOURCES

From *The Constitutions of Clarendon* (1164; The Avalon Project, Yale Law School Lillian Goodman Law Library, 2013), 135, http://avalon.law.yale.edu/medieval/constcla.asp

If a controversy concerning advowson and presentation of churches arise between laymen, or between laymen and clerks, or between clerks, it shall be treated of and terminated in the court of the lord king. *Article 1*

Clerks charged and accused of anything, being summoned by the Justice of the king, shall come into his court, about to respond there for what it seems to the king's court that he should respond there; and in the ecclesiastical court for what it seems he should respond there; so that the Justice of the king shall send to the court of the holy church to see in what manner the affair will there be carried on. And if the clerk shall be convicted, or shall confess, the church ought not to protect him further. *Article 3*

It is not lawful for archbishops, bishops, and persons of the kingdom to go out of the kingdom without the permission of the lord king. And if it please the king and they go out, they shall give assurance that neither in going, nor in making a stay, nor in returning, will they seek the hurt or harm of king or kingdom. *Article 4*

Reading Question

How does this text shape your understanding of the increasing order within the ecclesial structure and of the tension between the church and the crown over the administration of this order?

RELATED WORKS

Knowles, David. *Thomas Becket*. London: Black, 1970.

Thomas, à Becket. *The Correspondence of Thomas Becket, Archbishop of Canterbury, 1162–1170*. 2 vols. Ed. and trans. Anne J. Duggan. New York: Clarendon, 2000.

William of Ockham (289)

(c. 1288–c. 1348) A critic of the papacy who was denounced as a heretic by Pope John XXII. His nominalist philosophy argued against the existence of universals. He's best known for the idea called "Ockham's razor," in which "What can be done with fewer [assumptions] is done in vain with more."

PRIMARY SOURCES

From *The Summa Logicae* (c. 1323-1326, The Logic Museum, 2013), http://www.logicmuseum.com/wiki/Authors/Ockham/Summa_Logicae

For logic is of all the arts the most fitting tool, without which no science can be completely known, which is not consumed by repeated use, in the manner of material tools, but rather admits continual increase through the diligent exercise of any other science. For just as a mechanic who lacks a complete knowledge of his tool acquires a fuller knowledge by using it, so one who is erudite in the solid principles of logic, while he diligently devotes his work to the other sciences, at the same time acquires a greater skill at this art. Hence, I regard the common saying, "The art of logic is a slippery art", as appropriate only for those pay no attention to the study of wisdom.— *Summa Logicae*, Preface.

Reading Question

This text uses the categories of art and science perhaps somewhat differently than we do now. What can you glean from this passage about how these categories are defined for William of Ockham?

Related Works

Adams, Marilyn McCord. *William Ockham*. Publications in Medieval Studies. Notre Dame, IN: Medieval Institute, University of Notre Dame, 1987.

William of Ockham. *Philosophical Writings: A Selection*. Trans. and ed. Philotheus Boehner and Stephen F. Brown. Indianapolis: Hackett, 1990.

John Wyclif (287)

(c. 1328–84) A prominent English reformer who was a philosopher at Oxford University. He attacked some of the central doctrines of the medieval church, including transubstantiation. He also initiated a new translation of the Vulgate Bible, known as the Wyclif Bible. He attracted support at Oxford with his energetic lectures; his followers became known as Lollards, who advocated making the Bible available to all people in their own language.

Primary Sources

From Stephen Lahey, *Great Medieval Thinkers: John Wyclif* (New York: Oxford University Press, 2008), 227.

I have often confessed and acknowledge that numerically the same body of Christ that was assumed from the Virgin, that suffered on the cross that [lay] dead in the tomb during the holy triduum, that rose on the third day, that ascended into heaven after forty days, and that sits forever on the right hand of God the Father, this same, I say, the same body and the same substance is truly and really the sacramental bread or consecrated host that the faithful perceive in the hands of the priest. This was established because Christ, who cannot lie, asserts as much. I do not dare to say, though, that the body of Christ is essentially, substantially, corporeally, or identically this bread. Just as the body of Christ was extended, this bread [is], but the same body is not extensionally or dimensionally this bread. *Confessio*

Reading Questions

By what evidence does Wyclif support the presence of the body of Christ in the sacramental bread of the Eucharist? What distinction does Wyclif make between essential presence and existential presence? Do these arguments seem sound to you?

Related Works

Lahey, Stephen Edmund. *John Wyclif*. Great Medieval Thinkers. New York: Oxford University Press, 2008.

Wycliffe, John. *Wyclif: Select English Writings*. Ed. Herbert E. Winn. New York: AMS, 1976.

Chapter Summaries

16. The West in Crisis

During the early Middle Ages the Eastern and Western churches became increasingly divided, while Pope Gregory the Great attempted to respond to the invasions of the Lombards by working to convert them to catholic Christianity. Clovis, king of the Franks, converted in 500, leading to an important alliance between his people and the papacy.

Meanwhile, the prophet Muhammad's religious and political successes in Arabia led to the establishment of Islam, which became a significant threat to Christianity's influence.

Other developments in the church included the revival of the church in Gaul, work by Anglo-Saxons to bring the gospel back into continental Europe, and Pope Leo III's crowning of Emperor Charlemagne. The new Carolingian Empire soon erupted in civil wars and power struggles within the church between bishops, who wanted independence, and laymen, who owned much of the land and funded the building of churches. Some efforts at reform were also made during this period. Under the Saxon king Otto I, the church was granted more autonomy over its holdings.

17. The Eastern Church

The heritage of the Eastern Orthodox Church as it is known today stretches back to the very first centuries of Christianity. It was later greatly influenced by Constantine's work to reconcile his empire and the church through ecumenical councils.

The Eastern church was marked by a rich liturgy, a significant role played by monastics, and a concern for faith founded on proper beliefs. Under Emperor Leo III and later emperors, iconoclasm ruled the day. The theological divisions between East and West continued, with a focus particularly on the *filioque*—a phrase included in the Nicene Creed but excluded in the East's version.

18. Flowering: The Western Church

Renewal of the church took hold in the eleventh century through reform of the Cluniac order, leading to new life for the monastic tradition. At the same time, despite a compromise agreement, the struggle for power between emperor and pope continued.

A series of Crusades, begun in 1095 under Pope Urban II, had some success in stopping the Turks, who had conquered Jerusalem and were threatening Constantinople. But the later Crusades lost some of the ground gained by the first and also began to target those considered heretical by the church and even some Catholic rulers.

Christian theology at this time was marked by scholasticism, a scholarly approach to the study of the Bible influenced by Greek classical thought. Allegorical interpretation of Scriptures was emphasized.

Meanwhile, popular religion featured the cult of the Virgin Mary, traffic in holy relics, and pilgrimage to holy sites.

19. Monasticism in the West

The great monasteries of the eighth to tenth centuries were the cultural and educational centers of Europe. Their large libraries included illuminated manuscripts that preserved biblical and early Christian literature.

In the early tenth century attacks from Vikings and others destroyed abbeys and dispersed their communities. The French abbey of Cluny led a reform movement that created a complex, centralized administration of monasteries.

After a period of growth and renewal, monasticism began to decline around 1200. Legal fights and financial difficulties dominated life in many religious houses.

20. The Orthodox Church in Eastern Europe and Russia

Orthodox Christianity was first introduced to Slavic peoples by two brothers, Cyril and Methodius, who also created the first written Slavic language, now called Cyrillic. The Byzantine culture that spread along with orthodox Christianity was eventually brought to Bulgaria and later other Slavic nations.

The Russian Sergius of Radonezh headed a monastic community that is now the headquarters of the Russian Orthodox Church. His leadership inspired Russians to resist Mongol rule. Ultimately, under Ivan III, Moscow became the "Third Rome," after Constantinople fell to the Ottomans.

21. An Age of Unrest

As late medieval society entered a new unstable period of economic changes and political upheavals, popes continued to challenge the authority of kings. The papacy was forced into the "Avignon Captivity" for much of the fourteenth century. Later, cardinals divided over papal candidates and elected two men, creating the Great Schism, which affected both the church and the governments of Europe.

While individual spiritual practice became more common and mysticism flourished, many voices called for reform in the church and grew louder in their criticism of the papacy. The stage was set for the Reformation era.

Additional Readings

1. From "Jews, Muslims, and Christians," chapter 9 in *A People's History of Christianity*, vol. 4, *Medieval Christianity* (Fortress Press, 2007)

Teofilo F. Ruiz discusses the complex relationships among Jews, Muslims, and Christians in medieval Spain:

In early fourteenth-century Avila, almost all the artisan trades and small shops were run by either Muslims or Jews. In a town with just over four thousand inhabitants, Jews and Muslims ran over forty different shops, including those of a locksmith, cloth seller, weavers, painters, fruit dealers, and other essential goods and services. The Jew Mossé de Dueñas and his wife, Çid Buena, sold half of their house to the dean of the city's cathedral chapter. Two other Jews, Halaf and Alazar, sold property in Avila to the dean as well. Yuzef, a Muslim, sold his stores to a Christian. . . .

The flip side of these exchanges was dark indeed. From the early thirteenth century onward until the end of the Middle Ages, the legislation of the *Cortes*, enacted at almost every meeting of these parliamentary assemblies, promoted harsh measures against the Jews and, to a lesser extent, against the Muslims. These edicts sought to segregate religious minorities from Christians, demanding types of clothing and hairstyles that would make Jews and Muslims easily identifiable as such. Jews and Muslims could not serve as nannies to Christian children, and their economic activities were severely restricted. Jews suffered the most from this, as debts to them were cancelled or reduced. Urban representatives to the *Cortes* continuously requested an end to Jewish and Muslim exemption from municipal jurisdiction and taxation. In the *Siete Partidas*, the great Roman-based legal code from the second half of the thirteenth century, the sections dealing with Jews and Muslims were particularly restrictive. In *Partida* VII, title 24, while providing the usual bans on sexual intercourse with Christians or holding Christians as slaves, evokes some of the worse aspects of anti-Jewish rhetoric, even though tempered by the requirement of proof:

And because we have heard it said that in some places Jews celebrated, and still celebrate Good Friday . . . stealing children and fastening them to crosses, and making images of wax and crucifying them, when they cannot obtain children, we order that hereafter . . . [if] anything like this is done and can be proved, all persons who were present when the act was committed shall be seized, arrested and brought before the king; and after the king ascertains that they are guilty, he shall cause them to be put to death in a disgraceful manner.

Title 25 deals with Moors in only slightly kinder fashion. Although prohibitions on sexual intercourse remained, the thrust of the law was to foster gradual conversion of Muslims to Christianity and to prevent Christian conversion to Islam. The constant reissuing of these legal measures tells us that they were not easily enforced, but nonetheless something had changed for the worse. . . .

On the whole, as Castile and the Crown of Aragon sank into civil wars, demographic dislocations, social upheavals, and severe economic downturns, attitudes toward Jews and Muslims hardened. There were, of course, some important nuances. The antagonism against Jews was quite different from that against Muslims. Moreover, not all social groups shared equally in the hatred of religious minorities. One could say that the high nobility, clerical dignitaries, and the Crown were generally far less hostile than the lower classes. The bourgeoisie and urban middle class were in constant competition with Jews for control of financial resources, and they spearheaded the petitions against the Jews at the meetings of the *Cortes*.

QUESTIONS FOR DISCUSSION AND REFLECTION

How did the laws of the medieval Spanish parliament reflect the influence of the Crusades? (Review Part 3, chapter 18, pages 231–33.) What can you conclude from this text about the interaction of religion and economic power in medieval Spain?

2. From *Peter Abelard's "Ethics"* (Clarendon Press, 1971)

That a work is good by reason of a good intention

... When the same thing is done by the same man at different times, by the diversity of his intention, however, his action is now said to be good, now bad, and so it seems to fluctuate around the good and the bad, just as this proposition 'Socrates is seated' or the idea of it fluctuates around the true and the false, Socrates being at one time seated, at another standing. Aristotle says that the way in which this change in fluctuating around the true and the false happens here is not that what changes between being true and being false undergoes anything by this change, but that the subject, that is Socrates, himself moves from sitting to standing or vice versa.

Whence an intention should be said to be good

There are those who think that an intention is good or right whenever someone believes he is acting well and that what he does is pleasing to God, like the persecutors of the martyrs mentioned by Truth in the Gospel: 'The hour cometh that whosoever killeth you will think that he doth a service to God.' The Apostle had compassion for the ignorance of such as these when he said: 'I bear them witness that they have a zeal for God, but not according to knowledge,' that is, they have great fervour and desire in doing what they believe to be pleasing to God. But because they are led astray in this by the zeal or the eagerness of their minds, their intention is in error and the eye of their heart is not simple so it cannot see clearly, that is, guard itself against error. ... And so an intention should not be called good because it seems to be good but because in addition it is just as it is thought to be, that is, when, believing that one's objective is pleasing to God, one is in no way deceived in one's own estimation. Otherwise even the unbelievers themselves would have good works just like ourselves, since the deceived no less than we, believe they will be saved or will please God through their works.

QUESTIONS FOR DISCUSSION AND REFLECTION

What theological and ethical assumptions is Abelard questioning here? What features of his argument would you identify with scholasticism?

See also "Reading Historical Documents" (page 171 in this volume) for other questions to consider.

3. From Julian of Norwich, "In Our Mother Christ We Profit and Mature," chapter 11 in *Mystics, Visionaries, and Prophets: A Historical Anthology of Women's Spiritual Writings* (Fortress Press, 2004)

Editor Shawn Madigan tells us that little is known about Julian of Norwich, an anchorite and Christian mystic. She received revelations successively over the course of a day and night after nearly dying from an infection. She reflected on the meaning of the revelations for at least twenty years. According to Madigan, "The joyful hope that weaves through Julian's presentation of God was needed in this century. . . . To an age of anxiety about sudden death and the possibility of hell, Julian could write with assurance, 'God loves us and delights in us . . . all shall be well' " (191).

The following is an excerpt from "In Our Mother Christ We Profit and Mature" (197–200):

I saw the lord sitting in state and the servant standing respectfully before his lord, and in this servant there is a double significance, one outward, the other inward. Outwardly, he was simply dressed like a laborer, prepared to work, and he stood very close to the lord, not immediately in front of him but a little to one side, and that on the left; his clothing was a white tunic, scanty, old and all worn, dyed with the sweat of his body, tight fitting and short, as if it were a hand's breadth below his knee, looking threadbare as if it would soon be worn out, ready to go to rags and to tear.

And in this I was much amazed, thinking, "This is not fitting clothing for a servant so greatly loved to stand in before so honorable a lord." And, inwardly, there was shown in him a foundation of love, the love which he had for the lord, which was equal to the love which the lord had for him. . . .

In the servant is included the second person of the Trinity, and in the servant is included Adam, that is to say, all humanity. And therefore when I say "the Son," that means the divinity which is equal to the Father, and when I say "the servant," that means Christ's humanity, which is the true Adam. . . .

And so I saw that God rejoices that he is our Father, and God rejoices that he is our Mother, and God rejoices that he is our true spouse, and that our soul is his beloved wife. And Christ rejoices that he is our brother, and Jesus rejoices that he is our Savior. . . .

My understanding accepted that our substance is in God, that is to say, that God is God, and our substance is a creature in God. For the almighty Truth of the Trinity is our Father, for God made us and keeps us. And the deep Wisdom of the Trinity is our Mother, in whom we are enclosed. And the high Goodness of the Trinity is our Lord, and in him we are enclosed and he in us. We are enclosed in the Father and we are enclosed in the Son and we are enclosed in the Holy Spirit. And the Father is enclosed in us and the Son is enclosed in us and the Holy Spirit is enclosed in us.

Questions for Discussion and Reflection

How would you characterize Julian's idea of the Trinity? Can you identify any influences on her from leading Christian thinkers of her time mentioned in the main text?

See also "Reading Historical Documents" (page 171 in this volume) for other questions to consider.

Selected Online Resources

▶ The International Joan of Arc Society—links to articles, film clips and music, course syllabi, and bibliographies about Joan of Arc (1412–1431)
http://www.smu.edu/ijas/index.html

▶ "Crusades"—a University of Boise professor's collection of online material related to the Crusades, including essays, maps, and a bibliography
http://europeanhistory.boisestate.edu/crusades/contents.shtml

▶ "Jesuits and Dominicans Square Off Anew Over Savonarola"—an article from the *National Catholic Reporter* (January 22, 1999) about the controversy arising from an effort to beatify Savonarola
http://natcath.org/NCR_Online/archives2/1999a/012299/012299g.htm

▶ "The Murder of Thomas Becket, 1170"—a brief biographical essay followed by a contemporary account of the murder by a monk who claimed to have witnessed it
http://www.eyewitnesstohistory.com/becket.htm

▶ "Peter Abelard: *Historia Calamitatum*"—an autobiographical essay by Abelard (part of the online Medieval Sourcebook) in which he recounts his intellectual as well as personal adventures in Paris and elsewhere
http://www.fordham.edu/halsall/basis/abelard-histcal.asp

▶ "Icons and Iconoclasm in Byzantium"—brief discussion with links to photos of icons in the Metropolitan Museum of Art
http://www.metmuseum.org/toah/hd/icon/hd_icon.htm

▶ "Salisbury Cathedral"—extensive gallery of photographs of the interior and exterior of a medieval English cathedral
http://www.salisburycathedral.org.uk/gallery.php

▶ "Art of the Crusades Era"—photo essay on late Romanesque and early Gothic art as well as Islamic art of the period
http://www.umich.edu/~eng415/topics/art/art-article.html

Guide to Part 4: Reform and Renewal

Key Terms

The number in parentheses refers to the page where the term is explained. Those terms marked with asterisks also appear in the Glossary.

Catholic/Counter Reformation (293)* The revival and reform of the Roman Catholic Church as a reaction to the Reformation. Its reforms included those of the Council of Trent (1562–63).

Council of Constance (280) Assembly of Christian bishops held from 1414 to 1418, examining the administration of the Eucharist and other political matters, and accomplishing significant healing between branches of the church—culminating in an end to the three-popes controversy by the election of Pope Martin V.

***Devotio Moderna* (300)** The "modern way of serving God" (Latin). A spiritual revival that began within the Catholic Church in the late fourteenth century and strongly emphasized both personal devotion and social involvement.

humanism/humanist (296)* Way of life based on the belief that what is good for human beings is the highest good.

indulgence (304–6)* The remission by the Christian church of a period of correction in purgatory.

justification by faith (310–11)* The Protestant belief that salvation is achieved by repentance and faith in Jesus Christ.

Neoplatonism (298)* Religious and philosophical movement from the third to the sixth centuries CE. It used the teachings of Plato as a basis for ascetic practices and mystical experience. Its principal architect was Plotinus.

predestination (311)* The doctrine associated with Calvin that claims God has determined the fate of all creatures: eternal damnation or eternal reward has already been decided for every individual.

priesthood of believers (312) A principle of the Protestant Reformation rejecting the idea that authority rested in an exclusive priesthood. Rather than two levels of Christian, spiritual and lay, a common status before God is given to all people.

Protestantism (308)*   Christian faith and order as based on the principles of the Reformation. It emphasizes the sole authority of the Bible, justification by faith, and the priesthood of all believers. Since the nineteenth century it has also embraced liberal trends that have stressed the subjective side of religion.

purgatory (305)*   In Roman Catholic teaching, the temporary state of punishment and purification for the dead before their admission to heaven. Its existence was denied by the Protestant reformers.

Puritanism (323)*   Reform movement within Elizabethan and Stuart Protestantism.

Key Personalities

Numbers in parentheses refer to the pages where the text provides the individual's biographical details and historical significance.

Theodore Beza (316)

(1519–1605) A Reformation leader who succeeded John Calvin. He produced new versions of the Greek and Latin New Testament, which became a source for the King James Bible. Under his leadership, Geneva became the center of Reformed Protestantism.

PRIMARY SOURCES

From Theodore Beza, *The Life of John Calvin*, trans. Henry Beveridge, (Philadelphia: Westminster Press, 1909), 4-5.

> Let men, therefore, (both those who believe through ignorance, and those who so speak from malice,) cry out, that Luther,

Zuinglius, and Calvin, are regarded by us as gods, though we are continually charging the worshippers of saints with idolatry; let them, I say, cry out as much and as long as they please,—we are prepared with our answer, viz., that to commemorate the labours which holy men have undertaken in behalf of religion, together with their words and actions, (through the knowledge of which the good become better, while the wicked are reproved, our only aim in this kind of composition,) is a very different thing from doing as they do, when they either bring disgrace on the lives of men who were truly pious, by narratives not less impious than childish, (as an obscure individual called Abdias did with the history of the Apostles,) or compose fabulous histories filled with the vilest falsehoods, (they, in their barbarous jargon, call them Golden Legends, I call them abominable trash,) and endeavor, moreover, to bring back the idols of the ancient Gods, the only difference being a change of name.

Reading Questions

How would you characterize the tone of this text? What might Beza's words reveal to you about the overall tone of the Reformation debates?

RELATED WORKS

Beza, Theodore. *A Little Book of Christian Questions and Responses in Which the Principal Headings of the Christian Religion Are Briefly Set Forth.* Trans. Kirk M. Summers. Allison Park, PA: Pickwick, 1986.

Franklin, Julian H., trans. and ed. *Constitutionalism and Resistance in the Sixteenth Century: Three*

Treatises by Hotman, Beza, & Mornay. New York: Pegasus, 1969.

Martin Bucer (321)

(1491–1551) A reformer based in Strasbourg. He worked on uniting the German and Swiss Reformed churches and wrote a number of biblical commentaries.

PRIMARY SOURCES

From *Melancthon and Bucer* edited by Wilhelm Pauck, Library of Christian Classics (Philadelphia, Westminster Press, 1969), 236ff.

> Where, therefore the sovereignty of Christ is truly and fully received, there also what they have described should be restored, the administration of both sacraments according to the precepts of Christ and the example of the early apostolic Church. Hence for the more reverent and salutary presentation of these sacraments to the faithful, it is clearly fitting that they should not be presented except when the whole church or the greater part of it is gathered together and irreligious and unworthy persons removed, so that all present, as they know that through communion with Christ offered them in the Holy Supper. For those who do not seek to live and dwell in Christ the Lord nor for him to live and dwell in them (cf. John 15:4) ought not even to gaze upon these sacred mysteries but should be altogether excluded from the sacred assembly. *De Regno Christi*

Reading Questions

What, according to Bucer, makes a person worthy to receive the sacrament of communion? What values and priorities seem to be at stake for Bucer as he makes his arguments here?

RELATED WORKS

Bucer, Martin. *Common Places of Martin Bucer.* Trans. and ed. D. F. Wright. Appleford, UK: Sutton Courtenay, 1972.

Pauck, Wilhelm. *Melanchthon and Bucer.* Philadelphia: Westminster, 1969.

John Calvin (306–7)

(1509–64) French theologian who organized the Reformation from Geneva. He was influenced by the teachings of Luther. Considered a great systematizer, he encountered resistance when he tried to place all Genevans under the church's authority. In his theological writings he emphasized justification by faith and the sole authority of the Bible; he declared that each person's eternal destiny was decided irrevocably by God, and only those destined for salvation would come to faith.

PRIMARY SOURCES

From *Tracts Relating to the Reformation,* Volume 1, translated by Henry Beveridge (Edinburgh; Calvin Translation society, 1844) 183-184, 211, 215-216, 233-234 and *On the Christian Life,* trans. Henry Beveridge (1845; Christian Classics Ethereal Library, 2013), 36, http://www.ccel.org/ccel/calvin/chr_life .pdf and *Selected Works of John Calvin: Tracts and Letters,* edited by Henry Beveridge and Jules Bonnet (1545-1553; Center for Reformed Theology and Apologetics, 2013), http://www.reformed.org /ethics/index.html?mainframe=/ethics/calvin_to _somerset.html.

> When Luther at first appeared, he merely touched, with a gentle hand, a few abuses of the grossest description, now grown

intolerable. And he did it with a modesty which intimated that he had more desire to see them corrected, than determination to correct them himself. The opposite party forthwith sounded to arms; and when the contention was more and more inflamed, our enemies deemed it the best and shortest method to suppress the truth by cruelty and violence. Accordingly, when our people challenged them to friendly discussion, and desired to settle disputes by calm arguments, they were cruelly persecuted with sanguinary edicts, until matters have been brought to the present miserable pass. . .

The last and principle charge which they bring against us is, that we have made a schism in the church. And here they boldly maintain against us, that in no case is it lawful to break the unity of the church. How far they do us injustice, the books of our authors bear witness. Now, however, let them take this brief reply—that we neither dissent from the church, nor are aliens from her communion. . .

Let our opponents, then, in the first instance, draw near to Christ, and then let them convict us of schism, in daring to dissent from them in doctrine. But, since I have made it plain, that Christ is banished from their society, and the doctrine of his gospel exterminated, their charge against us simply amounts to this, that we adhere to Christ in preference to them. For what man, pray, will believe that those who refuse to be led away from Christ and his truth, in order to deliver themselves into the power of men, are thereby schismatics, and deserters from the communion of the church? . . .

In regard to ourselves, whatever be the event, we will always be supported, in the sight of God, by the consciousness that we have desired both to promote his glory and do good in his church; that we have labored faithfully for that end; that, in short, we have done what we could. Our conscience tells us, that in all our wishes, and all our endeavors, we have had no other aim. And we have essayed, by clear proof, to testify the fact. And, certainly, while we feel assured that we both care for and do the work of the Lord, we are also confident, that he will by no means be wanting, either to himself or to it. . .

But be the issue what it may, we will never repent of having begun, and of having proceeded thus far. The Holy Spirit is a faithful and unerring witness to our doctrine. We know, I say, that it is the eternal truth of God that we preach. We are, indeed, desirous, as we ought to be, that our ministry may prove salutary to the world; but to give it this effect belongs to God, not to us. If, to punish, partly the ingratitude, and partly the stubbornness of those to whom we desire to do good, success must prove desperate, and all things go to worse, I will say what it befits a Christian man to say, and what all who are true to this holy profession will subscript: We will die, but in death even be conquerors, not only because through it we shall have a sure passage to a better life, but because we know that our blood will be as seed to propagate the Divine truth which men now despise. *The Necessity of Reforming the Church*

Reading Questions

Review the article about John Calvin on pages 306-307 of your textbook. What do you learn there about the influence of Luther on Calvin? Can you detect any Lutheran influence in this text from Calvin?

. . . the Lord enjoins every one of us, in all the actions of life, to have respect to our own calling. He knows the boiling restlessness of the human mind, the fickleness with which it is borne hither and thither, its eagerness to hold opposites at one time in its grasp, its ambition. Therefore, lest all things should be thrown into confusion by our folly and rashness, he has assigned distinct duties to each in the different modes of life. And that no one may presume to overstep his proper limits, he has distinguished the different modes of life by the name of callings. Every man's mode of life, therefore, is a kind of station assigned him by the Lord, that he may not be always driven about at random. So necessary is this distinction, that all our actions are thereby estimated in his sight, and often in a very different way from that in which human reason or philosophy would estimate them. There is no more illustrious deed even among philosophers than to free one's country from tyranny, and yet the private individual who stabs the tyrant is openly condemned by the voice of the heavenly Judge. But I am unwilling to dwell on particular examples; it is enough to know that in every thing the call of the Lord is the foundation and beginning of right action. He who does not act with reference to it will never, in the discharge of duty, keep the right path. He will sometimes be able, perhaps, to give the semblance of something laudable, but whatever it may be in the sight of man, it will be rejected before the throne of God; and besides, there will be no harmony in the different parts of his life. Hence,

he only who directs his life to this end will have it properly framed; because free from the impulse of rashness, he will not attempt more than his calling justifies, knowing that it is unlawful to overleap the prescribed bounds. He who is obscure will not decline to cultivate a private life, that he may not desert the post at which God has placed him. Again, in all our cares, toils, annoyances, and other burdens, it will be no small alleviation to know that all these are under the superintendence of God. The magistrate will more willingly perform his office, and the father of a family confine himself to his proper sphere. Every one in his particular mode of life will, without repining, suffer its inconveniences, cares, uneasiness, and anxiety, persuaded that God has laid on the burden. This, too, will afford admirable consolation, that in following your proper calling, no work will be so mean and sordid as not to have a splendour and value in the eye of God. *On the Christian Life, Chapter 5*

Reading Questions

What does Calvin mean when he uses the word "calling" in this text? In what ways is this related to his role as a leader of the church? In what ways is it not?

. . . I come now to the last point, which concerns the chastisement of vice and the repression of scandals. I have no doubt that there are laws and statutes of the kingdom both good and laudable, to keep the people within the bounds of decency. But the great and boundless licentiousness which I see everywhere throughout the world, constrains me to beseech you, that you would earnestly turn your attention to keeping men within the restraint of sound and wholesome discipline. That, above all, you would hold yourself charged, for the honor of God, to punish those crimes of which men have been in the habit of making no very great account. I speak of this, because some times larcenies, assault, and extortions are more severely punished, because thereby men are wronged; whereas they will tolerate whoredom and adultery, drunkenness, and blaspheming of the name of God, as if these were things quite allowable, or at least of very small importance. Let us hear, however, what God thinks of them. He proclaims aloud, how precious his name is unto him. Meanwhile, it is as if torn in pieces and trampled under foot. It can never be that he will allow such shameful reproach to remain unpunished. More than this, Scripture clearly points out to us, that by reason of blasphemies a whole country is defiled. As concerning adulteries, we who call ourselves Christians, ought to take great shame to ourselves that even the heathen have exercised greater rigor in their punishment of such than we do, seeing even that some among us only laugh at them. When holy matrimony, which ought to be a lively image of the sacred union which we have with the Son of God, is polluted, and the covenant, which ought to stand more firm and indissoluble than any in this world, is disloyally rent asunder, if we do not lay to heart that sin against God, it is a token that our zeal for God is very low indeed. As for whoredom, it ought to be quite enough for us that St. Paul compares it to sacrilege, inasmuch as by its means the temples of God, which our bodies are, are profaned. Be it

remembered also, that whoremongers and drunkards are banished from the kingdom of God, on such terms that we are forbidden to converse with them, whence it clearly follows, that they ought not to be endured in the Church. We see herein the cause why so many rods of judgment are at this very day lifted up over the earth. For the more easily men pardon themselves in such enormities, the more certainly will God take vengeance on them. Therefore, to prevent his wrath, I entreat of you, Monseigneur, to hold a tight rein, and to take order, that those who hear the doctrine of the Gospel, approve their Christianity by a life of holiness. For as doctrine is the soul of the Church for quickening, so discipline and the correction of vices are like the nerves to sustain the body in a state of health and vigor. The duty of bishops and curates is to keep watch over that, to the end that the Supper of our Lord may not be polluted by people of scandalous lives. But in the authority where God has set you, the chief responsibility returns upon you, who have a special charge given you to set the others in motion, on purpose that every one discharge himself of duty, and diligently to look to it, that the order which shall have been established may be duly observed.

Now, Monseigneur, agreeably to the protestation which I made above, I shall make no further excuse, neither of the tiresomeness of my letter, nor on account of my having thus freely laid open to you what I had so much at heart. For I feel assured that my affection is well known to you, while in your wisdom, and as you are well versed in the Holy Scriptures, you perceive from what fountain I have drawn all that is herein contained. Wherefore, I do not fear to have been troublesome or importunate to you, in making manifest, according as I could, the hearty desire I have that the name of God may always be more and more glorified by you, which is my daily supplication; beseeching him that he would please to increase his grace in you, to confirm you by his Spirit in a true unconquerable constancy, upholding you against all enemies, having yourself with your whole household under his holy protection, enabling you successfully to administer the charge which is committed to you, that so the King may have whereof to praise this gracious God for having had such a governor in his childhood, both for his person and for his kingdom.

Whereupon I shall make an end, Monseigneur, very humbly commending me to your kind favor *From a letter (229) to Protector Somerset, 22ⁿᵈ October 1548*

Reading Questions

What do you imagine were Calvin's goals in writing this letter? What can you surmise about the community in which Calvin lived based on this text?

RELATED WORKS

Calvin, Jean. *Institution of the Christian Religion.* Trans. Ford Lewis Battles. Atlanta: John Knox, 1975.

Parker, T. H. L. *John Calvin: A Biography.* Rev. ed. Louisville, KY: Westminster John Knox, 2007.

John of the Cross (355)

(1542–91) Spanish mystic who co-founded a reformed Carmelite convent with Teresa of Avila (see below). His mystical writings discuss how the soul can achieve union with God.

PRIMARY SOURCES

From *The Ascent of Mount Carmel* (1578-1579; Christian Classics Ethereal Library, 2013), 64-65, http://www.ccel.org/ccel/john_cross/ascent.pdf

ALL the doctrine whereof I intend to treat in this Ascent of Mount Carmel is included in the following stanzas, and in them is also described the manner of ascending to the summit of the Mount, which is the high estate of perfection which we here call union of the soul with God. And because I must continually base upon them that which I shall say, I have desired to set them down here together, to the end that all the substance of that which is to be written may be seen and comprehended together; although it will be fitting to set down each stanza separately before expounding it, and likewise the lines of each stanza, according as the matter and the exposition require. The poem, then, runs as follows:

Wherein the soul sings of the happy chance which it had in passing through the dark night of faith, in detachment and purgation of itself, to union with the Beloved.

1. On a dark night, Kindled in love with yearnings—oh, happy chance!—

I went forth without being observed, My house being now at rest.

2. In darkness and secure, By the secret ladder, disguised—oh, happy chance!—

In darkness and in concealment, My house being now at rest.

3. In the happy night, In secret, when none saw me,

Nor I beheld aught, Without light or guide, save that which burned in my heart.

4. This light guided me More surely than the light of noonday,

To the place where he (well I knew who!) was awaiting me—A place where none appeared.

5. Oh, night that guided me, Oh, night more lovely than the dawn,

Oh, night that joined Beloved with lover, Lover transformed in the Beloved!

6. Upon my flowery breast, Kept wholly for himself alone,

There he stayed sleeping, and I caressed him, And the fanning of the cedars made a breeze.

7. The breeze blew from the turret As I parted his locks;

With his gentle hand he wounded my neck And caused all my senses to be suspended.

8. I remained, lost in oblivion; My face I reclined on the Beloved.

All ceased and I abandoned myself, Leaving my cares forgotten among the lilies.

Reading Questions

How does the introduction to this poem color your reading of the poem itself? What does this poem reveal to you about the themes of sixteenth century mysticism?

RELATED WORKS

Howells, Edward. *John of the Cross and Teresa of Avila: Mystical Knowing and Selfhood*. New York: Crossroad, 2002.

John of the Cross, Saint. *John of the Cross: Selected Writings*. Ed. Kieran Kavanaugh. New York: Paulist, 1987.

Thomas Cranmer (322)

(1489–1556) Archbishop of Canterbury under Henry VIII who helped overthrow papal authority in England and created a new order of English worship in his *Book of Common Prayer* of 1549 and 1552.

PRIMARY SOURCES

From Thomas Cranmer, *Preface to the Great Bible (1540)* in Gerald Bray, *Documents of the English Reformation*, (Minneapolis: Fortress Press 1994).

Wherefore, in few words to comprehend the largeness and utility of the Scripture, how it containeth fruitful instruction and erudition for every man; if any things be necessary to be learned, of the Holy Scripture we may learn it. If falsehood should be reproved, thereof we may gather wherewithal. If anything to be corrected and amended, if there need be any exhortation or consolation, of the Scripture we may well learn. In the Scriptures be the fat pastures of the soul; therein is no venomous meat, no unwholesome thing; they be the very dainty and pure feeding. He that is ignorant shall find there what he should learn. He that is a perverse sinner shall there find his damnation to make him to tremble for fear. He that laboreth to serve God shall find there his glory, and the promissions of eternal life, exhorting him more diligently to labor. Herein may princes learn how to govern their subjects; subjects, obedience, love and dread to their princes; husbands, how they should behave them unto their wives; how to educate their children and servants; and contrary the wives, children, and servants may know their duty to their husbands, parents, and masters. Here may all manner of persons, men, women, young, old, learned, unlearned, rich, poor, priests, laymen, lords, ladies, officers, tenants, and mean men, virgins, wives, widows, lawyers, merchants, artificers, husbandmen, and all manner of persons, of what estate or condition soever they be, may in this book learn all things what they ought to believe, what they ought to do, and what they should not do, as well concerning almighty God, as also concerning themselves and all other. Briefly, to the reading of Scripture none can be enemy, but that either be so sick that they love not to hear of any medicine, or else that be so ignorant that they know not Scripture to be the most healthful medicine.

Therefore, as touching this former part, I will here conclude and take it as a conclusion sufficiently determined and approved, that it is convenient and good the Scripture to be read of all sorts and kinds of people, and in the vulgar tongue, without further allegations and probations for the same . . . specifically now that the King's Highness, being supreme head next under Christ of this Church of England, hath approved with his royal assent the setting forth hereof, which only to all true and obedient subjects ought to be a sufficient reason for the allowance of the same, without further delay, reclamation, or resistance, although there were no preface nor other reason herein expressed.

Reading Questions

Can you construct a description of Cranmer's *theology of scripture*—the way in which he interprets the Bible and upholds its authority?

Related Works

Cranmer, Thomas. *Selected Writings*. Ed. Carl S. Meyer. London: SPCK, 1961.

MacCulloch, Diarmaid. *Thomas Cranmer: A Life*. New Haven, CT: Yale University Press, 1998.

George Fox (359–60)

(1624–91) An English dissenter and the founder of the Religious Society of Friends (the Quakers). A spiritual vision led him to proclaim Christ as liberator from sin. He advocated for religious freedom in England.

Primary Sources

From George Fox, *The Autobiography of George Fox*, edited by Rufus M. Jones, (Christian Classics Ethereal Library, 2013), 97-98, 104-106, http://www.ccel.org/ccel/fox_g/autobio.pdf

About this time the priests and professors fell to prophesying against us afresh. They had said long before that we should be destroyed within a month; and after that, they prolonged the time to half a year. But that time being long expired, and we mightily increased in number, they now gave forth that we would eat out one another. For often after meetings many tender people, having a great way to go, tarried at Friends' houses by the way, and sometimes more than there were beds to lodge in; so that some lay on the hay-mows. Hereupon Cain's fear possessed the professors and world's people; for they were afraid that when we had eaten one another out, we should all come to be maintained by the parishes, and be chargeable to them.

But after awhile, when they saw that the Lord blessed and increased Friends, as he did Abraham, both in the field and in the basket, at their goings forth and their comings in, at their risings up and their lyings down, and that all things prospered with them; then they saw the falseness of all their prophecies against us, and that it was in vain to curse whom God had blessed.

At the first convincement, when Friends could not put off their hats to peo-ple, or say You to a single person, but Thou and Thee;—when they could not bow, or use flattering words in salutation, or adopt the fashions and customs of the world, many Friends, that were tradesmen of sev-eral sorts, lost their customers at first, for the people were shy of them, and would not trade with them; so that for a time some Friends could hardly get money enough to buy bread.

But afterwards, when people came to have experience of Friends' honesty and faithfulness, and found that their yea was yea, and their nay was nay; that they kept to a word in their dealings, and would not cozen and cheat, but that if a child were

sent to their shops for anything, he was as well used as his parents would have been;—then the lives and conversation of Friends did preach, and reached to the witness of God in the people.

Then things altered so, that all the inquiry was, "Where is there a draper, or shop-keeper, or tailor, or shoemaker, or any other tradesman, that is a Quaker?" Insomuch that Friends had more trade than many of their neighbours, and if there was any trading, they had a great part of it. Then the envious professors altered their note, and began to cry out, "If we let these Quakers alone, they will take the trade of the nation out of our hands."

This has been the Lord's doing to and for His people! which my desire is that all who profess His holy truth may be kept truly sensible of, and that all may be pre-served in and by His power and Spirit, faithful to God and man. Faithful first to God, in obeying Him in all things; and next in doing unto all men that which is just and righteous in all things, that the Lord God maybe glorified in their practising truth, holiness, godliness, and righteous-ness amongst people in all their lives and conversation.

. . . The next morning I was moved of the Lord to write a paper to the Protector, Oliver Cromwell; wherein I did, in the pres-ence of the Lord God, declare that I denied the wearing or drawing of a carnal sword, or any other outward weapon, against him or any man; and that I was sent of God to stand a witness against all violence, and against the works of darkness; and to turn people from darkness to light; and to bring them from the causes of war and fighting, to the peaceable gospel. When I had written what the Lord had given me to write, I set my name to it, and gave it to Captain Drury to hand to Oliver Cromwell, which he did.

After some time Captain Drury brought me before the Protector himself at Whitehall. It was in a morning, before he was dressed, and one Harvey, who had come a little among Friends, but was disobedient, waited upon him. When I came in I was moved to say, "Peace be in this house"; and I exhorted him to keep in the fear of God, that he might receive wisdom from Him, that by it he might be directed, and order all things under his hand to God's glory.

I spoke much to him of Truth, and much discourse I had with him about religion; wherein he carried himself very moderately. But he said we quarrelled with priests, whom he called ministers. I told him I did not quarrel with them, but that they quarrelled with me and my friends. "But," said I, "if we own the prophets, Christ, and the apostles, we cannot hold up such teachers, prophets, and shepherds, as the prophets, Christ, and the apostles declared against; but we must declare against them by the same power and Spirit."

Then I showed him that the prophets, Christ, and the apostles declared freely, and against them that did not declare freely; such as preached for filthy lucre, and divined for money, and preached for hire, and were covetous and greedy, that

could never have enough; and that they that have the same spirit that Christ, and the prophets, and the apostles had, could not but declare against all such now, as they did then. As I spoke, he several times said, it was very good, and it was truth. I told him that all Christendom (so called) had the Scriptures, but they wanted the power and Spirit that those had who gave forth the Scriptures; and that was the reason they were not in fellowship with the Son, nor with the Father, nor with the Scriptures, nor one with another.

Many more words I had with him; but people coming in, I drew a little back. As I was turning, he caught me by the hand, and with tears in his eyes said, "Come again to my house; for if thou and I were but an hour of a day together, we should be nearer one to the other"; adding that he wished me no more ill than he did to his own soul. I told him if he did he wronged his own soul; and admonished him to hearken to God's voice, that he might stand in his counsel, and obey it; and if he did so, that would keep him from hardness of heart; but if he did not hear God's voice, his heart would be hardened. He said it was true.

Then I went out; and when Captain Drury came out after me he told me the Lord Protector had said I was at liberty, and might go whither I would.

Then I was brought into a great hall, where the Protector's gentlemen were to dine. I asked them what they brought me thither for. They said it was by the Protector's order, that I might dine with them. I bid them let the Protector know that I would not eat of his bread, nor drink of his drink. When he heard this he said, "Now I see there is a people risen that I cannot win with gifts or honours, offices or places; but all other sects and people I can." It was told him again that we had forsaken our own possessions; and were not like to look for such things from him.

Reading Questions

How does the text depict the lives of those who are religious dissenters? How does Fox differentiate himself (and those in his community) from other "sects and people"?

RELATED WORKS

Fox, George. *The Journal.* Ed. Nigel Smith. London: Penguin, 1998.

Hinds, Hilary. *George Fox and Early Quaker Culture.* Manchester, UK: Manchester University Press, 2011.

Ignatius of Loyola (347)

(1491–1556) The founder of the Jesuits. He became "Christ's soldier" in 1521 and wrote *Spiritual Exercises*, a four-week retreat focused on devotional meditation.

PRIMARY SOURCES

From Ignatius of Loyola, *The Spiritual Exercises,* trans. Father Elder Mullan, (1522-1524; Christian Classics Ethereal Library, 2013), 24, http://www.ccel.org/ccel/ignatius/exercises.pdf

Man is created to praise, reverence, and serve God our Lord, and by this means to save his soul.

And the other things on the face of the earth are created for man and that they may

help him in prosecuting the end for which he is created.

From this it follows that man is to use them as much as they help him on to his end, and ought to rid himself of them so far as they hinder him as to it.

For this it is necessary to make ourselves indifferent to all created things in all that is allowed to the choice of our free will and is not prohibited to it; so that, on our part, we want not health rather than sickness, riches rather than poverty, honor rather than dishonor, long rather than short life, and so in all the rest; desiring and choosing only what is most conducive for us to the end for which we are created. *Week One—Principle and Foundation*

Reading Question

What underlying assumptions about the worth and purpose of human life can you detect from this text? Do you agree with these assumptions?

RELATED WORKS

Ignatius, of Loyola. *The Constitutions of the Society of Jesus.* Trans. George E. Ganss. St. Louis: Institute of Jesuit Sources, 1970.

McManamon, John M. *The Text and Contexts of Ignatius Loyola's "Autobiography."* New York: Fordham University Press, 2013.

Martin Luther (304–5)

(1483–1546) Founder of the German Reformation; author of the Ninety-Five Theses, which criticized the church's sale of indulgences and its general materialism. He publicized his views in disputations and treatises and faced condemnation and ultimately excommunication. He translated the New

Testament into German and wrote or co-authored various doctrinal and creedal statements, such as the Small Catechism and the Schmalkald Articles, which became foundational to the Lutheran movement. He held that people could be justified before God only by faith in Jesus Christ, not by good works, and thus the mediating role of the priest and church are unnecessary.

PRIMARY SOURCES

From *Luther's Primary Works,* edited by Henry Wace and C.A. Buchheim (London: Hodder and Stoughton, 1896).

> The Romanists have very cleverly surrounded themselves with three walls, which have protected them till now in such a way that no one could reform them. As a result, the whole of Christendom has suffered woeful corruption. In the first place, when under threat of secular force, they have stood firm and declared that secular force had no jurisdiction over them; rather the opposite was the case, and the spiritual was superior to the secular. In the second place, when the Holy Scriptures have been used to reprove them, they have responded that no one except the pope was competent to expound Scripture. In the third place, when threatened with a council, they have pretended that no one but the pope could summon a council. In this way, they have adroitly nullified these three means of correction, and avoided punishment. Thus they still remain in secure possession of these three walls, and practice all the villainy and wickedness we see today. . .
>
> May God now help us, and give us one of those trumpets with which the walls of Jericho were overthrown; that we may blow away these walls of paper and straw, and set free the Christian, corrective measures to punish sin, and to bring the devil's deceits and wiles to the light of day. In this way, may we be reformed through suffering and again receive God's blessing.
>
> Let us begin by attacking the first wall. To call popes, bishops, priests, monks and nuns, the religious class, but princes, lords, artisans, and farm workers the secular class, is a specious device invented by certain time-servers; but no one ought to be frightened by it, and for good reason. For all Christians whatsoever really and truly belong to the religious class, and there is no difference among them except in so far as they do different work. That is St. Paul's meaning, in 1 Corinthians 12:12f., when he says, "We are all one body, yet each member hath his own work for serving others." This applies to us all, because we have one baptism, one gospel, one faith, and are all equally Christian. For baptism, gospel, and faith alone make men religious, and create a Christian people. When a pope or bishop anoints, grants, tonsures, ordains, consecrates, dresses differently from laymen, he may make a hypocrite of a man, or an anointed image, but never a Christian or a spiritually minded man. The fact is that our baptism consecrates us all without exception, and makes us all priests. As St. Peter says, 1 Peter 2:9, "You are a royal priesthood and a realm of priests," and Revelation, "Thou has made us priests and kings by thy blood" (Rev. 5:9f.). if we ourselves as Christians did not receive a higher

consecration than that given by pope or bishop, then no one would be made priest even by consecration at the hands of pope or bishop; nor would anyone be authorized to celebrate Eucharist, or preach, or pronounce absolution.

When a bishop consecrates, he simply acts on behalf of the entire congregation, all of whom have the same authority. They may select one of their number and command him to exercise this authority on behalf of the others. It would be similar if ten brothers, king's sons and equal heirs, were to choose one of themselves to rule the kingdom for them. All would be kings and of equal authority, although one would be appointed to rule. To put it more plainly, suppose a small group of earnest Christian laymen were taken prisoner and settled in the middle of a desert without any episcopally ordained priests among them; and they then agreed to choose one of themselves, whether married or not, and endow him with the office of baptizing, administering the sacrament, pronouncing absolution, and preaching; that man would be as truly a priest as if he had been ordained by all the bishops and popes. It follows that, if needs be, anyone may baptize or pronounce absolution, and impossible situation if we were not all priests. . .

Hence we deduce that there is, at bottom, really no other difference between laymen, priests, princes, bishops, or, in Romanist terminology, between religious and secular, than that of office or occupation, and not that of Christian status. All have spiritual status, and all are truly

priests, bishops, and popes. But Christians do not all follow the same occupation. Similarly, priests and monks, do not all work at the same tasks. . .

The second wall is more loosely built and less defensible. The Romanists profess to be the only interpreters of Scripture, even though they never learn anything contained in it their lives long. They claim authority for themselves alone, juggle with words shamelessly before our eyes, saying that the pope cannot err as to the faith, whether he be bad or good; although they cannot quote a single letter of Scripture to support their claim. Thus it comes about that so many heretical, unchristian, and even unnatural laws are contained in canon law—matters of which there is no need for discussion at the present juncture. Just because Romanists profess to believe that the Holy Spirit has not abandoned them, no matter if they are as ignorant and bad as they could be, they presume to assert whatever they please. In such a case, what is the need or the value of Holy Scripture? Let it be burned, and let us be content with the ignorant gentlemen at Rome who "possess the Holy Spirit within," who, however, in fact, dwells in pious souls only. Had I not read it, I should have thought it incredible that the devil should have produced such ineptitudes at Rome, and have gained adherents to them. But lest we fight them with mere words, let us adduce Scripture. St. Paul says, 1 Corinthians 14:30, "If something superior be revealed to any one sitting there and listening to another speaking God's word, the first speaker must be silent and give place." What would be the virtue of this commandment if only the speaker or the person in the highest position, were to be believed? Christ himself says, John 6:45, "that all Christians shall be taught by God." Then if the pope and his adherents were bad men, and not true Christians, i.e., not taught by God to have a true understanding; and if, on the other hand, a humble person should have the true understanding, why ever should we not follow him? Has not the pope made many errors? Who could enlighten Christian people if the pope erred, unless someone else, who had the support of Scripture, were more to be believed than he? . . .

The third wall falls without more ado when the first two are demolished; for, even if the pope acts contrary to Scripture, we ourselves are bound to abide by Scripture. We must punish him and constrain him, according to the passage, "If thy brother sin against thee, go and tell it him between thee and him alone; but if he hear thee not, take with thee one or two more; and if he hear them not, tell it to the church; and if he hear not the church, let him be unto thee as a gentile" (Matt. 18:15-17). This passage commands each member to exercise concern for his fellow; much more is it our duty when the wrongdoer is one who rules over us all alike, and who causes much harm and offense to the rest of us by his conduct. And if I am to lay a charge against him before the church, then I must call it together.

Romanists have no Scriptural basis for their contention that the pope alone has the right to summon or sanction a council. This is their own ruling, and only valid as long as it is not harmful to Christian's well-being or contrary to God's laws. If, however, the pope is in the wrong, this ruling becomes invalid, because it is harmful to Christian well-being not to punish him through a council. . .

It is empty talk when the Romanists boast of possessing an authority such as cannot be properly contested. No one in Christendom has authority to do evil, or to forbid evil from being resisted. The church has no authority except to promote the greater good. Hence, if the pope should exercise his authority to prevent a free council, and so hinder the reform in the church, we ought to pay no regard to him and his authority. If he should excommunicate and fulminate, that ought to be despised as the proceedings of a foolish man. Trusting in God's protection, we ought to excommunicate him in return and manage as best we can; for this authority of his be presumptuous and empty. *An Open Letter to the Christian Nobility*

Reading Questions

How would you summarize Luther's key critiques of the Roman Catholic Church from this text? Which of these seem most pertinent to you? Which argument, if any, could you expand upon?

Christian faith has appeared to many an easy thing; nay not a few even reckon it among the social virtues, as it were; and this they do because they have not made proof of it experimentally, and have never tasted of what efficacy it is. For it is not possible for any man to write well about it, or to understand well what is rightly written, who has not at some time tasted of its spirit, under the pressure of tribulation; while he who has tasted of it, even to a very small extent, can never write, think, speak, or hear about it sufficiently. For it is a living fountain, springing up unto eternal life, as Christ calls it in John 4.

Now, though I cannot boast of my abundance, and though I know how poorly I am furnished, yet I hope that, after having been vexed by various temptations, I have attained some little drop of faith, and that I can speak of this matter, if not with more elegance, certainly with more solidity, than those literal and too subtle disputants who have hitherto discoursed upon it without understanding their own words. That I may open then an easier way for the ignorant—for these alone I try to serve—I first lay down two propositions, concerning spiritual liberty and servitude.

A Christian man is the most free lord of all, and subject to none; a Christian man is the most dutiful servant of all and subject to everyone.

Although these statements appear contradictory, yet, when they are found to agree together, they will do so excellently for my purpose. They are both the statements of Paul himself, who says, "Though I be free from all men, yet have I made myself a servant unto all" (1 Cor. 9:19), and "Owe no man anything but to love one another" (Rom. 8:8). Now love is by its own nature dutiful and obedient to the beloved object. Thus even Christ, though Lord of

all things, was yet made of a woman; made under the law; at once free and a servant; at once in the form of God and in the form of a servant. *On Christian Liberty*

Reading Questions

Take note of a key Lutheran theme found in this text: that Christians are both free from all, and at the same time subject to all. How do you make sense of this paradox?

RELATED WORKS

Junghans, Helmar. *Martin Luther: Exploring His Life and Times, 1483–1546*. CD-ROM. Minneapolis: Fortress Press, 1998.

Lund, Eric, ed. *Documents from the History of Lutheranism, 1517–1750*. Minneapolis: Fortress Press, 2002.

Luther, Martin. *Luther's Ninety-Five Theses*. Trans. C. M. Jacobs. Ed. Harold J. Grimm. Philadelphia: Fortress Press, 1957.

Philipp Melanchthon (312)

(1497–1560) Succeeded Martin Luther as the leader of the Protestant reform movement. He supported and defended Luther publicly and worked with him on projects like the German version of the New Testament. He wrote what became the chief statement of faith in Lutheranism, *The Augsburg Confession*.

PRIMARY SOURCES

From *Loci Communes (1521)*, trans. Charles Leander Hill, (Boston: Meador Publishing Company 1944), 195ff.

Is there any reason why justification is attributed to faith alone? I answer that since we are justified by mercy of God alone, and since faith is plainly a knowledge of mercy by whatever promise you embrace it, our justification is attributed to faith alone. They who wonder why justification is attributed to the mercy of God also wonder why justification is attributed to the mercy of God and not rather to human merits. For to trust in divine mercy, is to have no respect for any of our works. He does injury to the mercy of God who denies that the saints are justified by faith. For since our justification is a work of divine mercy alone and not a merit of our own works, as Paul plainly teaches in Roms. 11, it is necessary for justification to be attributed to faith alone, by which alone without doubt, we receive the promised mercy.

What then about the works that precede justification, I mean the works of free will? They are all of them the accursed fruit of an accursed tree. And although they may be examples of the most beautiful virtues such as were Paul's before his conversion, nevertheless, they are nothing but deceit and mendacity, because they proceed from an impure heart.

Reading Questions

What, according to Melanchthon, is at stake in asserting justification by faith alone? What does he seem to reject here, and what does he embrace?

RELATED WORKS

Melanchthon, Philipp. *A Melanchthon Reader.* Trans. Ralph Keen. American University Studies, ser. 7: Theology and Religion, vol. 41. New York: Peter Lang, 1988.

Wengert, Timothy J. *Human Freedom, Christian Righteousness: Philip Melanchthon's Exegetical*

Dispute with Erasmus of Rotterdam. New York: Oxford University Press, 1998.

Teresa of Avila (354)

(1515–82). One of the best-known mystics from the sixteenth century. Founder of a reformed Carmelite convent, she wrote of achieving a "mystical marriage" with God.

PRIMARY SOURCES

From *The Interior Castle,* edited by Benedict Zimmerman, (1577; Christian Classics Ethereal Library, 2013), 18, 20-21, 178, http://www.ccel.org/ccel/teresa/castle2.pdf

He who bids me write this, tells me that the nuns of these convents of our Lady of Carmel need some one to solve their difficulties about prayer: he thinks that women understand one another's language best and that my sisters' affection for me would make them pay special attention to my words, therefore it is important for me to explain the subject clearly to them. Thus I am writing only to my sisters; the idea that any one else could benefit by what I say would be absurd. Our Lord will be doing me a great favour if He enables me to help but one of the nuns to praise Him a little better; His Majesty knows well that I have no other aim. If anything is to the point, they will understand that it does not originate from me and there is no reason to attribute it to me, as with my scant understanding and skill I could write nothing of the sort, unless God, in His mercy, enabled me to do so. *The Interior Castle, Introduction*

I thought of the soul as resembling a castle, formed of a single diamond or a very transparent crystal, and containing many rooms, just as in heaven there are many mansions. If we reflect, sisters, we shall see that the soul of the just man is but a paradise, in which, God tells us, He takes His delight. What, do you imagine, must that dwelling be in which a King so mighty, so wise, and so pure, containing in Himself all good, can delight to rest? Nothing can be compared to the great beauty and capabilities of a soul; however keen our intellects may be, they are as unable to comprehend them as to comprehend God, for, as He has told us, He created us in His own image and likeness.

As this is so, we need not tire ourselves by trying to realize all the beauty of this castle, although, being His creature, there is all the difference between the soul and God that there is between the creature and the Creator; the fact that it is made in God's image teaches us how great are its dignity and loveliness. It is no small misfortune and disgrace that, through our own fault, we neither understand our nature nor our origin. Would it not be gross ignorance, my daughters, if, when a man was questioned about his name, or country, or parents, he could not answer? Stupid as this would be, it is unspeakably more foolish to care to learn nothing of our nature except that we possess bodies, and only to realize vaguely that we have souls, because people say so and it is a doctrine of faith. Rarely do we reflect upon what gifts our souls may possess, Who dwells within them, or how extremely precious they are. Therefore we do little to preserve their beauty; all our care is concentrated on our bodies, which are but the coarse setting of the diamond, or the outer walls of the castle.

Let us imagine, as I said, that there are many rooms in this castle, of which some are above, some below, others at the side; in the centre, in the very midst of them all, is the principal chamber in which God and the soul hold their most secret intercourse. Think over this comparison very carefully; God grant it may enlighten you about the different kinds of graces He is pleased to bestow upon the soul. *The Interior Castle, Chapter 1*

ALTHOUGH, as I told you, I felt reluctant to begin this work, yet now it is finished I am very glad to have written it, and I think my trouble has been well spent, though I confess it has cost me but little. Considering your strict enclosure, the little recreation you have, my sisters, and how many conveniences are wanting in some of your convents, I think it may console you to enjoy yourselves in this interior castle which you can enter, and walk about at will, at any hour you please, without asking leave of your superiors. It is true you cannot enter all the mansions by your own power, however great it may appear to you, unless the Lord of the castle Himself admits you. Therefore I advise you to use no violence if you meet with any obstacle, for that would displease Him so much that He would never give you admission to them. He dearly loves humility: if you think yourselves unworthy to enter the third mansion, He will grant you all the sooner the favour of entering the fifth. Then, if you serve Him well there and often repair to it, He will draw you into the mansion where He dwells Himself, whence you need never depart unless called away by the Prioress, whose commands this sovereign Master wishes you to obey as if they were His own. If by her orders, you are often absent from His presence chamber, whenever you return He will hold the door open for you. When once you have learnt how to enjoy this castle, you will always find rest, however painful your trials may be, in the hope of returning to your Lord, which no one can prevent. Although I have only mentioned seven mansions, yet each one contains many more rooms, above, below, and around it, with fair gardens, fountains, and labyrinths, besides other things so delightful that you will wish to consume yourself in praising in return the great God Who has created the soul to His own image and likeness. If you find anything in the plan of this treatise which helps you to know Him better, be certain that it is sent by His Majesty to encourage you, and that whatever you find amiss in it is my own. In return for my strong desire to aid you in serving Him, my God and my Lord, I implore you, whenever you read this, to praise His Majesty fervently in my name and to beg Him to prosper His Church, to give light to the Lutherans, to pardon my sins and to free me from purgatory, where perhaps I shall be, by the mercy of God, when you see this book (if it is given to you after having been examined by theologians). If these writings contain any error, it is through my ignorance; I submit in all things to the teachings of the holy Catholic Roman Church, of which I am now a member, as I protest and promise I will be both in life and death. May our Lord God be for ever praised and blessed! Amen, Amen. *The Interior Castle, Epilogue.*

Reading Questions

What can you learn about the role and status of women in sixteenth-century religious life from this text? Does this text from Teresa of Avila serve to undermine your image of patriarchal authority, or reinforce that image? How does the description of her mystical experience translate into your conceptions of verifiable truth?

RELATED WORKS

du Boulay, Shirley. *Teresa of Avila: An Extraordinary Life.* Rev. ed. New York: BlueBridge, 2004.

Teresa, of Avila, Saint. *The Collected Works of Saint Teresa of Avila.* Trans. Kieran Kavanaugh and Otilio Rodriguez. Washington, DC: Institute of Carmelite Studies, 1976.

William Tyndale (331)

(c. 1492–1536) Known for his English translation of the New Testament, which was a major influence on the King James Bible. He aimed for accuracy in his translation by working with early Hebrew and Greek manuscripts.

PRIMARY SOURCES

From *The Works of William Tyndale,* (Luminarium: Anthology of English Literature, 2013), http://www .luminarium.org/renlit/tyndalebib.htm

> Which thing only moved me to translate the New Testament. Because I had perceived by experience, how that it was

impossible to stablish the lay people in any truth, except the scripture were plainly laid before their eyes in their mother tongue, that they might see the process, order, and meaning of the text. *Tyndale's Preface to the Pentateuch*

What shall we then saye vnto these thinges? yf god be on oure syde: who can be agaynst vs? which spared not his awne sonne, but gave him for vs all: how shall he not with him geve vs all thinges also? Who shall laye eny thinge to the charge of goddes chosen? it is god that iustifieth: who then shall condempne? it is Christ which is deed, yea rather which is rysen agayne, which is also on the ryght honde of God, and maketh intercession for vs.

Who shall seperate vs from the love of god? shall tribulacion? or anguysshe? or persecucion? other honger? other nakednesse? other parell? other swearde? As it is written: For thy sake are we kylled all daye longe, and are counted as shepe apoynted to be slayne. Neverthelesse in all these thinges we overcome strongly thorow his helpe that loved vs. Yea and I am sure that nether deeth, nether lyfe, nether angels, nor rule, nether power, nether thinges present, nether thinges to come, nether heyth, nether loweth, nether eny other creature shalbe able to departe vs from the love of God, shewed in Christ Iesu oure lorde. *Tyndale Bible, Romans*

Reading Questions

How does Tyndale's translation style strike you? How do these texts affect your understanding of biblical translation?

I believe, most excellent Sir, that you are not unacquainted with the decision reached concerning me. On which account, I beseech your lordship, even by the Lord Jesus, that if I am to pass the winter here, to urge upon the lord commissary, if he will deign, to send me from my goods in his keeping a warmer cap, for I suffer greatly from cold in the head, being troubled with a continual catarrh, which is aggravated in this prison vault. A warmer coat also, for that which I have is very thin. Also cloth for repairing my leggings. My overcoat is worn out; the shirts also are worn out. He has a woolen shirt of mine, if he will please send it. I have also with him leggings of heavier cloth for overwear. He likewise has warmer nightcaps: I also ask for leave to use a lamp in the evening, for it is tiresome to sit alone in the dark. But above all, I beg and entreat your clemency earnestly to intercede with the lord commissary, that he would deign to allow me the use of my Hebrew Bible, Hebrew Grammar, and Hebrew Lexicon, and that I might employ my time with that study. Thus likewise may you obtain what you most desire, saving that it further the salvation of your soul. But if, before the end of winter, a different decision be reached concerning me, I shall be patient, and submit to the will of God to the glory of the grace of Jesus Christ my Lord, whose spirit may ever direct your heart. Amen. *Tyndale's Letter from Vilvorde Prison, 1535.*

Reading Questions

What sort of picture does this text paint for you about Tyndale's time in prison?

RELATED WORKS

Daniell, David. *William Tyndale: A Biography*. New Haven, CT: Yale University Press, 1994.

Tyndale, William. *The Obedience of a Christian Man*. Ed. David Daniell. London: Penguin, 2000.

Huldrych (Ulrich) Zwingli (315)

(1484–1531) Swiss reformer based in Zurich. He lectured on the New Testament and wrote a systematic theology that was highly influential on the development of Protestant thought.

PRIMARY SOURCES

From *The Latin Work of Huldreich Zwingli*, V2 edited by William John Hinke (Philadlphia: The Heidelberg Press, 1922), 46ff; and *Selected Works of Huldreich Zwingli*, trans. Samuel Macauley Jackson (Philadelphia: University of Pennsylvania Press, 1901), 25ff.

Seventhly—I believe, indeed I know, that all the sacraments are so far from conferring grace that they do not even convey or dispense it. In this matter, most powerful Emperor, I may seem to thee perhaps too bold. But my opinion is firm. For as grace comes from or is given by the Divine Spirit (when I speak of grace I use the Latin term for pardon, i.e., indulgence or spontaneous favor), so this gift pertains to the spirit alone. Moreover, a channel or vehicle is not necessary to the Spirit, for He Himself is the virtue and energy whereby all things are borne, and has no need of being borne; neither do we read in the Holy Scriptures that visible things, as are the sacraments, carry certainly with them the Spirit, but if visible things have ever been borne with the Spirit, it has been the Spirit, not the visible things that have done the bearing. . .

From this it follows (as I willingly and gladly admit in regard to the subject of the sacraments) that the sacraments are given as a public testimony of that grace which is previously present to every individual. Thus baptism is administered in the presence of the church to one who, before receiving it, either confessed the religion of Christ or has the word of promise, whereby he is known to belong to the church . . . by baptism, therefore, the church publicly receives one who has previously been received through grace. Hence baptism does not convey grace but the church certifies that grace has been given to him to whom it has been administered. . .

I believe therefore, O Emperor, that a sacrament is a sign of a sacred thing. i.e., of grace that has been given. I believe that it is a visible figure or form of the invisible grace, provided and bestowed by God's bounty, i.e., a visible example which presents an analogy to something done by the Spirit. . .

Eighthly—I believe that in the Holy Eucharist, i.e., the supper of thanksgiving, the true body of Christ is present by the contemplation of faith. This means that they who thank the Lord for the benefits bestowed on us in His Son acknowledge that He assumed flesh, in it truly suffered, truly washed away our sins by His blood; and thus everything done by Christ becomes as it were present to them by the contemplation of faith. But that the body of Christ in essence and really, i.e., the natural body itself, is either present in the supper or masticated with our mouth and teeth, as the Papists or some who look back to the fleshpots of Egypt assert, we not only deny, but constantly maintain to be an error, contrary to the Word of God. . .

Let them who wish go now and condemn us for heresy, only let them know that by the same process they are condemning the opinions of the theologians, contrary to the decrees of the pontiffs. For from these facts it becomes very evident that the ancients always spoke figuratively when they attributed so much to the eating of the body of Christ in the Supper; meaning, not that sacramental eating could cleanse the soul but faith in God through Jesus Christ, which is spiritual eating, whereof this external eating is but symbol and shadow. *An Account of the Faith of Huldrych Zwingli, 1530.*

Reading Questions

How would you summarize Zwingli's theology of the sacraments based on this text? Can you piece together the counter-argument against which he writes?

To the Most Reverend Father and Lord in Christ, Hugo of Hohenlandenberg, Bishop of Constance, the undersigned offer obedient greeting.

Your Excellency will perhaps wonder, Most Reverend Father, what this unusual action of writing a letter to yourself means, and not without reason. . . For we do not come to your Excellency in regard to anything very troublesome, but to find help. For we are so sure that you are both a most pious lord and a most loving father that

there is nothing we do not promise ourselves from you. . .

We think that your most Reverend Fatherhood is not unaware how unsuccessfully and scantily the prescriptions in regard to chastity that have come down to our times from our predecessors have been kept by the general run of priests, and oh, that they could have vouchsafed us strength to keep their commands as easily as they gave them! . . .

We, then, having tried with little enough success alas! to obey the law (for the disease must be boldly disclosed to the physician), have discovered that the gift [of chastity] has been denied unto us, and we have meditated long within ourselves how we might remedy our ill-starred attempts at chastity.

. . . if we run through the whole of the New Testament we find nowhere anything that favours free concubinage, but everything in approval of marriage. Therefore it appears to us most true and most right that for a Christian no third possibility besides chastity or marriage is left, and that he should live chastely if that is given unto him from above, or marry a wife if he be on fire with passion, and this we shall show more clearly in a little while from the truly sacred writings. Hence we beseech your mercy, wisdom and learning, illustrious Leader, to show yourself the first to lay hold upon the glory of taking the lead over all the bishops of Germany in right thinking upon Christianity, since you see Christ bestowing especial favour upon this age of our ours and revealing himself more clearly than for several ages since, while from the whole great body of bishops scarcely one or two thus far have shown themselves fairly on the side of the revivified Christianity, and while others continue to thrust ill-feigned chastity upon the unfortunate general body of our fellow bishops, do you suffer those who are consumed with passion to marry wives, since this, as has been shown, will be lawful according to Christ and according to the laws of men. From the whole vast crowd we are the first to venture to come forward, relying upon your gentleness, and to implore that you grant us this thing, not, as we think, without due consideration . . .

O happy the invincible race of Hohen-landenberg, if you shall be the first of all the bishops in Germany to apply healing to our wounds and restore us to health! For what historian will ever pass over the achievement unmentioned? What scholar will not trumpet it abroad? What poet will not sing it to coming generations? What embalming will not protect it from decay and destruction? The door of well doing is surely open before you. You have only to take care lest you do not hold your hands firmly clasped, and so let the offered opportunity slip through them. For we presage that things are going to put on a new face whether we will or no, and when this happens we shall lament in vain having neglected the opportunity of winning glory. We have on the side of our request that Creator who made the first human beings male and female; we have the practice of the Old Testament, which is much more strict than the New,

under which, however, even the highest priests took upon their necks the gentle yoke of matrimony; we have Christ, who makes chastity free, nay, bids us marry, that his little children may not be offended, and our petition meets with loud approval on all sides. . .

If, however, you cannot possibly be persuaded to grant it, we beseech you at least not to forbid it, according to the suggestion of another than ourselves . . . and in fact you will have to refrain at least from interfering. For there is a report that most of the ecclesiastics have already chosen wives, not only among our Swiss, but among all peoples everywhere, and to put this down will certainly be not only beyond your strength but beyond that of one far more mighty, if you will pardon our saying so. *Letter to Bishop Constance, July 2nd 1522. Zwingli joined 10 others in signing this letter, written the same year he secretly married Anna Reinhard.*

Reading Questions

Does this letter from Zwingli challenge any assumptions for you about the behavior of clergy, either from the sixteenth century or now?

RELATED WORKS

Aland, Kurt. *Four Reformers: Luther, Melanchthon, Calvin, Zwingli.* Trans. James L. Schaaf. Minneapolis: Augsburg, 1979.

Zwingli, Ulrich. *Huldrych Zwingli.* Ed. G. R. Potter. Documents of Modern History. New York: St. Martin's, 1978.

Chapter Summaries

22. Seeds of Renewal

The Reformation did not appear out of the blue. Humanism, the beginnings of biblical criticism as a scholarly and religious endeavor, and the invention of the printing press were all factors leading to a revolution within the church.

The Reformers responded to what they saw as corruption in the church, including negligence, ignorance, and sexual immorality among the clergy.

Humanism came of age with Petrach, whose writings influenced European literature for generations. His views polarized Christian opinion between the old scholasticism and the new humanism.

It would be hard to exaggerate the importance of Johannes Gutenberg's invention: the use of movable metal type to print words on a page. The printing press allowed the Reformers to spread their message far and wide.

It could be argued that Erasmus made the Reformation inevitable: his satirical writings highlighted the corruption of Rome and the need for enlightened thought in Christian practice.

23. Reformation

The central figure of the Reformation, Martin Luther, is famous for his Ninety-Five Theses, which he originally intended as a discussion of the theology behind indulgences. But Luther was destined to lead a new movement. He preached the authority of the Bible over tradition, justification by faith alone, and the need for all Christians to take responsibility for their relationship with God and with society.

Other key figures, such as Philipp Melanchthon and John Calvin, were leaders in the movement for reform and made significant contributions to Protestant theology. The struggle between the church at Rome and the Reformers led to the Thirty Years' War, and it also changed shape as it affected kingdoms across Europe. The Reformers gained strength wherever a ruler took their side, as in England under Queen Elizabeth I.

24. A Flood of Bibles

Because of the Reformers' desire to make the Bible accessible to all Christians, many new translations of Scripture in the vernacular were made and distributed through the mass print production that was now available.

Bible versions flourished during this period, from Hebrew Old Testaments to Greek New Testaments to the Latin Bible known as the Vulgate. The Luther Bible, in German, is the preeminent vernacular translation of the era.

25. The Radical Reformation

The belief that the civil government should not hold ultimate sway over the church helped motivate many groups, after working to purify the church from within, to leave and establish new churches. The Anabaptists and the Puritans are two results of the Radical Reformation.

The Anabaptists rejected infant baptism and practiced baptism of adults on confession of faith. They promoted the primacy of discipleship: the active engagement with Christian beliefs on a daily basis. They were led by Ulrich Zwingli in Zurich, where he attempted to persuade the authorities through his preaching of the rightness of their belief.

The first English Baptist movement came out of the English Separatists. They were involved in debates about the relationship between church and state as well as in millenarian speculations. While rejecting state interference in the running of the church, the Baptists created structures for mutual assistance among congregations.

26. The Catholic Reformation

Also called the Counter Reformation, the Catholic Reformation was both a response to the Protestants and the continuous effort of many to reform the church from within. One of the most significant responses to the Protestants was the Council of Trent, called by Pope Paul III.

Other popes who worked to reform the papal office were Clement VII, Paul III, and Paul VI. All were caught up in political upheavals and affected by their joint status as temporal ruler of the Papal States and spiritual leader of the Catholic Church.

The Catholic Reformation led to the revival of the Inquisition as well as the establishment of the Society of Jesus, also known as the Jesuits. While working to counteract the Protestant movement, the Jesuits contributed to the development of higher education and global missions.

Catholic mysticism in Spain was revived during this time. Such an emphasis on personal spiritual experience was often viewed as a threat by church authorities. One of these mystics, Teresa of Avila, was assisted by her follower John of the Cross in founding a reformed Carmelite order.

The Catholic Reformation resulted in some European countries resisting the establishment of Protestantism as the official state church. It ultimately ended the cultural and religious unity of medieval Europe.

27. Art and the Spirit

Art from the Roman Catholic tradition during the High Renaissance was produced by some of the greatest artists of the Western world, including Michelangelo, Titian, Dürer, and Rembrandt.

Additional Readings

1. From *Luther's Last Battles: Politics and Polemics, 1531–46* (reprint, Fortress Press, 2005)

Mark U. Edwards Jr. analyzes Luther's primary anti-Jewish treatises, *On the Jews and Their Lies*, *On the Ineffable Name and on Christ's Lineage*, and *On the Last Word of David*. Edwards considers these essays to be three parts of one major statement, his "last testament against the Jews and the Jewish interpretation of the Old Testament" (128). According to Edwards (131–42), in the first treatise, after a list of indictments,

> Luther swung immediately into a series of harsh recommendations to secular authorities on how to deal with the Jews. Their synagogues and schools should be burned and whatever would not burn should be buried. Their homes should be destroyed. All their prayer books and Talmudic writing should be taken from them. Their rabbis should be forbidden to teach. . . . They should be expelled after a portion of their wealth had been confiscated. Luther rejected angrily the argument that the Jews were an indispensable financial resource to governments. The benefit failed to outweigh the blasphemy and harm done by the Jews. . . .
>
> By the mid-1530s Luther had abandoned his belief that Jewish blasphemy against Christ and God was confined to the privacy of the synagogue. Having encountered Jewish propaganda and received reports of active Jewish proselytizing, Luther became convinced that the Jews and their blasphemy were a threat to the public good. His demands—that the synagogues be burned and buried, that Jewish prayer books and the Talmud be destroyed, that rabbis be forbidden to teach, and that Jewish worship be forbidden—stem from his belief that Jewish teaching and preaching contained blasphemy.
>
> These harsh recommendations were for Luther an expression of "rough mercy" [*scharfe Barmherzigkeit*] that might save a few Jews from the flames of hell. . . .
>
> The central concern of the late treatises was not, however, these political and economic expressions of "rough mercy." Luther's late anti-Jewish writings were attempts to defend and maintain theologically and exegetically the Christian sense of the Old Testament and to refute competing Jewish exegesis. . . .
>
> The attractiveness of this "theological" explanation of Luther's attitude toward the Jews obviously goes beyond its ability to account for Luther's beliefs and behavior. For one thing, it makes clearer the inappropriateness of *racial* anti-Semites claiming Luther as a patron of their cause. Luther identified a Jew by his religious beliefs, not by his race. . . .
>
> From an historical perspective, however, this "theological" evaluation of Luther's attitude toward the Jews is unsatisfactory. Sixteenth-century readers of Luther's treatises, and even Luther himself, could not have distinguished between what [the scholar Wilhelm] Maurer termed the "essential theology" of the tracts and the "remnants of medieval tradition" that they also contained. For Luther and for his contemporaries the "remnants" of prejudice and discriminatory treatment were in logic and in

practice tied to the theological description of the Jews as a God-forsaken people suffering under divine wrath. Theology and practice reinforced each other. . . .

To insist on the importance of context for a proper understanding of Luther's anti-Jewish treatises is not merely good history. It also makes it more difficult for modern anti-Semites to exploit the authority of Luther's name to support their racist beliefs. . . . But we cannot have it both ways. If the anti-Jewish treatises cannot be divorced from their context without serious distortion, then the same should be true for his other writings. It is not intellectually honest to pick and choose.

QUESTIONS FOR DISCUSSION AND REFLECTION

Based on this passage, what is your understanding of Luther's motivations and goals in his anti-Jewish writings? What does Edwards argue for in regards to interpreting Luther's work and ideas? Do you agree with Edwards's thesis?

2. From Ignatius Loyola, *The Spiritual Exercises* (1548), in *A Reformation Reader: Primary Texts with Introductions* (Fortress Press, 1999)

Editor Denis R. Janz explains that Ignatius appended to his spiritual guidebook a list of "Rules for Thinking with the Church," which was intended to attack what Ignatius saw as the Protestant mind-set. The following are the first nine rules, focused on what is worthy of praise (371):

The following rules should be observed to foster the true attitude of mind we ought to have in the church militant.

1. We must put aside all judgment of our own, and keep the mind ever ready and prompt to obey in all things the true spouse of Christ our Lord, our holy mother, the hierarchical church.

2. We should praise sacramental confession, the yearly reception of the most blessed Sacrament, and still more weekly Communion, provided requisite and proper dispositions are present.

3. We ought to praise the frequent hearing of mass, the singing of hymns, psalmody, and long prayers whether in church or outside; likewise, the hours arranged at fixed times for the whole Divine Office, for every kind of prayer, and for the canonical hours.

4. We must praise highly religious life, virginity, and continence; and matrimony ought not be praised as much as any of these.

5. We should praise vows of religion, obedience, poverty, chastity, and vows to perform other works of supererogation conducive to perfection. However, it must be remembered that a vow deals with matters that lead us closer to evangelical perfection. Hence, whatever tends to withdraw one from perfection may not be made the object of a vow, for example, a business career, the married state, and so forth.

6. We should show our esteem for the relics of the saints by venerating them and praying to the saints. We should praise visits to the station churches, pilgrimages, indulgences, jubilees, crusade indults, and the lighting of candles in churches.

7. We must praise the regulations of the church with regard to fast and abstinence, for example, in Lent, on ember days, vigils, Fridays, and Saturdays. We should praise works of penance, not only those that are interior but also those that are exterior.

8. We ought to praise not only the building and adornment of churches, but also images and veneration of them according to the subject they represent.

9. Finally, we must praise all the commandments of the church, and be on the alert to find reasons to defend them, and by no means in order to criticize them.

QUESTIONS FOR DISCUSSION AND REFLECTION

What Protestant critiques or concerns do you recognize in this list? What would you identify as Ignatius's priorities in attacking Protestantism and defending the Catholic faith? How would you describe his characterization of the Protestant mindset?

See also "Reading Historical Documents" (page 171 in this volume) for other questions to consider.

3. From *Daughters of Light: Quaker Women Preaching and Prophesying in the Colonies and Abroad, 1700–1775* (University of North Carolina Press, 1999)

Rebecca Larson writes about the role of Quaker women as traveling ministers in England and the American colonies in the early eighteenth century (186–88):

> Friends' habits of being self-disciplined, frugal, industrious, and plain were directly related to the "divine messages" vocalized by the travelling ministers—female as well as male—and to the individuals' adherence to their own "inner promptings." When Mary Weston travelled through some English counties in 1735, her companion, Elizabeth Hutchinson of Cork, Ireland, exhorted Friends to "a diligent Improvement of their Time . . . the Lord . . . [having] entrusted every one with a Gift to improve to his Honour." The emphasis on productive pursuits—"Improve thy time to the glory of Him who gave thee a being"—tended to produce diligent Quaker works, enabling many Friends' businesses to flourish. Instead of viewing rational capitalism and religious mysticism as irreconcilable opposites, Friends believed that order and economy were evidence of adhering to the Inward Light, since "Truth" was neither confused nor excessive. . . . After her non-Quaker alcoholic husband died, Elizabeth Ashbridge was saddled with his debts, although the creditors had no legal claim on her. Since some said they would not have trusted her husband but for Elizabeth's sake, Elizabeth "took the whole debt on herself, and beside supporting herself reputably, paid off nearly the whole debt during her widowhood, during which time she also frequently travelled in the ministry."
>
> Recognizing "no dividing-line between the religious and the mundane," Friends tried to infuse their temporal occupations with their spiritual values, providing a unique avenue of influence for spiritually authoritative Quaker women. . . .
>
> Respecting "divine leadings," Friends in public office were receptive to religious advice from Quaker women ministers, like Ann Roberts of Pennsylvania, who felt "led by the Spirit," at times, to

encourage them to be faithful in executing their duties, to adhere to Quaker testimonies, and to rely on God.

Questions for Discussion and Reflection

What values does Larson highlight in her discussion of Quaker women ministers? Are any of those shared with other Christian sects from the Reformation era?

Selected Online Resources

▶ Project Wittenberg—extensive collection of texts and other links about Lutheran history and theology
http://www.iclnet.org/pub/resources/text/wittenberg/wittenberg-home.html

▶ "The Reformation"—a History Channel website with short articles, videos, and illustrations about the Reformation's major figures, themes, and events
http://www.history.com/topics/reformation

▶ "Martin Luther"—a PBS website with essays, "Luther Trivia," and videos about Martin Luther's life and writings
http://www.pbs.org/empires/martinluther/

▶ "Philipp Melanchthon in Germany"—short essays about Melanchthon's life, writing, and historical context, accompanied by illustrations
http://www.melanchthon.de/e/

▶ "John Calvin: Protestant Reformer"—a biographical essay accompanied by photos of relevant museums and places from his life, published by a European tour company
http://www.reformationtours.com/site/490868/page/669536

▶ "Anne Hutchinson"—site devoted to the American Puritan preacher Anne Hutchinson
http://www.annehutchinson.com

▶ "George Fox: An Autobiography"—the journal of the Quaker founder
http://www.strecorsoc.org/gfox/title.html

▶ "The Spiritual Exercises of St. Ignatius of Loyola"—the complete text of Loyola's 1548 *Spiritual Exercises*
http://www.sacred-texts.com/chr/seil/

Guide to Part 5: Reason, Revival, and Revolution

Key Terms

The number in parentheses refers to the page where the term is explained. Those terms marked with asterisks also appear in the Glossary.

deism, deists (413)* Followers of a movement for natural religion that flourished in seventeenth-century England. They rejected the idea of revelation and held that the Creator did not interfere in the workings of the universe.

empiricism (411) Derived from the Greek word for "experience." Stresses the part played by experience in knowledge; represented by such British figures as Locke, Berkeley, and Hume.

Evangelical Revival (386) A period of religious revival in Britain, spurred by the Great Awakening in the North American colonies.

Great Awakening (386) A period of religious renewal begun in Northampton, Massachusetts, under Jonathan Edwards in 1734, coming to fruition in New England between 1740 and 1743, the time of George Whitefield's visit to the area.

natural theology (418) A branch of theology based on reason and experience that looks for a basis in innate or "natural" human reason for accepting specific theological beliefs.

Pietist (392–93)* Someone with strong feelings of religious devotion. It originally referred to an important seventeenth-century Lutheran reform movement in Germany.

Propaganda (370)* Sacred Congregation for the Propagation of the Faith, a Roman Catholic body concerned with mission in non-Christian countries. It dates from the Counter-Reformation and is now known as the Congregation for the Evangelization of Peoples.

Quietism (417) The belief that, to attain perfection, people must be passive, so far abandoning themselves to God that they do not even care for their own salvation.

rationalism (408) A viewpoint that regards reason as the chief source and test of knowledge, holding that the universe is by nature rational and that human reason has the power to grasp this nature.

Key Personalities

Numbers in parentheses refer to the pages where the text provides the individual's biographical details and historical significance.

René Descartes (408–9)

(1596–1650) The first great rationalist; famous for his formula *Cogito ergo sum* ("I think; therefore I am"). He used it as the basis of his proof for the existence of God.

PRIMARY SOURCES

From Rene Descartes, *The Discourse on Method* (1637; Internet Sacred Text Archive, 2013), http://www.sacred-texts.com/phi/desc/disc.txt.

> Good sense is, of all things among men, the most equally distributed; for every one thinks himself so abundantly provided with it, that those even who are the most difficult to satisfy in everything else, do not usually desire a larger measure of this quality than they already possess. And in this it is not likely that all are mistaken the conviction is rather to be held as testifying that the power of judging aright and of distinguishing truth from error, which is properly what is called good sense or reason, is by nature equal in all men; and that the diversity of our opinions, consequently, does not arise from some being endowed with a larger share of reason than others, but solely from this, that we conduct our thoughts along different ways, and do not fix our attention on the same objects. For to be possessed of a vigorous mind is not enough; the prime requisite is rightly to apply it. The greatest minds, as they are capable of the highest excellences, are open likewise to the greatest aberrations; and those who travel very slowly may yet make far greater progress, provided they keep always to the straight road, than those who, while they run, forsake it. *Discourse on Method, Preface*
>
> Finally, if there be still persons who are not sufficiently persuaded of the existence of God and of the soul, by the reasons I have adduced, I am desirous that they should know that all the other propositions, of the truth of which they deem themselves perhaps more assured, as that we have a body, and that there exist stars and an earth, and such like, are less certain; for, although we have a moral assurance of these things, which is so strong that there is an appearance of extravagance in doubting of their existence, yet at the same time no one, unless his intellect is impaired, can deny, when the question relates to a metaphysical certitude, that there is sufficient reason to exclude entire assurance, in the observation that when asleep we can in the same way imagine ourselves possessed of another body and that we see other stars and another earth, when there is nothing of the kind. For how do we know that the thoughts which occur in dreaming are false rather than those other which we experience when awake, since the former are often not less vivid and distinct than the latter? And though men of the highest genius study this question as long as they please, I do not believe that they will be able to give any reason which can be sufficient to remove this doubt, unless they

presuppose the existence of God. *Discourse on Method, Part IV*

Reading Questions

Based on what you observe in these texts, how might Descartes define the word "truth"? What is the crux of Descartes' argument in favor of the existence of God?

RELATED WORKS

Descartes, René. *The Essential Descartes.* Ed. Margaret D. Wilson. New York: New American Library, 1969.

Tierno, Joel Thomas. *Descartes on God and Human Error.* Atlantic Highlands, NJ: Humanities, 1997.

Jonathan Edwards (390)

(1703–58) The most significant figure of the Great Awakening. His Calvinistic theology, focused on predestination, brought him into controversy with his Congregational church. He worked as a missionary before becoming a university president. In his major work *Freedom of the Will* he denies that human beings are free to choose, emphasizing his Calvinistic beliefs.

PRIMARY SOURCES

From *Sinners in the Hands of an Angry God,* a sermon by Jonathan Edwards, (1741; Christian Classics Ethereal Library, 2013), 7-8, http://www.ccel.org/ccel/edwards/sermons.pdf

. . . whatever some have imagined and pretended about promises made to natural men's earnest seeking and knocking, it is plain and manifest, that whatever pains a natural man takes in religion, whatever prayers he makes, till he believes in Christ, God is under no manner of obligation to keep him a moment from eternal destruction.

So that, thus it is that natural men are held in the hand of God, over the pit of hell; they have deserved the fiery pit, and are already sentenced to it; and God is dreadfully provoked, his anger is as great towards them as to those that are actually suffering the executions of the fierceness of his wrath in hell, and they have done nothing in the least to appease or abate that anger, neither is God in the least bound by any promise to hold them up one moment; the devil is waiting for them, hell is gaping for them, the flames gather and flash about them, and would fain lay hold on them, and swallow them up; the fire pent up in their own hearts is struggling to break out: and they have no interest in any Mediator, there are no means within reach that can be any security to them. In short, they have no refuge, nothing to take hold of; all that preserves them every moment is the mere arbitrary will, and uncovenanted, unobliged forbearance of an incensed God.

Reading Questions

How do you react to the rhetoric in this preaching? What effect do you imagine it had on listeners?

RELATED WORKS

Edwards, Jonathan. *Sinners in the Hands of an Angry God and Other Puritan Sermons.* Mineola, NY: Dover, 2005.

Nichols, Stephen J. *Jonathan Edwards: A Guided Tour of His Life and Thought.* Phillipsburg, NJ: P & R, 2001.

Immanuel Kant (416)

(1724–1804) Philosopher known for his *Critique of Pure Reason* (1781), he pointed out the weaknesses in traditional arguments for the existence of God.

PRIMARY SOURCES

From Immanuel Kant, *What is Enlightenment* (1784; Internet Modern History Sourcebook, 2013), http://www.fordham.edu/halsall/mod/kant-whatis.asp

> Enlightenment is man's release from his self-incurred tutelage. Tutelage is man's inability to make use of his understanding without direction from another. Self-incurred is this tutelage when its cause lies not in lack of reason but in lack of resolution and courage to use it without direction from another. Sapere aude! "Have courage to use your own reason!"—that is the motto of enlightenment.
>
> Laziness and cowardice are the reasons why so great a portion of mankind, after nature has long since discharged them from external direction, nevertheless remains under lifelong tutelage, and why it is so easy for others to set themselves up as their guardians. It is so easy not to be of age. If I have a book which understands for me, a pastor who has a conscience for me, a physician who decides my diet, and so forth, I need not trouble myself. I need not think, if I can only pay—others will easily undertake the irksome work for me. . .

Reading Questions

How does the "motto of the enlightenment," *sapere aude*, characterize the general themes of the Enlightenment era? In what ways do you see these themes reflected in this text from Kant?

RELATED WORKS

Kant, Immanuel. *Critique of Pure Reason*. Trans. and ed. Paul Guyer and Allen W. Wood. Cambridge: Cambridge University Press, 1998.

Paulsen, Friedrich. *Immanuel Kant: His Life and Doctrine*. Trans. J. E. Creighton and Albert Lefevre. New York: Scribner's, 1910.

Blaise Pascal (409)

(1623–62) A mathematician, physicist, and religious writer. A mystical vision in 1654 led him to write about Augustine's doctrine of grace and an apologetics, never completed. His collection of notes, *Pensées* (Thoughts), is a classic apologetics that promotes faith as the foundation of Christianity above all else, including reason.

PRIMARY SOURCES

From Blaise Pascal, *Pensees* (1660; Christian Classics Ethereal Library, 2013), 38-40, http://www.ccel.org/ccel/pascal/pensees.pdf

> . . . Men despise religion; they hate it and fear it is true. To remedy this, we must begin by showing that religion is not contrary to reason; that it is venerable, to inspire respect for it; then we must make it lovable, to make good men hope it is true; finally, we must prove it is true. . .
>
> . . . The immortality of the soul is a matter which is of so great consequence to us and which touches us so profoundly that we must have lost all feeling to be indifferent as to knowing what it is. All our actions and thoughts must take such different courses, according as there are or are not eternal joys to hope for, that it is impossible to take one step with sense and judgment unless we regulate our course by our view

of this point which ought to be our ultimate end. . .

. . . But as for those who pass their life without thinking of this ultimate end of life, and who, for this sole reason that they do not find within themselves the lights which convince them of it, neglect to seek them elsewhere, and to examine thoroughly whether this opinion is one of those which people receive with credulous simplicity, or one of those which, although obscure in themselves, have nevertheless a solid and immovable foundation, I look upon them in a manner quite different.

This carelessness in a matter which concerns themselves, their eternity, their all, moves me more to anger than pity; it astonishes and shocks me; it is to me monstrous. I do not say this out of the pious zeal of a spiritual devotion. I expect, on the contrary, that we ought to have this feeling from principles of human interest and self-love; for this we need only see what the least enlightened persons see.

We do not require great education of the mind to understand that here is no real and lasting satisfaction; that our pleasures are only vanity; that our evils are infinite; and, lastly, that death, which threatens us every moment, must infallibly place us within a few years under the dreadful necessity of being for ever either annihilated or unhappy.

There is nothing more real than this, nothing more terrible. Be we as heroic as we like, that is the end which awaits the world. Let us reflect on this and then say whether it is not beyond doubt that there is no good

in this life but in the hope of another; that we are happy only in proportion as we draw near it; and that, as there are no more woes for those who have complete assurance of eternity, so there is no more happiness for those who have no insight into it. *Pensees, Chapter IV*

Reading Questions

What do you think Pascal is getting at when he suggests that people both hate religion and fear that it is true? Reflect on Pascal's assertion that his concern for the "ultimate end of life" is not out of piety, but "from principles of human interest and self-love." What does this suggest about why Pascal values religion?

RELATED WORKS

Connor, James A. *Pascal's Wager: The Man Who Played Dice with God.* San Francisco: HarperSanFrancisco, 2006.

Pascal, Blaise. *Apology for Religion, Extracted from the Pensées.* Ed. H. F. Stewart. Cambridge, UK: Cambridge University Press, 1942.

Junípero Serra (378)

(1713–84) The Spanish Franciscan founder of a string of missions along the coast of Northern California, from San Diego to just north of San Francisco. Beginning in 1749, he worked as a missionary in Mexico, where he was elected father president of the Sierra Gorda missions. His successful conversion of thousands of Native Americans earned him a place of honor within the Catholic tradition along with criticism from Native scholars and their colleagues for his attempts to destroy Native people's culture, including their family structures and traditional way of life.

PRIMARY SOURCES

From *Writings of Junípero Serra*, edited by Antoníne Tibesar, (Washington: Academy of American Franciscan History, 1955), 63.

. . . It was for me a day of great joy, because just after the Masses, while I was praying, retired inside of the little brush hut, they came to tell me that Indians were coming and were close by. I gave praise to the Lord, kissing the ground, and thanking His Majesty for the fact that, after so many years of looking forward to it, He now permitted me to be among the pagans in their own country. I came out at once, and found myself in front of twelve of them, all men and grown up, except two who were boys, one about ten years old and the other fifteen. I saw something I could not believe when I had read of it, or had been told about it. It was this: they were entirely naked, as Adam in the garden, before sin. So they go, and so they presented themselves to us. We spoke a long time with them, and not for one moment, while they saw us clothed, could you notice the least sign of shame in them for their own lack of dress. One after the other, I put my hands upon the head of each one of them, in sign of affection. I filled both their hands with dried figs, which they immediately began to eat. We received with show of much appreciation the presents they offered us, viz.: a net of roasted mescales, and four fishes of more than medium size. But the poor fellows had not bothered to clean them, still less to salt them, and the cook declared that they were of very little use. Father Campa also

gave them raisins. The Governor gave them tobacco in the leaf, and all the soldiers gave them a big welcome and plenty of food. Meanwhile, with the help of the interpreter, I gave them to understand that now, in that very spot, a Father would stay with them; that he was this one—and I pointed him out—and that his name was Father Miguel; that they should come to him, they and their friends, and visit him; that they should tell the others not to have any fear or timidity; that the Father would be their best friend; and these gentlemen, the soldiers, who are to stay with the Father, would do them much good and no harm; that they, in return, must not steal the cattle that grazed in the fields, but when in need they should call on the Father and ask him for what they wanted; and he would always give them what he could. These and other such sentiments they seemed to understand fairly well, and they gave evidence that they agreed with it all. Thus I was convinced that, before long, they would be caught in the apostolic and evangelical net. *The Diary of Father Junipero Serra, May 15, 1769.*

Reading Questions

What does this excerpt from the diary of Father Junipero Serra reveal to you about the Californian religious frontier in the eighteenth century? What assumptions does Father Serra seem to hold with regard to native peoples?

RELATED WORKS

Geiger, Maynard J. *The Life and Times of Fray Junípero Serra, O.F.M.; or, The Man Who Never Turned Back, 1713-1784, a Biography*. 2 vols.

Washington, DC: Academy of American Franciscan History, 1959.

Hackel, Steven W. *Junípero Serra: California's Founding Father*. New York: Hill and Wang, 2013.

Philipp Spener (393)

(1635–1705) The founder of Lutheran Pietism. He is best known as the author of *Pia Desideria* (*Holy Desires*), his plan to remedy the spiritual decay in the church. He was mostly in line with Lutheran theology, except for his millenarian beliefs.

Primary Sources

From Philip Jacob Spener, *Pia Desideria*, trans. and ed. Theodore G. Tappert, (Philadelphia: Fortress Press, 1964), 36-38.

Let us, all of us together, now do diligently what we have been appointed to do, namely, to feed the flock which God has bought with his own blood and therefore at a very great price

Let us remember, dear Fathers and Brethren, what we promised to God when we were set apart for our ministries and what must consequently be our concern.

Let us remember the rigorous reckoning which faces us at the hands of him who will call us to account for the souls which have in any way been neglected.

Let us remember that in the last judgment we shall not be asked how learned we were and whether we displayed our learning before the world; to what extent we enjoyed the favor of men and knew how to keep it; with what honors we were exalted and how great a reputation in the world we left behind us; or how many treasures of earthly goods we amassed for our children

and thereby drew a curse upon ourselves. Instead, we shall be asked how faithfully and with how childlike a heart we sought to further the kingdom of God; with how pure and godly a teaching and how worthy an example we tried to edify our hearers amid the scorn of the world, denial of self, taking up the cross, and imitation of our Savior; with what zeal we opposed not only error but also wickedness of life; or with what constancy and cheerfulness we endured the persecution or adversity thrust upon us by the manifestly godless world or by false brethren, and amid such suffering praised our God.

Let us therefore be diligent in investigating ever more deeply our own shortcomings and those of the rest of the church in order that we may learn to know our sicknesses, and then with a fervent invocation of God for the light of his Spirit let us also search and ponder over the remedies.

Let us not leave it at that, however, but let everybody seek, as he is able in his own congregation, to introduce what we have found to be beneficial and necessary. For what is the value of consultation except to serve as a testimony against us whenever we do no desire to live up to what we have found to be good?

If we have to suffer somewhat at the hands of people who disagree with us, let us take it as a reassuring sign that our work is pleasing to the Lord, inasmuch as he allows it to be put to such a test, and meanwhile let us not grow weary on this account and let up in our zeal.

Let us begin by putting ourselves at the disposal especially of those who are still willing to accept what is done for their edification. If everybody in his own congregation makes provision for these above all others, they may little by little grow to such a measure of godliness that they will be shining examples to others. In time, then, by God's grace we may also gradually attract those who at present seem to be lost in order that they, too, may finally be one. All of my suggestions are aimed quite exclusively at first helping those who are tractable, at doing all that is needful for their edification. Once this is accomplished and made the foundation, sternness toward the disobedient may bear more fruit.

Let us not abandon all hope before we have set our hands to the task. Let us not lay down our rod and staff if we do not have the desired success at once. What is impossible for men remains possible for God. Eventually God's hour must come, if only we wait for it. Our fruit, like other fruit, must be borne in patience, and the fruit in others must be cultivated by us with perseverance. The work of the Lord is accomplished in wondrous ways, even as he is himself wonderful. For this very reason his work is done in complete secrecy, yet all the more surely, provided we do not relax our efforts. If God does not give you the pleasure of seeing the result of your work quickly, perhaps he intends to hide it from you, lest you become too proud of it. Seeds are there, and you may think they are unproductive, but do your part in watering them, and ears will surely sprout and in time become ripe.

Reading Questions

Based on the guidance he provides in this text, can you construct a list of Spener's grievances against the church? What shortcomings is he working to correct here? Do you find his entreaties here to be effectual?

RELATED WORKS

Spener, Philip Jacob. *Pia Desideria.* Trans. and ed. Theodore G. Tappert. Philadelphia: Fortress Press, 1964.

Strom, Jonathan, ed. *Pietism and Community in Europe and North America, 1650-1850.* Boston: Brill, 2010.

John Wesley (397)

(1703–91) Founder of the Methodist movement, along with his brother, Charles. He traveled through Britain preaching the "new birth" anywhere a church would allow him the pulpit. Opposition grew, so he began to preach outdoors, where working-class Britons were converted by his message. Although loyal to the Church of England, he was eventually forced to ordain his own ministers. He is responsible for the development of the religious tract and also edited the Christian Library, a collection of theological and devotional books accessible to nonspecialists.

PRIMARY SOURCES

From *The Journal of John Wesley,* (Christian Classics Ethereal Library, 2013), 58-59, http://www.ccel.org/ccel/wesley/journal.pdf

Thursday, [March] 29.—I left London and in the evening expounded to a small company at Basingstoke, Saturday, 31. In the evening I reached Bristol and met Mr. Whitefield there. I could scarcely reconcile myself at first to this strange way of preaching in the fields, of which he set me an example on Sunday; I had been all my life (till very lately) so tenacious of every point relating to decency and order that I should have thought the saving of souls almost a sin if it had not been done in a church.

April 1.—In the evening (Mr. Whitefield being gone) I began expounding our Lord's Sermon on the Mount (one pretty remarkable precedent of field-preaching, though I suppose there were churches at that time also), to a little society which was accustomed to meet once or twice a week in Nicholas Street.

Monday, 2.—At four in the afternoon, I submitted to be more vile and proclaimed in the highways the glad tidings of salvation, speaking from a little eminence in a ground adjoining to the city, to about three thousand people. The Scripture on which I spoke was this (is it possible anyone should be ignorant that it is fulfilled in every true minister of Christ?): "The Spirit of the Lord is upon me, because he hath anointed me to preach the gospel to the poor; he hath sent me to heal the broken-hearted, to preach deliverance to the captives, and recovering of sight to the blind, to set at liberty them that are bruised, to proclaim the acceptable year of the Lord" [see Isa. 61:1, 2; Luke 4:18, 19].

Sunday, 8.—At seven in the morning I preached to about a thousand persons at Bristol, and afterward to about fifteen hundred on the top of Hannam Mount in Kingswood. I called to them, in the words of the evangelical prophet, "Ho! every one that thirsteth, come ye to the waters; . . . come, and buy wine and milk without money and without price" [Isa. 55:1]. About five thousand were in the afternoon at Rose Green (on the other side of Kingswood); among whom I stood and cried in the name of the Lord, "If any man thirst, let him come unto me and drink. He that believeth on me, as the Scripture hath said, out of his belly shall flow rivers of living water" [John 7:38].

Tuesday, 17.—At five in the afternoon I was at a little society in the Back Lane. The room in which we were was propped beneath, but the weight of people made the floor give way; so that in the beginning of expounding, the post which propped it fell down with a great noise. But the floor sank no farther; so that, after a little surprise at first, they quietly attended to the things that were spoken.

Monday, May 7.—I was preparing to set out for Pensford, having now had leave to preach in the church, when I received the following note:

"Sir, Our minister, having been informed you are beside yourself, does not care that you should preach in any of his churches."

I went, however; and on Priestdown, about half a mile from Pensford, preached Christ our "wisdom, righteousness, sanctification, and redemption. *Journal of John Wesley, March-May 1739.*

Reading Questions

How does this excerpt from the journal of John Wesley portray the life of a traveling preacher? What is unique about Wesley's message?

RELATED WORKS

Wesley, John. *John Wesley: An Autobiographical Sketch of the Man and His Thought, Chiefly from His Letters.* Ed. Ole E. Bergen. Textus Minores, vol. 35. Leiden: Brill, 1966.

Wesley, John. *John Wesley: A Representative Collection of His Writings.* Ed. Albert C. Outler. New York: Oxford University Press, 1964.

George Whitefield (390–91)

(1714–70) An English Revivalist preacher who traveled to the United States. His sermons were marked by plain, colloquial language, and his great voice lent power to his open-air preaching. His work can be compared to the Wesley brothers and their Methodism. His theology focused on Puritan themes: original sin, justification by faith, and regeneration. In addition to traveling and preaching, he founded a school and published a magazine.

PRIMARY SOURCES

From *The Selected Sermons of George Whitefield* (Christian Classics Ethereal Library, 2013), 247-248, http://www.ccel.org/ccel/whitefield/sermons.pdf

Some, and I fear a multitude which no man can easily number, there are amongst us, who call themselves Christians, and yet seldom or never seriously think of Jesus Christ at all. They can think of their shops and their farms, their plays, their balls, their assemblies, and horse-races (entertainments which directly tend to exclude religion out of the world); but as for Christ, the author and finisher of faith, the Lord who has bought poor sinners with his precious blood, and who is the only thing worth thinking of, alas! he is not in all, or at most in very few of their thoughts. But believe me, O ye earthly, sensual, carnally-minded professors, however little you may think of Christ now, or however industriously you may strive to keep him out of your thoughts, by pursuing the lust of the eye, the lust of the flesh, and the pride of life, yet there is a time coming, when you will wish you had thought of Christ more, and of your profits and pleasures less. For the gay, the polite, the rich also must die as well as others, and leave their pomps and vanities, and all their wealth behind them. And O! what thoughts will you entertain concerning Jesus Christ, in that hour?

But I must not purpose these reflections: they would carry me too far from the main design of this discourse, which is to show, what those who are truly desirous to know how to worship God in spirit and in truth, ought to think concerning Jesus Christ, whom God hath sent to be the end of the law for righteousness to all them that shall believe.

I trust, my brethren, you are more noble than to think me too strict or scrupulous, in thus attempting to regulate your thoughts about Jesus Christ: for by our thoughts, as well as our words and actions, are we to be judged at the great day. And in vain do we hope to believe in, or worship Christ aright, unless our principles, on which our faith and practice are founded, are agreeable to the form of sound words delivered to us in the scriptures of truth.

Besides, many deceivers are gone abroad into the world. Mere heathen morality, and not Jesus Christ, is preached in most of our churches. And how should people think rightly of Christ, of whom they have scarcely heard? Bear with me a little then, whilst, to inform your consciences, I ask you a few questions concerning Jesus Christ. For there is no other name given under heaven, whereby we can be saved, but his.

First, What think you about the person of Christ? "Whose Son is he?" This is the question our Lord put to the Pharisees in the words following the text; and never was it more necessary to repeat this question than in these last days. For numbers that are called after the name of Christ, and I fear, many that pretend to preach him, are so far advanced in the blasphemous chair, as openly to deny his being really, truly, and properly God. But no one that ever was partaker of his Spirit, will speak thus lightly of him. No; if they are asked, as Peter and his brethren were, "But whom say ye that I am?" they will reply without hesitation, "Thou art Christ the Son of the ever-living God." For the confession of our Lord's divinity, is the rock upon which he builds his church. Was it possible to take this away, the gates of hell would quickly prevail against it. My brethren, if Jesus Christ be not very God of very God, I would never preach the gospel of Christ again. For it would not be gospel; it would be only a system of moral ethics. Seneca, Cicero, or any of the Gentile philosophers, would be as good a Savior as Jesus of Nazareth. It is the divinity of our Lord that gives a sanction to his death, and makes

him such a high-priest as became us, one who by the infinite mercies of his suffering could make a full, perfect sufficient sacrifice, satisfaction and oblation to infinitely offended justice. And whatsoever minister of the church of England, makes use of her forms, and eats of her bread, and yes holds not this doctrine (as I fear too many such are crept in amongst us) such a one belongs only to the synagogue of Satan. He is not a child or minister of God: no; he is a wolf in sheep's clothing; he is a child and minister of that wicked one the devil. *What Think Ye of Christ?*

Reading Questions

How does Whitefield define the difference between those who are true believers and those who are children of the devil? What is the purpose, do you suppose, of this kind of separating language? How do you compare the preaching style of Whitefield with that of Jonathan Edwards?

RELATED WORKS

Belden, Albert David. *George Whitefield, the Awakener: A Modern Study of the Evangelical Revival.* New York: Macmillan, 1953.

Whitefield, George. *Sermons of George Whitefield.* Ed. Evelyn Bence. Peabody, MA: Hendrickson, 2009.

Nikolaus von Zinzendorf (394)

(1700–60) The key figure in the renewal of Moravianism in the eighteenth century. He was also a pioneer of ecumenism and the first to use the word "ecumenical" in the modern sense.

RELATED WORKS

Wagner, Walter H. *The Zinzendorf-Muhlenberg Encounter: A Controversy in Search of Understanding.* Nazareth, PA: Moravian Historical Society, 2002.

Zinzendorf, Nicolaus Ludwig. *A Collection of Sermons from Zinzendorf's Pennsylvania Journey, 1741–42.* Trans. Julie Tomberlin Weber. Ed. Craig D. Atwood. Bethlehem, PA: Moravian Church in North America, 2001.

Chapter Summaries

28. Expansion Worldwide

Catholic missions were a major part of European colonization efforts from the beginning. Under the Sacred Congregation for the Propagation of the Faith, missionaries were sent east to Macao and Vietnam and south to what are now Zaire and Angola.

Jesuit missions spread quickly through South America with the use of "reductions" to organize the native people for more effective evangelizing. Protestant missions operated through trading companies in India, Sri Lanka, South Africa, and New England. Moravian missionaries were successful in many areas of the world, including North America, the Virgin Islands, and South Africa. Rivalries among secular governments were present in various colonized lands, but especially Africa, where the slave trade flourished and prevented most missions from succeeding.

29. Awakening

The movement known as the Great Awakening was the counterpart to Britain's Evangelical (or Methodist) Revival.

Many of the early colonists of the United States were fleeing persecution for their Protestant beliefs; most of these were Calvinists. These facts are behind the significant cultural and societal event known as the Great Awakening.

The earliest Protestants in America were Anglican, soon followed by Congregationalists and Presbyterians. Baptists first arrived on the continent in 1639 under the leadership of Separatist Roger Williams.

Preachers such as Jonathan Edwards and George Whitefield led the way to renewed faith and spiritual practice among the early Americans. Edwards preached a series of sermons in 1734 that led to a revival in a large area surrounding Northampton, Massachusetts. Whitefield's six-week tour, featuring many open-air preaching events, sparked an awakening that spread from town to town.

In Europe the Awakening had a slightly different face, from its Pietist identity in Germany to its Methodist version in England. Methodism also became a strong force in the American colonies, particularly under the leadership of Francis Asbury.

The Moravians, led by Nikolaus von Zinzendorf, provided a haven for Protestant refugees from all over Germany. They were particularly active during the Revival and were influential in the conversion of John Wesley, the co-founder of Methodism.

30. Reason and Unreason

Rationalism was a significant movement in the early modern era. While Descartes ultimately used his philosophy to prove the existence of God, his ideas challenged traditional concepts of humankind's relationship to the divine and promoted the importance of the individual.

Philosophers of the seventeenth and eighteenth centuries developed important ideas about the nature of reality, human existence, and the power of reason—all key themes of the Enlightenment and aspects of the thinkers' search for the ultimate truth.

By contrast, groups such as the Pietists and Quakers emphasized faith, devotion, and other non-rational values. George Fox, the first Quaker leader, preached to thousands on the liberating power of Christ; he emphasized a simple lifestyle without the need for church structures. His followers were persecuted in both England and the colonies.

Unitarianism taught the oneness of God and therefore rejected the idea of the Trinity. Unitarian ideas spread throughout Protestant churches but eventually led to the founding of a separate church, which later split over issues of dogma.

31. The Russian Church

The Russian church, meanwhile, was experiencing its own controversy between the Possessors and the Non-Possessors. The traditional leadership of the church, the patriarchate, was replaced by the Most Holy Synod in 1721 by Czar Peter the Great. His innovations led to a split within the Orthodox church, and in later years sectarian movements continued to grow.

Additional Readings

1. From "A Report on Whitefield in New York: *The New England Weekly Journal*, 1739," in *The Great Awakening: Documents on the Revival of Religion, 1740–1745* (Atheneum, 1970)

The following is an excerpt from a newspaper article dated December 4, 1739 (22–23) on the open-air preaching of George Whitefield:

In the Afternoon he preached in the Fields to many Hundreds of People.

Among the Hearers, the Person who gives this Account, was one. I fear Curiosity was the Motive that led me and many others into that Assembly. I . . .had obtained a settled Opinion, that he was a

Good Man. Thus far was I prejudiced in his Favour. But then having heard of much Opposition, and many Clamours against him, I tho't it possible that he might have carried Matters too far. . . . With these Prepossessions I went into the Fields; when I came there, I saw a great Number of People consisting of *Christians* of all Denominations, some *Jews*, and a few, I believe, that had no Religion at all. . . . Mr. *Whitefield* . . . prayed most excellently, in the same manner (I guess) that the first Ministers of the *Christian Church* prayed, before they were shackled with Forms. The Assembly soon appeared to be divided into two Companies, the one of which I considered under the Name of God's *Church*, and the other the *Devil's Chappel*. The first were collected round the Minister, and were very serious and attentive. The last had placed themselves in the skirts of the Assembly, and spent most of their Time in Giggling, Scoffing, Talking and Laughing. I believe the Minister saw them, for in his Sermon, observing the Cowardice and Shamefacedness of *Christians* in Christ's Cause, he pointed towards this Assembly, and reproached the former with the boldness and Zeal with which the Devil's Vassals serve him. Towards the last Prayer, the whole Assembly appeared more united, and all became hush'd and still; a solemn Awe and Reverence appeared in the Faces of most, a mighty Energy attended the Word. I heard and felt something astonishing and surprizing, but, I confess; I was not at that Time fully rid of my Scruples. But as I tho't I saw a visible Presence of God with Mr. *Whitefield*, I kept my Doubts to my self.

QUESTIONS FOR DISCUSSION AND REFLECTION

Did anything surprise you about this account of Whitefield's preaching? What was most striking about it? How does the fact it is written by a reporter who was not a follower of Whitefield affect your evaluation of the account?

See also "Reading Historical Documents" (page 171 in this volume) for other questions to consider.

2. From *Missionary Conquest: The Gospel and Native American Cultural Genocide* (Fortress Press, 1993)

In chapter 1 of his book, George E. Tinker analyzes the ideology of the Spanish missionaries who "devoted their lives to Indian evangelization" (2); he explains that his primary objectives "are to demonstrate the inevitable confusion of virtually every missionary between the gospel he, or occasionally she, proclaimed to the Indian people and the missionary's own European or Euroamerican culture, and to trace the resulting devastation of Indian peoples and their cultures" (4). In a section on the ideology of white superiority as it relates to cultural genocide, he writes (8–10):

The prevailing and thoroughly entrenched philosophical presupposition that fueled all European attitudes toward Indians was one of pronounced cultural and intellectual superiority. The notion of European superiority over native peoples goes back to the very beginnings of the European invasion, as Columbus's own diary entry for October 12, 1492, documents. . . . [From the diary:] "They ought to make good and skilled servants, for they repeat very quickly whatever we say to them. I think they can easily be made Christians, for they seem to have no religion. . . ."

. . . This European/Euroamerican notion of superiority works its way out in at least two general branches of a historical trajectory—a trajectory that used inherent superiority as a rationalization for conquest and even genocide. It became a justification for slavery and the *encomienda* system among Spanish immigrants and, later, an excuse for punishing the "hostiles" in the western United States in order to tame their perceived savagery. The other branch of the same trajectory led to a much more sympathetic concern for "the Indians," but one that saw the resolution of "the Indian problem" in the replacement of Indian culture with European culture, sometimes blatantly referred to as "Christian culture" or "Christian civilization." It was this second branch of the trajectory that energized the missionary endeavor, but around an arrogance that never questioned its clear goal of Christianizing and civilizing the savages. . . .

My points is not just to chastise the missionaries. Not only would that serve little purpose, but it would be asking these forebears in the faith to have done the impossible—namely, to have demonstrated an awareness beyond what was culturally possible at that time. Instead, my investigation has a primary objective and two closely related subordinate objectives. First, this analysis is part of an ongoing process of owning our history, honestly knowing our past, so that our future may be freed from living in a cover-up mode and our decisions for the future may be most creative and life-giving. It is equally crucial for white Americans to recognize occasions of oppressing others in their past and for Native American peoples to identify the sources of the oppression they have experienced and continue to experience. Both Indian and white must confront the lie [of white superiority] . . . that finally results in both the oppressor and the oppressed blaming the oppressed for their own oppression. Naming the oppression suffered by Indian peoples is easy. Las Casas wrote in the sixteenth century to expose Spanish atrocities. . . . Modern writers continue to expose the past and present oppression and exploitation of Native Americans. . . . Yet the churches have somehow avoided recognition of their participation in this history of destruction and oppression.

My second objective is to provide a better understanding of what is at stake in the evangelization process. If we concede good intentions to the missionaries in general, we also must be careful to recognize them as people of their own times, incapable of the hindsight of critical analysis with which we are more likely to be blessed. That they confused their spiritual proclamation of the gospel of Jesus Christ with the imposition of new and strange cultural models for daily life is today inexcusable. But a century and more ago, the distinction between gospel and Euroamerican culture was far less clear. . . . Moreover, the missionaries most often came to an Indian nation after the effects of conquest had already become visible, increasing the missionaries' sense of their own cultural superiority. De Smet's criticism of the squalor of some Indian nations is an example. In his rather devastating critique of the Potawatomis, for instance, De Smet seemed blind to the fact that he was witnessing a people in postconquest depression and not the independent, self-sufficient nation they must have been before European contact. As he moved west among nations that had been less affected at that point by the European invasion, he was invariably more impressed. In the nineteenth century, the widespread notion of divinely appointed Manifest Destiny, along with convictions that America was God's "New

Israel" and the European immigrants its chosen people, infected the missionaries as much as it did others. Even today the distinction becomes blurred on occasion. Thus, it would have been impossible for these earlier missionaries to see and acknowledge their own sin in this regard. Unfortunately the results were inevitably devastating for Indian people, utterly contradicting the intentions of the missionaries themselves.

Questions for Discussion and Reflection

What is the core of Tinker's critique of missionaries and their attitude toward Native Americans? What other significant point does he make here about the historical context of missionaries in early American history? If you were to read an account from a Spanish missionary in early nineteenth-century California, how would Tinker's insight affect your interpretation?

3. From *Russian Mystics* (Cistercian Publications, 1977)

Sergius Bolsharkoff describes the life and mystic experiences of Russian Orthodox bishop Tikhon, who lived from 1724 to 1783 (66–68):

> The bishop began his night vigils after his first mystical experience. . . . [Tikhon recalled:] "One night in May was pleasant, quiet and clear. I went out of my room to the balcony which faced the North. I stood and meditated on eternal beatitude. Suddenly heaven opened and I saw such a sea of light that no corruptible tongue nor mind could ever comprehend it. This wondrous vision started in me a burning desire for the solitary life. Long after that vision I was full of joy and even now when I remember it I feel in my heart a peculiar gaiety and joy."
>
> . . . Tikhon lived in Zadonsk in great simplicity. He slept on the carpet with two pillows, without a blanket, covering himself with a fur overcoat. His cassock was the poorest, as well as his socks and shoes. He often used to walk in peasant footgear. . . . The walls of his cell were bare but for pictures of Christ's passion and of a dead man in the coffin. Tikhon often looked at the latter picture and sang: "Tell me, Lord, my end and what is the number of my days, to give an account of them." Even this humble life seemed too lofty for him. He often said: "If it were possible I would lay down my episcopacy and not only that dignity but also my cowl and would say to others I am a simple peasant. I would go then to the remotest monastery as a laborer, saw wood, carry water, bake bread. It is misery that here in Russia, this is impossible to do!"
>
> . . . In Zadonsk St Tikhon experienced several raptures and visions. In 1775 he prayed, "Lord, show me the place prepared for those who love you and what is pity." And coming before the alter he prayed. Then he saw heaven open and the entire monastery illuminated and there was a voice saying: "Look what is prepared for those who love God." He beheld a scene of indescribable beauty and fell in fear to the earth. He could only crawl back to his cell with difficulty.

QUESTIONS FOR DISCUSSION AND REFLECTION

What does this portrait of Tikhon emphasize about the man and about the orthodox faith? Compare the accounts of his mystical experience with those of other mystics, such as Julian of Norwich. What similar elements can you identify?

Selected Online Resources

▶ "Religion and the Founding of the American Republic: Religion in Eighteenth-Century America"—an illustrated essay from the Library of Congress
http://www.loc.gov/exhibits/religion/rel02.html

▶ "The Great Awakening"—essays, illustrations, and bibliographies on the figures and events of the Great Awakening
http://www.great-awakening.com/

▶ "The Great Awakening: Biographies"—links to biographical essays on Jonathan Edwards, William Tennent, Gilbert Tennent, and George Whitefield
http://greatawakeningdocumentary.com/exhibits/show/biographies

▶ "The Competing Legacies of Junípero Serra" by Steven W. Hackel—discussion of Serra's complex reputation and symbolic value as missionary to Native peoples of California, with illustrations
http://www.common-place.org/vol-05/no-02/hackel/index.shtml

▶ "Philip Jacob Spener's Contribution to the Protestant Doctrine of the Church"—an extensive scholarly essay on Spener's influence and historical and religious context
http://www.xenos.org/essays/spen_a.htm

▶ "Moravian Women during the Eighteenth Century"—an essay by the scholar Beverly Smaby about the role of women in the Moravian church during Zinzendorf's lifetime
http://zinzendorf.com/pages/index.php?id=moravian-women

▶ "The J. S. Bach Home Page"—landing page with links to biography, illustrations, extensive information on his music, related sites (some with sample music files)
http://www.jsbach.org

Guide to Part 6: Cities and Empires

Key Terms

The number in parentheses refers to the page where the term is explained.

camp meeting (459)   Religious revival carried into the frontier wherein members of individual congregations from a region traveled to a central location, pooled resources, and crossed denominational boundaries to reach the masses.

crusade among equals (459)   The ministry of untrained and unpaid farmer-ministers who gathered in small groups of several families and organized their own churches, before moving westward to spread the revival fire.

theory of evolution (465)   A scientific theory holding that plant and animal life evolves naturally with the fittest surviving, made most known by Charles Darwin and his *Origin of the Species*. Also has roots in ancient Greek philosophy.

Idealism (468)   Instead of starting with the individual "I," the Idealists began with the absolute "I": all reality is the manifestation of the Absolute Spirit. God does not exist over and above the world, as in Christian orthodoxy, but is the "world spirit" that is to be found in the depths of the world's processes. The world is a manifestation of God.

Industrial Revolution (440)   Beginning in 1760, a period of rapid industrialization and urbanization.

Oxford Movement (450)   A movement within the Anglican church, also known as the Tractarian Revival, with roots in the High Church movement of the seventeenth century, that sought to revive lost Christian traditions from the first four centuries and resulted in the formation of Anglo-Catholicism.

papal infallibility (434)   A dogma of the Catholic Church that teaches the pope is infallible (incapable of error) when speaking *ex cathedra* on matters of faith and practice.

Ultramontanism (429)   Derived from a term meaning "beyond the mountains," a movement within the Catholic church that places the highest recognition of authority on the pope in Rome.

Key Personalities

Numbers in parentheses refer to the pages where the text provides the individual's biographical details and historical significance.

Samuel Crowther (489)

(c. 1806–91) The outstanding African Christian leader of his time. Having escaped being enslaved, he was baptized in Sierra Leone and became a teacher for the Church Missionary Society. He became the first African Anglican bishop in 1864.

PRIMARY SOURCES

From Samuel Crowther, *Journal of an Expedition up the Niger and Tshadda Rivers* 2nd ed. (London: Cass, 1970).

> I believe the time is fully come when Christianity must be introduced on the banks of the Niger: the people are willing to receive any who may be sent among them. The English are still looked upon as their friends, with whom they themselves desire to have connexion as with the first nation in the world. Could the work have begun since 1841, how imperfect soever it might have been, yet it would have kept up the thread of connexion with England and the countries on the banks of the Niger. God has provided instruments to begin the work, in the liberated Africans in the Colony of Sierra Leone, who are the natives of the banks of this river. *A Letter to Rev. H. Venn, December 2, 1854.*
>
> *July 23: Sunday.* Had service on board at half-past ten, and preached from St. John i. 29. The boat was just ready for me after service, to go on shore to see and speak a few words with the chief on religious subject, and also to ask his permission to address the people in the town, when his canoe appeared from the creek, with numerous attendants, so I postponed my going till his return; but he remained so long on board, that there was no prospect of his soon going away. When Captain Taylor had done with him, I took the opportunity to speak with him at length on the subject of the Christian religion, Simon Jonas interpreting for me. The quickness with which he caught my explanation of the all sufficient sacrifice of Jesus Christ, the Son of God, for the sin of the world, was gratifying. . . He frequently repeated the names, "Oparra Tshuku! Oparra Tshuku!" Son of God! Son of God! As I did not wish to tire him out, I left my discourse fresh in his mind. The attention of his attendants, with the exception of a few, was too much engaged in begging and receiving presents, to listen to all I was talking about. I gave Tshukuma a Yoruba primer, in which I wrote his name; and left some with Simon Jonas, to teach the children, or any who should feel disposed to learn, the Alphabet and words of two letters. Tshukuma and his attendants were perfectly at home in the steamer, and it was not till a gentle hind was given them, that the gentlemen wanted to take their dinner, that he ordered his people to make ready for their departure, at half-past four o'clock. *The Diaries of Samuel Crowther, 1854.*

Reading Questions

How does Crowther seem to characterize the native Africans in comparison to the English? What are the basic goals of Crowther's mission?

Related Works

Crowther, Samuel. *Journal of an Expedition up the Niger and Tshadda Rivers.* 2nd ed. London: Cass, 1970.

Crowther, Samuel, and John Christopher Taylor. *The Gospel on the Banks of the Niger: Journals and Notices of the Native Missionaries Accompanying the Niger Expedition of 1857-1850.* London: Dawsons, 1968.

Charles Darwin (465–66)

(1809–82). The father of the theory of evolution. He landmark work *On the Origin of Species* promoted his theory of natural selection.

Primary Sources

From Charles Darwin, *On the Origin of Species*, (London: John Murray 1859), 126ff.

> If during the long course of ages and under varying conditions of life, organic beings vary at all in the several parts of their organization, and I think this cannot be disputed; if there be, owing to the high geometrical powers of increase of each species at some ages, season, or year, a severe struggle for life, and this certainly cannot be disputed; then, considering the infinite complexity of the relations of all organic beings to each other and to their conditions of existence, causing an infinite diversity in structure, constitution, and habits, to be advantageous to them I think it would be a most

> extraordinary fact if no variation ever had occurred useful to each being's own welfare, in the same way as so many variations have occurred useful to man. But if variations useful to any organic being do occur, assuredly individuals thus characterized will have the best chance of being preserved in the struggle for life; and from the strong principle of inheritance they will tend to produce offspring similarly characterized. This principle of preservation, I have called, for the sake of brevity, Natural Selection. *On the Origin of Species, Chapter IV.*

Reading Questions

How does this description from Darwin of his concept of natural selection cohere with what you have heard and read about the theory of evolution? What seems new and what is familiar about the way Darwin lays out his argument here?

Related Works

Browne, Janet. *Charles Darwin: A Biography.* 2 vols. New York: Knopf, 1995–2002.

Darwin, Charles. *The Origin of Species by Means of Natural Selection.* Ed. W. R. Thompson. New York: Dutton, 1956.

David Livingstone (484–85)

(1813–73) Medical missionary and explorer from Scotland. He strongly opposed the slave trade and proposed trade and agriculture as a substitute economic system, to be accompanied by the gospel message.

Primary Sources

From David Livingstone, *Missionary Travels and Researches in South Africa*, (Project Gutenberg

EBook, 2013), http://www.gutenberg.org/files/1039/1039-h/1039-h.htm

Sending the Gospel to the heathen must, if this view be correct, include much more than is implied in the usual picture of a missionary, namely, a man going about with a Bible under his arm. The promotion of commerce ought to be specially attended to, as this, more speedily than any thing else, demolishes that sense of isolation which heathenism engenders, and makes the tribes feel themselves mutually dependent on, and mutually beneficial to each other. With a view to this, the missionaries at Kuruman got permission from the government for a trader to reside at the station, and a considerable trade has been the result; the trader himself has become rich enough to retire with a competence. Those laws which still prevent free commercial intercourse among the civilized nations seem to be nothing else but the remains of our own heathenism. My observations on this subject make me extremely desirous to promote the preparation of the raw materials of European manufactures in Africa, for by that means we may not only put a stop to the slave-trade, but introduce the negro family into the body corporate of nations, no one member of which can suffer without the others suffering with it. Success in this, in both Eastern and Western Africa, would lead, in the course of time, to a much larger diffusion of the blessings of civilization than efforts exclusively spiritual and educational confined to any one small tribe. These, however, it would of course be extremely desirable to carry on at the same time at large central and healthy stations, for neither civilization nor Christianity can be promoted alone. In fact, they are inseparable.

Reading Questions

What characteristics of a missionary does Livingstone lift up here as exemplary? What characteristics does he eschew?

Related Works

Livingstone, David. *Livingstone's Travels*. Ed. James I. Macnair with Ronald Miller. New York: Macmillan, 1954.

Tomkins, Stephen. *David Livingstone: The Unexplored Story*. London: Lion, 2013.

D. L. Moody (460)

(1837–99) Noted American evangelist as well as businessman. He was converted by his Sunday school teacher and joined the Congregational Church, to which he actively recruited new members. His evangelistic fame began in England on tour, and afterward he devoted his life to revivals. He founded two schools and a summer Bible conference.

Primary Sources

From D.L. Moody, *To the Work! To the Work! Exhortations to Christians,* (Chicago: F.H. Revell, 1884), 8 ff.

What does 'Revival' mean? It simply means a recalling from obscurity—a finding some hidden treasure and bringing it back to the light. I think that every one of us must acknowledge that we are living in a time of need. I doubt if there is a family in the world that has not some relative whom they would like to see brought into the fold of God, and who needs salvation.

Men are anxious for a revival in business. I am told that there is a widespread and general stagnation in business. People are very anxious that there should be a revival of trade this winter. There is a great revival in politics just now. In all departments of life you find that men are very anxious for a revival in the things that concern them most.

If this is legitimate—and I do not say but it is perfectly right in its place—should not every child of God be praying for and desiring a revival of godliness in the world at the present time. Do we not need a revival of downright honesty, of truthfulness, of uprightness, and of temperance? Are there not many who have become alienated from the Church of God and from the house of the Lord, who are forming an attachment to the saloon? Are not our sons being drawn away by hundreds and thousands, so that while you often find the churches empty, the liquor shops are crowded every Sabbath afternoon and evening. I am sure the saloon-keepers are glad if they can have a revival in their business; they do not object to sell more whisky and beer. Then surely every true Christian ought to desire that men who are in danger of perishing eternally should be saved and rescued. . .

People are so afraid of excitement. When I went over to England in 1867, I was asked to go and preach at the Derby racecourse. I saws more excitement there in one day than I have seen at all the religious meetings I ever attended in my life put together. And yet I heard no one complaining of too much excitement. I heard of a minister, not long ago, who was present at a public dance till after five o'clock in the morning. The next Sabbath he preached against the excitement of revivals—the late hours, and so on. Very consistent kind of reasoning, was it not? . . .

There are many professed Christians who are all the time finding fault and criticizing. . . You may find hundreds of such fault-finders among professed Christians; but all their criticism will not lead one solitary soul to Christ. I never preached a sermon yet that I could not pick to pieces and find fault with. I feel that Jesus Christ ought to have a far better representative than I am. But I have lived long enough to discover that there is nothing perfect in this world. If you are to wait until you can find a perfect preacher, or perfect meetings, I am afraid you will have to wait till the millennium arrives. What we want is to be looking right up to Him. Let us get done with fault-finding. . . my friends, it is so easy to find fault; it takes neither brains nor heart. *To the Work!*

Reading Questions

How is your response to this description of revivalism and preaching from Moody colored by having read excerpts from the sermons of Jonathan Edwards and George Whitefield? What do you note as unique about Moody's perspective?

RELATED WORKS

Evensen, Bruce J. *God's Man for the Gilded Age: D. L. Moody and the Rise of Modern Mass Evangelism*. New York: Oxford University Press, 2003.

Moody, Dwight Lyman. *Commending the Faith: The Preaching of D. L. Moody.* Ed. Garth Rosell. Peabody, MA: Hendrickson, 1999.

John Henry Newman (455)

(1801–90) The leader of the Oxford Movement and later a Roman Catholic cardinal. He was the son of an Evangelical, but even after his conversion experience, he felt drawn to the Catholic tradition. He believed the church's authority was guaranteed by apostolic descent, and his *Tract 90* was one of his last efforts to justify the Church of England. He converted to Catholicism in 1845 and became a cardinal in 1877.

PRIMARY SOURCES

From John Henry Cardinal Newman, *Apologia pro Vita Sua* (London: Longmans, Green, and Co., 1908), 241ff.

To consider the world in its length and breadth, its various history, the many races of man, their starts, their fortunes, their mutual alienation, their conflicts; and then their ways, habits, governments, forms of worship; their enterprises, their aimless courses, their random achievements and acquirements, the impotent conclusion of long-standing facts, the tokens so faint and broken of a superintending design, the blind evolution of what turn out to be great powers or truths, the progress of things, as if from unreasoning elements, not towards final causes, the greatness and littleness of man, his far-reaching aims, his short duration, the curtain hung over his futurity, the disappointments of life, the defeat of good, the success of evil, physical pain, mental anguish, the prevalence and intensity of sin, the pervading idolatries, the corruptions, the dreary hopeless irreligion, that condition of the whole race, so fearfully yet exactly described in the Apostle's words, "having no hope and without God in the world,"—all this is a vision to dizzy and appall; and inflicts upon the mind the sense of a profound mystery, which is absolutely beyond human solution. . .

And now, supposing it were the blessed and loving will of the Creator to interfere in this anarchical condition of things, what are we to suppose would be the methods which might be necessarily or naturally involved in His purpose of mercy? Since the world is in so abnormal a state, surely it would be no surprise to me, if the interposition were of necessity equally extraordinary—or what is called miraculous. But that subject does not directly come into the scope of my present remarks. Miracles as evidence, involve a process of reason, or an argument; and of course I am thinking of some mode of interference which does not immediately run into argument. I am rather asking what must be the face-to-face antagonist, by which to withstand and baffle the fierce energy of passion and the all-corroding, all-dissolving scepticism of the intellect in religious inquiries? I have no intention at all of denying, that truth is the real object of our reason, and that, if it does not attain to truth, either the premis or the process is in fault; but I am not speaking here of right reason, but of reason as it acts in fact and concretely in fallen man. I know that even the unaided reason, when correctly exercised, leads to a belief in God, in the immortality of the soul, and in a future retribution; but I am considering the faculty of reason actually and historically; and in this point of view, I do not think I am wrong in saying that its tendency is towards a simple unbelief in matters of religion. No truth, however sacred, can stand against it, in the long run; and hence it is that in the pagan world, when our Lord came, the last traces of the religious knowledge of former times were all but disappearing from those portions of the world in which the intellect had been active and had had a career. . .

Supposing then it to be the Will of the Creator to interfere in human affairs, and to make provisions for retaining in the world a knowledge of Himself, so definite and distinct as to be proof against the energy of human scepticism, in such a case,—I am far from saying that there was no other way,—but there is nothing to surprise the mind, if He should think fit to introduce a power into the world, invested with the prerogative of infallibility in religious matters. Such a provision would be a direct, immediate, active, and prompt means of withstanding the difficulty; it would be an instrument suited to the need; and, when I find that this is the very claim of the Catholic Church, not only do I feel no difficulty in admitting the idea, but there is a fitness in it, which recommends it to my mind.

Reading Questions

How do you respond to Newman's argument here about the necessity of the church? From which sources of evidence is the argument drawn—reason, experience, tradition, observation?

RELATED WORKS

Ker, Ian. *John Henry Newman: A Biography.* 1988; reprint, Oxford: Oxford University Press, 2009.

Newman, John Henry. *Apologia pro vita sua and Six Sermons.* Ed. Frank M. Turner. New Haven, CT: Yale University Press, 2008.

Pope Pius IX (433)

(1792–1878) The longest-serving pope in history. He summoned the first Vatican Council to meet in Rome and also proclaimed the doctrines of the immaculate conception (the belief that the Virgin Mary was conceived immaculately) and of papal infallibility (see Key Terms).

PRIMARY SOURCES

From *The Immaculate Conception: Ineffabilis* Deus, Apostolic Constitution issued by Pope Pius IX on December 8, 1854, (Papal Encyclicals Online, 2013), http://www.papalencyclicals.net/Pius09/p9ineff.htm.

From the very beginning, and before time began, the eternal Father chose and prepared for his only-begotten Son a Mother in whom the Son of God would become incarnate and from whom, in the blessed fullness of time, he would be born into this world. Above all creatures did God so loved [sic] her that truly in her was the Father well pleased with singular delight. Therefore, far above all the angels and all the saints so wondrously did God endow her with the abundance of all heavenly gifts poured from the treasury of his divinity that this mother, ever absolutely free of all stain of sin, all fair and perfect, would possess that fullness of holy innocence and sanctity than which, under God, one cannot even imagine anything greater, and which, outside of God, no mind can succeed in comprehending fully.

And indeed it was wholly fitting that so wonderful a mother should be ever resplendent with the glory of most sublime holiness and so completely free from all taint of original sin that she would triumph utterly over the ancient serpent. To her did the Father will to give his only-begotten Son—the Son whom, equal to the Father and begotten by him, the Father loves from his heart—and to give this Son in such a way that he would be the one and the same common Son of God the Father and of the Blessed Virgin Mary. It was she whom the Son himself chose to make his Mother and it was from her that the Holy Spirit willed and brought it about that he should be conceived and born from whom he himself proceeds. . .

Wherefore, in humility and fasting, we unceasingly offered our private prayers as well as the public prayers of the Church to God the Father through his Son, that he would deign to direct and strengthen our mind by the power of the Holy Spirit. In like manner did we implore the help of the entire heavenly host as we ardently invoked the Paraclete. Accordingly, by the inspiration of the Holy Spirit, for the honor of the Holy and undivided Trinity, for the glory and adornment of the Virgin Mother of God, for the exaltation of the Catholic Faith, and for the furtherance of the Catholic religion, by the authority of Jesus Christ our Lord, of the Blessed Apostles Peter and Paul, and by our own: "We declare, pronounce, and define that

the doctrine which holds that the most Blessed Virgin Mary, in the first instance of her conception, by a singular grace and privilege granted by Almighty God, in view of the merits of Jesus Christ, the Savior of the human race, was preserved free from all stain of original sin, is a doctrine revealed by God and therefore to be believed firmly and constantly by all the faithful."

Hence, if anyone shall dare—which God forbid!—to think otherwise than as has been defined by us, let him know and understand that he is condemned by his own judgment; that he has suffered shipwreck in the faith; that he has separated from the unity of the Church; and that, furthermore, by his own action he incurs the penalties established by law if he should are [sic] to express in words or writing or by any other outward means the errors he think in his heart.

Reading Questions

How would you characterize the writing style, tone, and function of a papal encyclical? What does this text reveal to you about the authority of the church—particularly the pope—when it comes to defining doctrine?

RELATED WORKS

Hales, E. E. Y. *Pio Nono: A Study in European Politics and Religion in the Nineteenth Century.* New York: P. J. Kenedy, 1954.

Hasler, August Bernhard. *How the Pope Became Infallible: Pius IX and the Politics of Persuasion.* Trans. Peter H. Heinegg. Garden City, NY: Doubleday, 1981.

Friedrich Schleiermacher (468)

(1768–1834) German theologian and a pioneer of biblical criticism. A Pietist, he was ardently patriotic and believed the unification of the Protestant church would be part of German national renewal. He saw the essence of religion in experience and declared that believers are absolutely dependent on God.

PRIMARY SOURCES

From Friedrich Schleiermacher, *Pioneer of Modern Theology,* edited by Keith W. Clements (Fortress Press: Minneapolis, 1991),70.

> Let us then, I pray you, examine whence exactly religion has it's rise. Is it from some clear intuition, or from some vague thought? Is it from the different kinds of sects of religion found in history, or from some general idea which you have perhaps conceived arbitrarily? Some doubtless will profess the latter view. But here as in other things the ready judgment may be without ground, the matter being superficially considered and no trouble being taken to gain an accurate knowledge. Your general idea turns on fear of an eternal being, or, broadly, respect for his influence on the occurrences of this life called by you providence, on expectation of a future life after this one, called by you immortality. These two conceptions which you have rejected, are, you consider, in one way or another, the hinges of all religion. But say, my dear sirs, how you have found this; for there are two points of view from which everything taking place in man or proceeding from him may be regarded. Considered from the centre outwards, that is according to its inner quality, it is an expression of human nature, based in one of its necessary modes of acting or impulses or whatever else you like to call it, for I will not now quarrel with your technical language. On the contrary, regarded from the outside, according to the definite attitude and form it assumes in particular cases, it is a product of time and history. From what side have you considered religion that great spiritual phenomenon, that you have reached the idea that everything called by this name has a common content? You can hardly affirm that it is by regarding it from within. If so, my good sirs, you would have to admit that these thoughts are at least in some way based in human nature. And should you say that as no found they have sprung only from misinterpretations or false references of a necessary human aim, it would become you to seek in it the true and eternal, and to unite your efforts to ours to free human nature from the injustice which it always suffers when aught in it is misunderstood or misdirected.

Reading Questions

According to Schleiermacher, what is the basis or source of religious activity? In your estimate, does this argument serve to undermine or increase the value of religion?

RELATED WORKS

Redeker, Martin. *Schleiermacher: Life and Thought.* Trans. John Wallhausser. Philadelphia: Fortress Press, 1973.

Schleiermacher, Friedrich. *On Religion: Speeches to Its Cultured Despisers.* Trans. John Oman. Louisville, KY: Westminster/John Knox, 1994.

Chapter Summaries

32. Europe in Revolt

The French Revolution brought the church under control of the government more thoroughly than ever before. The papacy was powerless to stop the changes—including the requirement that clergy swear allegiance to the French constitution. And although Napoleon Bonaparte reached a concordat with Pope Pius VII, the state retained the right to veto the appointments of both bishops and clergy.

The conservative reaction was to reassert the divine right of kings and the authority of the church over all. But when Friedrich Wilhelm III of Prussia decreed the union of the Lutheran and Reformed churches in Germany, he was strongly opposed by both denominations. And while ultramontanism sought to confirm the power of the pope, the Roman church continued to struggle with secular movements and authorities. Ultimately it lost much ground under hostile French and Italian governments.

33. The First Industrial Nation

During the Industrial Revolution an evangelical fervor swept over Britain. The revival resulted in renewed evangelism and the establishment of organizations such as the Salvation Army. Moreover, a concern to improve society and human living standards led to widespread opposition to slavery as well as some attempts to improve conditions in factories and elsewhere.

City churches in England often focused on missions to the poor, although some seemed to have little purpose except to perpetuate the self-satisfaction of the middle and upper classes. Meanwhile, other movements like the Tractarian Revival, or Oxford Movement, looked to the medieval heritage of the church in aiming to reform the Anglican church from within.

34. A Crusade Among Equals

In the United States a second Great Awakening developed, particularly on the frontier through camp meetings. Abolitionism was an important movement that crossed denominational boundaries, although many Christians were also slaveholders or supporters of slavery.

35. A World Come of Age

One of the greatest controversies of the nineteenth century was the conflict between the traditional Christian view of creation and Charles Darwin's theory of evolution. Darwin's ideas were argued over and supported not only by scientists and religious scholars but also by political philosophers such as Karl Marx and business leaders.

Modern philosophy and biblical criticism were just two of the forces that forced the church into a defensive posture. Archaeology helped to confirm the accuracy of much historical information in the Bible; at the same time new interpretive methods challenged long-held beliefs about the meanings of Scripture.

36. Outposts of Empire

The missionary society, a new organization in the eighteenth century, was the outcome of a renewed priority, that of preaching the gospel to the world. While the Catholic Church was the first to send missions to many countries, among the Protestants the Evangelicals became eager to bring their message to foreign peoples.

The relationship between the colonial powers and the missions was ambiguous at best. While, at first, governments made grants to churches to help with projects such as education, later missionaries questioned their nations' activities overseas, including involvement in the slave trade. Ultimately, however, churches embraced the view that Christianity, commerce, and civilization were inextricably linked.

One result of the expanding missionary movement was the need for more translations of the Bible. Hence the Bible societies were born. These organizations often funded emerging churches as well as supplying them with copies of Scripture. They were typically ecumenical efforts.

Additional Readings

1. From "Memoirs of the Life, Religious Experience, Ministerial Travels and Labours of Mrs. Zilpha Elaw, an American Female of Colour; Together with Some Account of the Great Religious Revivals in America [Written by Herself]" in *Sisters of the Spirit: Three Black Women's Autobiographies of the Nineteenth Century* (Indiana University Press, 1986)

Zilpha Elaw begins her 1846 memoir with a letter to the "faithful Brethren in Christ, who have honoured my ministry with their attendance, in London and other localities of England" (51–52; note that the bracketed biblical references were inserted by the volume editor, William L. Andrews):

Dear Brethren and Friends,

After sojourning in your hospitable land, and peregrinating among you during these last five years; in the course of which period, it has been my happiness to enjoy much spiritual intercourse with may of you in your family circles, your social meetings, and in the house of God, I feel a strong desire again to cross the pathless bosom of the foaming Atlantic and rejoin my dear friends in the occidental land of my nativity; and, in the prospect of an early departure from your shores, I feel that I cannot present you with a more appropriate keepsake, or a more lively memento of my Christian esteem, and affectionate desires for your progressive prosperity and perfection in the Christian calling, than the following contour portrait of my regenerated constitution—exhibiting, as did the bride of Solomon, comeliness with blackness [Song of Sol. 1:5]; and, as did the apostle Paul, riches with poverty, and power in weakness [2 Cor. 12:9]—a representation, not, indeed, of the features of my outward person, drawn and coloured by the skill of the pencilling artist, but of the lineaments of my inward man, as inscribed by the Holy Ghost, and, according to my poor ability, copied off for your edification.

. . . My dear brethren and sisters in the Lord. . . . I affectionately exhort you to walk worthy of the high vocation wherewith you are called, shunning, carefully, the destructive vices which so deplorably abound in and disfigure the Christian community, in this day of feverish restlessness and mighty movement. Remember, dear brethren, that they who will be rich, fall into temptation, and a snare, and numerous foolish and hurtful lusts, which will eventually drown them in perdition. Cease, therefore, from earthly accumulations; but lay up for yourselves treasures in heaven. Renounce the love of money; for it is the root of all evil [1 Tim. 6:10]. Love not the world; for the love of God is not in those who love the world. Look deep into the principles which form the under current, regardless of the artificial surface-polish of society; and abhor the pride of respectability; for that which is highly esteemed amongst men, is an abomination in the sight of God.

QUESTIONS FOR DISCUSSION AND REFLECTION

How would you describe the tone of Elaw's letter? What are the main themes of her message to her "Brethren" in England? What do the elements of her writing (word choice, sentence structure, and so forth) tell you about her concerns and her social and historical context?

See also "Reading Historical Documents" (page 171 in this volume) for other questions to consider.

2. From *Mission and Menace: Four Centuries of American Religious Zeal* (Fortress Press, 2008)

In chapter 5, "The Second Great Awakening: Manifest Destiny, Reform, and the Pre-Millennial Reaction," Robert Jewett writes about some of the features and effects of the Second Great Awakening (87–90):

In the first three decades of the nineteenth century, a Second Great Awakening swept over the country, with particular strength in the expanding West. It produced a radical democratization of American religion and spawned an awesome number of new denominations and reform movements. In Nathan Hatch's estimation, "Christendom had probably not witnessed a comparable period of religious upheaval since the Reformation—and never such an explosion of entrepreneurial energy." It started in the summer of 1801 in an extraordinary outdoor revival over a seven-day period in Cane Ridge, Kentucky. Between ten thousand and twenty thousand people took part, with services marked by mass hysteria and lasting all day and night with preaching by Presbyterian, Baptist, and Methodist evangelists. "Observers noted that some worshipers wept uncontrollably while others appeared to laugh, twitch, and run in circles. Some even fell to their knees and barked like dogs."

In the same year there were important steps in missionary planning by the well-established Presbyterians and Congregationalists, who agreed to cooperate in organizing churches in the West and allowing clergy from either denomination to serve. Nevertheless, because of their affinity with revivalist techniques and lower educational requirements for their ministers, the Baptists and the Methodists were able to function more effectively in the thinly settled and rapidly moving frontier. They carried the revival to every part of the country. The Baptists grew from 460 congregations in 1780 to over 12,000 by 1860. . . .

The Methodists were even more successful with their system of training lay preachers who served as circuit riders, moving from settlement to settlement on the frontier, holding services, and organizing small groups of converts that would meet regularly even when the preacher could only be present when he made his rounds. Under the leadership of Bishop Francis Asbury, who followed an even more grueling itinerary than his pastors, the church devoted itself "to condescend to men of low estate," primarily on the frontier. Itinerancy was advocated as a recovery of the ethos of the early church, which had been shaped by traveling evangelists. A dramatic account by James Girth tells of his circuit riding in 1834, preaching several times a day, sleeping in homes of converts, baptizing their children, and helping with their work. He refers to a "camp meeting," which would be an outdoor revival service, and a "prayer meeting," which would be an informal service with a smaller group of believers. His sermons ended with a call for "mourners" to come forward to confess their sins and receive grace.

. . . Both the Baptists and the Methodists stressed the need for taking personal responsibility for one's salvation, and they were adept at using the revivalist methods developed in the Great Awakening. The Methodists were in tune with the optimistic, post-millennial civil religion, stressing the perfectibility of believers and their free will to accept salvation and make decisions for the betterment of their lives. Nevertheless, a contemporaneous description of a Methodist meeting in North Carolina in 1807 reveals a revivalist intensity that was often troubling to outsiders:

> About a week past there was a methodist conference in this place which lasted 7 or 8 days & nights with very little intermission, during which there was a large concourse of people of various colors, classes & such, assembled for various purposes. Confusion, shouting, praying, singing, laughing, talking, amorous engagements, falling down, kicking, squealing and a thousand other ludicrous things prevailed most of the time and frequently of nights, all at once—In short, it was the most detestible farcical scene that ever I beheld.

The conference's tolerance of religious and cultural diversity evident in this description embodies the "liberty" extolled by Methodist evangelists, who resonated with the democratic civil religion claimed by the country as a whole.

. . . The main force in the Second Great Awakening was the Protestant clergy from the denominations that had benefited most from the first awakening: the Baptists, the Methodists, and to a lesser extent the Presbyterians. . . . In place of a single towering figure who covered the entire country, such as George Whitefield, there were hundreds of evangelical revivalist preachers—male, female, black, Native, and white—who had learned to use the revivalist techniques Whitefield had developed. Sermons were extemporaneous; services were held out where the people were, in camp meetings or town halls; advertising was used, and printed tracts were distributed; and the calls to individual religious decision were supported by new forms of the Jeremiad sermon.

QUESTIONS FOR DISCUSSION AND REFLECTION

Based on this chapter excerpt, how would you describe what Jewett calls the "democratic civil religion claimed by the country as a whole" during the Second Great Awakening? What role did things like camp meetings and circuit riders play in the development of Protestant denominations in the United States?

3. From *Women and the Work of Benevolence: Morality, Politics, and Class in the 19th-Century United States* (Yale University Press, 1990)

Lori D. Ginzburg explores the role of middle-class Protestant women in nineteenth-century America as social reformers. She points to the significant role of Christian ideas and virtues in the way women's roles were defined:

> By the nineteenth century, piety and moral virtue had come to be associated with female qualities. Women had long dominated Protestant church congregations, participating in the process by which Christianity gradually recast an older image of women as lustful seducers of men. . . . Women's adherence to, indeed identification with, traditional Christian virtues—humility, modesty, submission, piety—would "exalt [them] to an equal rank with man in all the felicities of the soul, in all the advantages of religious attainment, in all the prospects and hopes of immortality. . . ."
>
> The ideology of female moral superiority was a central component of nineteenth-century domesticity, or the "cult of true womanhood." It was among women's duties to be religious, insisted Lydia Sigourney, who claimed women's greater fitness of guarding the morals of home and society. Women, she wrote, were "sheltered from temptation"; this, added to "our physical weakness, our trials, and our inability to protect ourselves, prompt that trust in Heaven, that implicit leaning upon a Divine arm." Women both embodied and utilized "the highest natural faculty or element of the human soul . . . moral sense." The message was clear: women were protected by their religious training from abandoning themselves to the lusts and corruptions of men; they were in turn duty bound to cling to religion as the only safeguard against vice.
>
> . . . That women were less often discovered in a degraded condition fueled the belief that women bore a responsibility to teach virtue to others. . . . Women, numerous observers insisted, could affect all aspects of life, from church attendance to drinking, from education to laws. "It is woman's womanhood, her instinctive femininity, her highest morality that society now needs to counteract the excess of masculinity that is everywhere to be found in our unjust and unequal laws," claimed Jane Frohock in 1856.
>
> . . . Women . . . would activate an influence that was very nearly divine in nature. In theory, the more invisible—that is to say, characteristically feminine—this influence was, the more effective. "Woman is to win every thing by peace and love," intoned Catharine Beecher. Indeed, women's agency was so gentle, pervasive, and unseen that the world would hardly know it was being subverted. A Michigan abolitionist explained that "woman's influence, distilling like the dew of Heaven, gentle, constant and no less effectual, fertilizes and refreshes where it goes, and steals over the heart with irresistless power, which prompts to action."

According to this reading, how did women's benevolent roles reflect Christian social ideals? How did women themselves use religious ideas in their public exhortations to other women?

Selected Online Resources

▶ "Into the Wilderness: Circuit Riders Take Religion to the People"—illustrated article on the role of circuit riders in early American Methodist history
http://www.learnnc.org/lp/editions/nchist-newnation/4451

▶ "Newman Reader: Works"—a list of links (ordered chronologically) to the text of the works of John Henry Newman
http://www.newmanreader.org/works/index.html

▶ "Boston Collaborative Encyclopedia of Western Theology: Friedrich Schleiermacher"—extensive biographical essay with information on major works, plus a bibliography
http://people.bu.edu/wwildman/bce/mwt_themes_470_schleiermacher.htm

▶ "Samuel Crowther: The Slave Boy Who Became Bishop of the Niger"—images and text from a nineteenth-century biography of the African bishop
http://anglicanhistory.org/africa/crowther/page1892/

▶ Livingstone Online—an extensive collection of Livingstone's publications and letters (including images of the original manuscripts), along with essays on his life and work
http://www.livingstoneonline.ucl.ac.uk/index.php

▶ "Africans in America"—covers the history from 1450 to 1865 with information on people, events, the complex role of Christianity, and the birth of the black church
http://www.pbs.org/wgbh/aia/home.html

▶ "Hannah More: Biography and Bibliography"—information about an important English abolitionist with links to primary sources and information on her contemporaries
http://www.brycchancarey.com/abolition/more.htm

▶ "The Second Great Awakening: A Christian Nation?"—video and transcript of the forty-fifth Henry J. Miller Distinguished Lecture at the Georgia State University College of Law given by Geoffrey R. Stone, a University of Chicago professor
http://digitalarchive.gsu.edu/cgi/viewcontent.cgi?article=2593&context=gsulr

Guide to Part 7: A Century of Conflict

Key Terms

The number in parentheses refers to the page where the term is explained. Those terms marked with asterisks also appear in the Glossary.

Barmen Declaration (504–5) Document spelling out the theological basis of the Confessing Church (an alternative church government structure), written by Karl Barth in May 1934. Called the German church back to the central truths of Christianity and rejected the totalitarian claims of the state in religious and political matters.

civil religion (522)* Religion as a system of beliefs, symbols, and practices that legitimate the authority of a society's institutions and bind people together in the public sphere.

Confessing Church (504) An alternative church government structure in Nazi Germany set up not as a rival church but in order to defend the orthodox Christian faith against the influence of the state.

fascism (499) Right-wing totalitarianism that counters personal frustration, alienation, and social and economic tension by stressing class unity, reaffirming traditional values, and glorifying the national identity.

feminist theology (541–42)* A movement developed first in the United States that uses the experience of being female in a male-dominated society as a basis for critical reflection on Christian thought, tradition, and practice.

Fundamentalism (528)* The doctrine that the Bible is verbally inspired and therefore inerrant and infallible on all matters of doctrine and history. The bases of fundamentalism were set out in twelve volumes, *The Fundamentals*, published between 1910 and 1915.

German Christian movement (502) Those Protestant Christians in Germany who overlooked the anti-Semitic and pagan side of Nazism and praised Hitler's anti-communism and call for "positive Christianity." Arose in the 1930s and eventually formed a pro-Nazi party within the church.

hermeneutics (546)   Rules of interpretation.

just war (524)   Rooted in Roman Stoic philosophy, a Christian approach to the problem of war, formed in the late fourth century by Ambrose and Augustine. Provides a series of criteria by which the permissibility of war in a particular situation can be weighed.

Lateran Agreements of 1929 (499)   Agreements between the papacy and the kingdom of Italy, wherein the papacy gave up its territorial claims in Italy, recognized the Italian ruling dynasty, agreed to keep out of politics, and permitted state approval of nominations to bishoprics. Italy, in turn, recognized Vatican City as an independent, sovereign state with the pope as its ruler, established Catholicism as the sole religion of the state, and gave legal standing to Catholic religious orders and associations.

National Socialism (500)   The other name for Nazism, a form of fascism with a utopian antimodernism that rejected the assumptions underlying the Enlightenment and glorified a primitive, idealized past.

nonviolent action (525)   Popularized by leaders such as Dr. Martin Luther King Jr., strategies for group action that emphasize noncooperation, boycott, and public demonstration as a means of protest.

pacifism (524–25)   Complete opposition to war and violence espoused by some early Christians and later others (e.g., Quakers), who practiced a simple obedience to the words of Jesus: "Love your enemies" (Matthew 5:44); "Put your sword back in its place" (Matthew 26:52).

Pentecostal Churches (551)*   Churches that have formed from a renewal movement that started in the United States in the early 1900s. They teach the experience of baptism in the Holy Spirit, which shows itself in speaking in tongues and other spiritual gifts.

quest of the historical Jesus (537)   Scholarly pursuit involving biblical and historical criticism that looks for the picture of Jesus as he really was, behind the theology of the New Testament.

totalitarianism (499)   A much-debated political concept. Distinguished by such features as an official ideology that covers all vital aspects of human existence and looks toward a perfect state of humankind; a single, mass party led by a dictator or small group that is dedicated to the ideology and controls most aspects of life.

Key Personalities

Numbers in parentheses refer to the pages where the text provides the individual's biographical details and historical significance.

Karl Barth (503)

(1886–1968) Swiss Calvinist theologian who reacted against Liberal Protestantism in theology and declared theology's central theme to be the Word of God. Living through World War I as a pastor in Switzerland made him highly critical of liberal Christianity. He was the chief creator of the Barmen Declaration, which argued that the church owed its allegiance to God, not to government. His *Church Dogmatics* is one of the most important works of twentieth-century theology.

PRIMARY SOURCES

From Karl Barth, *The Call to Discipleship*, Facets, (Minneapolis: Fortress Press, 2003).

At this point we must think of the concrete form of the demand with which Jesus in the gospels always approached those whom he called to discipleship. It is common to every instance that the goal is a form of action or abstention by which his disciples will reveal and therefore indicate to the world the break in the human situation, the end of the irresistible and uncontested dominion of the given factors and orders and historical forces, as it has always been brought about by the dawn and irruption of the kingdom. It is common to every instance that the obedience concretely demanded of, and to be achieved by, the disciple, always means that he must move out of conformity with what he hitherto regarded as the self-evident action and abstention of Lord Everyman and into the place allotted to him . . . at this particular place he is freed from the bonds of that which is generally done or not done, because and as he is bound now to Jesus. . .

For us Westerners, at any rate, the most striking of these main lines is that on which Jesus, according to the Gospel tradition, obviously commanded many people, as the concrete form of their obedient discipleship, to renounce their general attachment to the authority, validity, and confidence of possessions, not mere inwardly but outwardly, in the venture and commitment of a definite act. . .

Along a second line the instructions given by Jesus have to do no less directly with the destruction by the coming of the kingdom of what is generally accepted as honour or fame among men: "Blessed are you when people revile you and persecute you and utter all kinds of evil against you falsely on my account" (Matt 5:11). . .

Along a further line, the command of Jesus, and the obedience which has to be shown to it, takes the concrete form of an attestation of the kingdom of God as the end of the fixed idea of the necessity and beneficial value of force. . .

If along the third main line of the texts in question we have to do with the overcoming, proclaimed with the incursion of the kingdom of God, of the false separation between man and man revealed in the friend-foe relationship and concretely expressing itself in the exercise of force, along a fourth line we have, conversely the dissolution of self-evident attachments between one person and another.

Reading Questions

What three demands of obedience does Barth discuss here? Why do you suppose Barth suggests that a renunciation of one's attachment to possessions would be most striking to Westerners?

RELATED WORKS

Barth, Karl. *The Call to Discipleship*. Facets. Minneapolis: Fortress Press, 2003.

Barth, Karl. *Karl Barth's "Church Dogmatics": An Introduction and Reader*. Ed. R. Michael Allen. London: T&T Clark, 2012.

Green, Clifford J. *Karl Barth: Theologian of Freedom*. The Making of Modern Theology. Minneapolis: Fortress Press, 1991.

Dietrich Bonhoeffer (535)

(1906–45) German theologian who was hanged by the Nazis for his part in a conspiracy to assassinate Hitler. He promoted the idea of "religionless" Christianity—that is, Christianity involved in the world. He argued that conventional Christian thinking led to "cheap grace," while faith in fact calls for costly discipleship. The themes and ideas in his large body of work, which include theological monographs as well as his letters from prison, are highly influential on modern Christian theology.

PRIMARY SOURCES

From Dietrich Bonhoeffer, *The Cost of Discipleship*, (New York: Simon & Schuster, 1995), 43-45.

> Cheap grace is the deadly enemy of our Church. We are fighting today for costly grace.
>
> Cheap grace means grace sold on the market like cheapjacks' wares. The sacraments, the forgiveness of sins, and the consolations of religion are thrown away at cut prices. Grace is represented as the Church's inexhaustible treasury, from which she showers blessings with generous hands, without asking questions or fixing limits. Grace without price; grace without cost! The essence of grace, we suppose, is that the account has been paid in advance; and, because it has been paid, everything can be had for nothing. Since the cost was infinite, the possibilities of using and spending it are infinite. What would grace be if it were not cheap?
>
> Cheap grace means grace as a doctrine, a principle, a system. It means forgiveness of sins proclaimed as a general truth, the love of God taught as the Christian "conception" of God. An intellectual assent to that idea is held to be of itself sufficient to secure remission of sins. . .
>
> Cheap grace means the justification of the sin without the justification of the sinner. Grace alone does everything, they say, and so everything can remain as it was before. . .
>
> Cheap grace is the preaching of forgiveness without requiring repentance, baptism without church discipline, Communion without confession, absolution without personal confession. Cheap grace is grace without discipleship, grace without the cross, grace without Jesus Christ, living and incarnate.
>
> Costly grace is the treasure hidden in the field; for the sake of it a man will gladly go and sell all that he has. It is the pearl of great price to buy which the merchant will sell all his goods. It is the kingly rule of Christ, for whose sake a man will pluck out the eye which causes him to stumble; it is the call of Jesus Christ at which the disciple leaves his nets and follows him.
>
> Costly grace is the gospel which must be *sought* again and again, the gift which must be *asked* for, the door at which a man must *knock*.
>
> Such grace is *costly* because it calls us to follow, and it is *grace* because it calls us to follow *Jesus Christ*.

Reading Questions

What, according to Bonhoeffer, differentiates between that which is cheap and that which is costly? What seems to be at stake for Bonhoeffer as he makes this argument?

RELATED WORKS

Bonhoeffer, Dietrich. *Dietrich Bonhoeffer Works*. 16 vols. Minneapolis: Fortress Press, 1996–2013.

Dramm, Sabine. *Dietrich Bonhoeffer and the Resistance*. Trans. Margaret Kohl. Minneapolis: Fortress Press, 2009.

Green, Clifford J., and Guy C. Carter, eds. *Interpreting Bonhoeffer: Historical Perspectives, Emerging Issues*. Minneapolis: Fortress Press, 2013.

Till, Eric, director. *Bonhoeffer: Agent of Grace*. DVD. 90 mins. Minneapolis: Fortress Press, 2004.

Hélder Câmara (570)

(1909–99) Catholic archbishop in Brazil. He is known for his nonviolent defense of the rights of poor people and his opposition to conservatives in both government and church.

PRIMARY SOURCES

From Helder Camara, *The Spiral of Violence*, (London: Sheed & Ward, 1971), 60-63.

Without being blind to the problems created by the differences in race, language, country and religion; without forgetting hatred, struggles, coldness and egoism, is it a dream or an illusion to think that there are, everywhere, people who have made up their minds to demand, in a peaceful but resolute way, justice as condition of peace?

Whatever the colour of your skin, the shape of your lips or your nose, whatever your height, you are neither a sub-man nor a superman; you are a human creature. You have a head, a heart, hopes, dreams. More important still; the creator and Father has a whole plan of human fulfillment which involves you.

If you belong to a tribe, a family, a race, you belong too to the human family. The injustices you encounter in your own environment exist everywhere.

If you have a special love for your own race, for your people, come and join all those who are resolved to build a more united and human world. Whatever your language, little known or well known, primitive or rich—we shall be able to understand you.

A look, a smile, gestures of peace and friendship, attention and delicacy, these are the universal language, capable of demonstrating that we are much closer to one another than we imagined. Everywhere kindness touches, injustice wounds, peace is an ideal.

Keep your language. Love its sounds, its modulation, its rhythm. But try to march together with men of different languages, remote from your own, who wish like you for a more just and human world. . . .

Whatever your religion, try to demand that, instead of separating men, it helps to unite them.

War of religions! Is this not the tragedy to end all tragedies, a contradiction in terms, an absurdity! God is Love. Religion must gather men, draw them together

In the teachings of your faith, what are the principles, the directives which call for justice and peace?

If your life has taken you far from religious practice or even from faith, perhaps you still love truth. Perhaps you are capable of suffering for justice. Then you will be able to help a great deal and serve as an example in difficult times!

Beyond the barriers let us unite!

Reading Questions

How do you respond to the exhortations from Archbishop Camara in this text? Do the words of Camara cohere with or challenge your assumptions about the role of clergy and church leadership?

RELATED WORKS

Câmara, Hélder. *The Desert Is Fertile*. Trans. Dinah Livingstone. London: Sheed & Ward, 1974.

Moosbrugger, Bernhard, and Gladys Weigner. *A Voice of the Third World: Dom Helder Camara*. New York: Paulist, 1972.

Sigmund Freud (533)

(1856–1939) Father of modern psychology. Influenced by positivism and a belief in the important role of self-knowledge in treating psychological disorders, he argued that religion is "the universal obsessional neurosis of humanity."

PRIMARY SOURCES

From Sigmund Freud, *Civilization and Its Discontents*, trans. James Strachey, (New York: W.W. Norton, 1961), 21.

> In my *Future of an Illusion* (1927) I was concerned much less with the deepest sources of the religious feeling than with what the common man understands by his religion—with the system of doctrines and promises which on the one hand explains to him the riddles of this world with enviable completeness, and, on the other, assures him that a careful Providence will watch over his life and will compensate him in a future existence for any frustrations he suffers here. The common man cannot imagine this Providence otherwise than in the figure of an enormously exalted father. Only such a being can understand the needs of the children of men and be softened by their prayers and placated by the signs of their remorse. The whole thing is so patently infantile, so foreign to reality, that to anyone with a friendly attitude to humanity it is painful to think that the great majority of mortals will never be able to rise above this view of life. It is still more humiliating to discover how large a number of people living today, who cannot but see that this religion is not tenable, nevertheless try to defend it piece by piece in a series of pitiful rearguard actions. One would like to mix among the ranks of the believers in order to meet these philosophers, who think they can rescue the God of religion by replacing him by an impersonal, shadowy and abstract principle, and to address them with the warning words: 'Thou shalt not take the name of the Lord thy God in vain!'

Reading Questions

What are the underlying assumptions behind Freud's description of the human tendency toward religious belief? How do you respond to Freud's attitude toward religion?

RELATED WORKS

Freud, Sigmund. *Beyond the Pleasure Principle*. Trans. James Strachey. International Psycho-Analytical Library, no. 4. New York: Liveright, 1950.

Freud, Sigmund. *Civilization and Its Discontents.* Trans. Joan Riviere. International Psycho-Analytical Library, no. 17. London: Hogarth, 1951.

Gay, Peter. *Freud: A Life for Our Time.* New York: Norton, 2006.

Billy Graham (514–15)

(1918–) The most successful Christian mass evangelist in history. He used modern mass communications and organization to promote his message about individual conversion to Christ. A prolific author, he promoted evangelism through books, institutes, congresses, and films.

PRIMARY SOURCES

From *Just as I am: The Autobiography of Billy Graham*, (New York: HarperCollins, 1997), 750.

> No, I don't know the future, but I do know this: the best is yet to be! Heaven awaits us, and that will be far, far more glorious than anything we can ever imagine. I know that soon my life will be over. I thank God for it, and for all He has given me in this life. But I look forward to Heaven. I look forward to the reunion with friends and loved ones who have gone on before. I look forward to Heaven's freedom from sorrow and pain. I also look forward to serving God in ways we can't begin to imagine, for the Bible makes it clear that Heaven is not a place of idleness. And most of all, I look forward to seeing Christ and bowing before Him in praise and gratitude for all He has done for us, and for using me on this earth by His grace—just as I am.

Reading Question

Do you find the figure of Billy Graham, and this excerpt in particular, to be representative of the American religious experience?

RELATED WORKS

Graham, Billy. *The Early Billy Graham: Sermon and Revival Accounts.* Ed. Joel A. Carpenter. New York: Garland, 1988.

Miller, Steven P. *Billy Graham and the Rise of the Republican South.* Politics and Culture in Modern America. Philadelphia: University of Pennsylvania Press, 2009.

Pope John XXIII (563)

(1881–1963) Known for his efforts to modernize the Catholic Church. He issued eight encyclicals, which included updates to social teaching and arguments against the arms race and for reconciliation. His signal achievement is the Second Vatican Council (Vatican II).

PRIMARY SOURCES

From *Gaudet Mater Ecclesia (Mother Church Rejoices)*: Opening Address of John XXIII at the Council, (1962; Conciliaria, 2013), http://conciliaria.com/2012/10/mother-church-rejoices-opening-address-of-john-xxiii-at-the-council/#more-2134

> Mother Church rejoices that, by the singular gift of Divine Providence, the longed-for day has finally dawned when—under the auspices of the Virgin Mother of God, whose maternal dignity is commemorated on this feast—the Second Vatican Ecumenical Council is being solemnly opened here beside St. Peter's tomb. . . .
>
> In calling this vast assembly of bishops, the latest and humble successor of the Prince of the Apostles who is addressing you intended to assert once again the Church's magisterium [teaching authority], which is unfailing and perdures until the end of time, in order that this magisterium,

taking into account the errors, the requirements and the opportunities of our time, might be presented in exceptional form to all men throughout the world. . .

Illuminated by the light of this council, the Church—we confidently trust—will become greater in spiritual riches and, gaining the strength of new energies therefrom, she will look to the future without fear. In fact, by bringing herself up-to-date where required, and by the wise organization of mutual cooperation, the Church will make men, families and peoples really turn their minds to heavenly things.

And thus the holding of the council becomes a motive for wholehearted thanksgiving to the Giver of every good gift, in order to celebrate with joyous canticles the glory of Christ Our Lord, the glorious and immortal King of ages and of peoples.

There is, moreover, venerable brothers, another subject which it is useful to propose for your consideration. Namely, in order to render our joy more complete, we wish to narrate before this great assembly our assessment of the happy circumstances under which the ecumenical council commences.

In the daily exercise of our pastoral office, we sometimes have to listen, much to our regret, to voices of persons who, though burning with zeal, are not endowed with too much sense of discretion or measure. In these modern times they can see nothing but prevarication and ruin. They say that our era, in comparison with past eras, is getting worse and they behave as though they had learned nothing from history, which is, none the less, the teacher of life. They behave as though at the time of former councils everything was a full triumph for the Christian idea and life and for proper religious liberty.

We feel we must disagree with those prophets of gloom, who are always forecasting disaster, as though the end of the world was at hand.

In the present order of things, Divine Providence is leading us to a new order of human relations which, by men's own efforts and even beyond their very expectations, are directed toward the fulfillment of God's superior and inscrutable designs. And everything, even human differences, leads to the greater good of the Church *Opening Address of John XXIII at the Second Vatican Council, October 11, 1962.*

Reading Questions

How does this opening address from Pope John XXIII set out the goals of the Second Vatican Council? After reading about the results of Vatican II on pages 539-540 of your textbook, do you think these goals were met?

RELATED WORKS

Hebblethwaite, Peter. *Pope John XXIII, Shepherd of the Modern World*. Garden City, NY: Doubleday, 1985.

Purdy, William A. *The Church on the Move: The Characters and Policies of Pius XII and John XXIII*. New York: John Day, 1966.

Martin Luther King Jr. (521)

(1929–68) Civil rights leader who promoted nonviolence and successfully led mass movements to challenge Jim Crow laws in the United States. His speeches and writing focused on Christian principles applied to social problems.

PRIMARY SOURCES

From Martin Luther King Jr., *Strength to Love* (Minneapolis: Fortress Press, 2010), 159-161.

> As I delved deeper in to the philosophy of Gandhi, my skepticism concerning the power of love gradually diminished, and I came to see for the first time that the Christian doctrine of love, operating through the Gandhian method of nonviolence, is one of the most potent weapons available to an oppressed people in their struggle for freedom. At that time, however, I acquired only an intellectual understanding and appreciation of the position, and I had no firm determination to organize it in a socially effective situation.
>
> When I was in Montgomery, Alabama, as a pastor in 1954, I had not the slightest idea that I would later become involved in a crisis in which nonviolent resistance would be applicable. After I had lived in the community about a year, the bus boycott began. The Negro people of Montgomery, exhausted by the humiliating experiences that they had constantly faced on the buses, expressed in a massive act of noncooperation their determination to be free. They came to see that it was ultimately more honorable to walk the streets in dignity than to ride the buses in humiliation. At the beginning of the protest, the people called on me to serve as their spokesman. In accepting this responsibility, my mind, consciously or unconsciously, was driven back to the Sermon on the Mount and the Gandhian method of nonviolent resistance. This principle became the guiding light of our movement. Christ furnished the spirit and motivation and Gandhi furnished the method.
>
> The experience in Montgomery did more to clarify my thinking in regard to the question of nonviolence than all of the books that I had read. As the days unfolded, I became more and more convinced of the power of nonviolence. Nonviolence became more than a method to which I gave intellectual assent; it became a commitment to a way of life. . .
>
> I would not wish to give the impression that nonviolence will accomplish miracles overnight. Men are not easily moved from their mental ruts or purged of their prejudiced and irrational feelings. When the underprivileged demand freedom, the privileged at first react with bitterness and resistance. Even when the demands are couched in nonviolent terms, the initial response is substantially the same . . . but the nonviolent approach does something to the hearts and souls of those committed to it. It gives them new self-respect. It calls up resources of strength and courage that they did not know they had. Finally, it so stirs the conscience of the opponent that reconciliation becomes a reality. *Pilgrimage to Nonviolence.*

Reading Questions

What relationship do you discover in this text between a nonviolent approach to racial segregation and King's commitment to his Christian faith?

What, according to this text, is most effective about nonviolent action?

Related Works

Baldwin, Lewis V. *Never to Leave Us Alone: The Prayer Life of Martin Luther King Jr.* Minneapolis: Fortress Press, 2010.

Echols, James, ed. *I Have a Dream: Martin Luther King Jr. and the Future of Multicultural America.* Minneapolis: Fortress Press, 2004.

King, Martin Luther, Jr. *The Measure of a Man.* Facets. Minneapolis: Fortress Press, 2001.

Jürgen Moltmann (543)

(1926–) Leading contemporary theologian who urges Christians to practical action based on faith. As a prisoner of war in Britain during World War II, he experienced a spiritual awakening and returned to Germany to study theology. His works reflect theological vision and concern for human affairs; he sees God present and witness to human suffering.

Primary Sources

From Jürgen Moltmann, *God for a Secular Society: The Public Relevance of Theology*, trans. Margaret Kohl, (Minneapolis: Fortress Press, 1999),172ff.

After Auschwitz can we go on believing in an almighty, good God in heaven? After Auschwitz, can even evil still work for good?

That is the way some people ask about God: their questions are theoretical questions. How can God permit this if he is just? They have the impression that God is a cold, blind force of Destiny, for whom the dying and death of his human children is a matter of indifference. People think about God like this because they are afraid of becoming like that themselves—untouched, cold and cynical toward suffering. But isn't this so called theodicy question wrongly framed? Why did God permit this? Given a negative slant, this is an onlooker's question, the question of onlookers who ask 'why' after the event, and yet know perfectly well that any answer that begins 'because' would make a mockery of the sufferers and would blaspheme God. Given a positive turn, this question of theodicy is not the question which the people involved ask. It is the question of the people who mourn for them: 'My God, why, why. . . ?' We cannot answer that question in this world, but we cannot let it drop either. We have to exist in the question and with it, as with an open wound in our lives.

The question asked by the sufferers themselves is not 'Why does God permit this?' it is more immediate than that. Their question is 'My God, where are you?', or, more generally, 'Where is God?'

The first question—why does God permit this?—is the question how God can be justified in view of the immeasurable suffering in the world. The second question—the question of the people involved—is the cry for God's companionship in the suffering of the world, a suffering which he condemns. The premise of the first question, the 'why', is an apathetic God who is supposed to justify himself in the face of human suffering. The second question, the 'where', seeks a God who shares our suffering and carries our griefs.

But then there is still a third question about God, which we often suppress with the help of the first. It is God's question about men and women. It is not the question about the victims. It is the question about the perpetrators and those who have to live in the long shadows of Auschwitz. This question is what we call the question of justification, meaning by that, not that God has to justify himself to the world for its suffering, but that the evil-doers, the murderers and those who have to live in their shadows, have to justify themselves before God. Can the godless become just? Is there reconciliation for the perpetrators and those who come after them? Is conversion to life possible? After Auschwitz, do we still have a human future worth living for? In this context we don't cry 'Where is God?'. We hear the eternal voice which cries 'Adam, where are you?' and "Cain, where is your brother Abel?' and 'What have you done?'. *God for a Secular Society*

Reading Questions

What, according to Moltmann, is the significance of Auschwitz and the Holocaust for theology? Do you agree with Moltmann's assessment of the importance of "the question of justification"? How might you begin to respond to these questions?

RELATED WORKS

Moltmann, Jürgen. *A Broad Place: An Autobiography*. Trans. Margaret Kohl. Minneapolis: Fortress Press, 2009.

Moltmann, Jürgen. *The Coming of God: Christian Eschatology*. Trans. Margaret Kohl. Minneapolis: Fortress Press, 2004.

Moltmann, Jürgen. *God for a Secular Society: The Public Relevance of Theology*. Trans. Margaret Kohl. Minneapolis: Fortress Press, 1999.

Wolfhart Pannenberg (542–43)

(1928–) Among the most eminent theologians of the contemporary era. He sees God as the God of all history and of promise. His concern for history runs as a thread throughout his work, beginning with the history of Jesus as history "from below." His writing includes a three-volume systematics that emphasizes the Holy Trinity and his belief that humankind is destined for fellowship with God.

PRIMARY SOURCES

From Wolfhart Pannenberg, *Basic Questions in Theology; Collected Essays Volume 1*, trans. George K Helm, (Minneapolis: Fortress Press, 1971), 15.

History is the most comprehensive horizon of Christian theology. All theological questions and answers are meaningful only within the framework of the history which God has with humanity and through humanity with his whole creation—the history moving toward a future still hidden from the world but already revealed in Jesus Christ. *Redemptive Event and History*

Reading Question

How are history and theology related, according to Pannenberg?

RELATED WORKS

Eilers, Kent. *Faithful to Save: Pannenberg on God's Reconciling Action*. T&T Clark Studies in Systematic Theology, vol. 10. London: T&T Clark, 2011.

Pannenberg, Wolfhart. *Christianity in a Secularized World*. New York: Crossroad, 1989.

Pannenberg, Wolfhart. *Ethics*. Trans. Keith Crim. Philadelphia: Westminster, 1981.

Albert Schweitzer (527)

(1875–1965) A theologian, philosopher, and medical missionary. His *Quest of the Historical Jesus* (1906) is a landmark work in the field of historical Jesus studies. He was a strong advocate for peace among nations and against the atomic bomb.

PRIMARY SOURCES

From Albert Schweitzer, *The Quest of the Historical Jesus: The First Complete Edition*, ed. John Bowden, (Minneapolis: Fortress Press, 2001), xliv-xlv.

The main question for today and tomorrow is how to explain the relation of Christian faith to historical truth, and what is the result of that relation. It follows from historical study of Jesus, the primitive Christianity and the origin of dogma that Christians are faced with the difficult task of giving an account of the growth of their religion, and of conceding that its present form is the result of a development which it has undergone. No other religion has had to meet such a demand, nor would it have been equal to it. . .

Historical research not only compels us to recognize change; it also shows us what is actually happening, viz., that the type of idea employed for the expression of religious truth becomes increasingly spiritual.

The gospel of the Kingdom of God came into the world in its late-Jewish form, which it could not retain. The kingdom, expected to come immediately in supernatural fashion, failed to appear, and so did the Son of man who was to arrive on the clouds of heaven. Grappling with this compelled believers to take a more and more spiritual view of the Kingdom of God and the messiahship of Jesus, the former becoming a spiritual and ethical ideal to be realized in this world, and Jesus the spiritual Messiah who laid its foundation through his ethical preaching. So obvious is this view to faith that it is taken to be the view of Jesus himself, and his preaching is understood in this sense. All this involves overlooking the words of the first two Gospels, which are based on a different presupposition.

Respect for historical truth, however, compels our faith to give up this naivety, and to admit that it has been subject to development. It can do this without being untrue to itself or to Jesus. It has become what it is under the pressure of a higher necessity, under the influence of the Spirit of Jesus. . .

Historical truth not only creates difficulties for faith; it also enriches it, by compelling it to examine the importance of the work of the Spirit of Jesus for its origin and continuance. The gospel of Jesus cannot simply be taken over; it must be appropriated in his Spirit. What the Bible really offers us is his Spirit, as we find it in him and in those who first came under its power. Every conviction of faith must be tested by him. Truth in the highest sense is what is in the Spirit of Jesus.

It is the essence of Protestantism that it is a church which does not believe in the church, but in Christ. That lays upon it the necessity of being truthful in all things. If it ceases to have an unshakable need for truthfulness it is only a shadow of itself—useless to the Christian religion and to the world to which it is called. *Preface to the Sixth Edition (1950).*

Reading Questions

Why is it important to discover truths about the historical person of Jesus, according to Schweitzer?

Do you agree with Schweitzer that historical truth is both challenging and enriching to religious faith?

RELATED WORKS

Brabazon, James. *Albert Schweitzer: A Biography.* 2nd ed. Syracuse, NY: Syracuse University Press, 2000.

Schweitzer, Albert. *The Quest of the Historical Jesus: The First Complete Edition.* Ed. John Bowden. Minneapolis: Fortress Press, 2001.

Chapter Summaries

37. An Age of Ideology

While Benito Mussolini and the Roman Catholic Church came to terms in the Lateran Agreements of 1929, the relationship between Adolf Hitler and the German churches was much less stable. Christian conservatives believed that Nazism might bring national regeneration and thus helped establish the German Christian church, a pro-Nazi movement; the Confessing Church rejected the state's authority over the church while continuing to profess loyalty to the government. In general Christians throughout Europe did not actively protest Nazi persecution of Jews and others during the Holocaust.

Joseph Stalin systematically worked to destroy the church in Russia using secret police and labor camps, which were also his tools to end all dissent. While Patriarch Tikhon attempted to take a stand against moves to disempower the church, ultimately he was arrested and swore loyalty to the regime in order to be freed.

Pius XII has been criticized for not speaking out against Nazi aggression. He was caught between his abhorrence of fascism and his concern for the health of the institutional church.

After World War II the Chinese leader Mao Ze-dong expelled all foreign missionaries and promoted his nationalist views that centered around a peasant-based revolution. In other Communist countries around the world, Christianity was restricted to various degrees. The era of glasnost brought an end to most restrictions in Russia and elsewhere.

Christians played a significant role in the fight against apartheid in South Africa. Similarly, Christian leaders and laypeople were active in the civil rights movement in the United States.

38. An Age of Anxiety

From the Social Gospel movement to fundamentalism, a diverse range of movements developed in twentieth-century Christianity. New kinds of biblical interpretation, such as form criticism, raised new questions about Scripture. Psychological insights from Sigmund Freud eventually influenced pastoral counseling practices. Ethics and theology developed further through the work of theologians like Dietrich Bonhoeffer, who advocated a "costly discipleship" for Christians.

Modern biblical scholarship was marked by new studies in archeology and world mythology; the "history of religions" school brought insights from other ancient cultures to a fresh analysis of Christian origins.

Modern Christian theology took many forms, from the work of Karl Barth, who emphasized the sovereignty of God, to that of Paul Tillich, who used existentialism to connect Christian ideas with secular concerns.

The Second Vatican Council was a watershed event in the history of the modern Catholic Church. It promoted conclusions in four areas: liturgy; the church; revelation, scripture, and dogma; and the church in the modern world. Ecumenism was commended, as was biblical interpretation using methods also employed by Protestants.

Feminist theology was an important new movement that brought critique and renewal to Christian scholarship and church life. Theologians like Elisabeth Schüssler Fiorenza have written scholarly works that challenge traditional assumptions within the field of biblical studies. Womanist theologians have developed critical lenses incorporating liberatory views of the Bible and an explicitly anti-racist approach.

39. Pentecostalism and the Charismatic Movement

While active congregations are spread throughout the United States, Pentecostals show impressive numbers in Latin America and Africa. Their emphasis on the gifts of the Spirit is one of their particular contributions to the worldwide church.

Pentecostalism is a "fourth strand" in Christianity—not a single denomination or a sect. Pentecostals generally hold orthodox Christian beliefs, although some baptize in the name of Jesus only. Their view of Christ encapsulates four roles: savior, baptizer in the Spirit, healer, and soon-coming king. They believe that speaking in tongues is a sign of Spirit-baptism.

The Charismatic movement emerged in the late 1960s. It gained momentum from people disillusioned with a society that supported the Vietnam War. By the 1980s it had increasing world influence, especially in Latin America.

African independent churches are an important contemporary development in the global church. They range widely in style and structure as well as doctrine. Some reject European leadership but have a similar organization; some are charismatic and often called "prophet-healing." African independent churches are typically Bible-centered and incorporate pre-Christian features such as healing traditions. They often combine ritual ceremonies with charismatic activities like dance.

40. The Arts in the Christian West

The central paradoxes of Christianity have driven an enormous range of expression in music, visual art, drama, and literature. While iconoclasm has been a factor in the Orthodox Church, even some Protestant traditions have shied away from visual depictions of Christian beliefs. Nevertheless, through the centuries artists have been inspired by biblical stories, Christian figures in history and tradition, and core values of the faith.

41. Organizing for Unity

Ecumenism is an important twentieth-century movement to bring world religions into dialogue with each other.

The ecumenical movement began within the Student Volunteer Movement as a shared concern for evangelism and was first organized in 1910 at the International Missionary Conference in Edinburgh.

After the work of the council Vatican II, Roman Catholics were encouraged to join in ecumenical dialogue. Evangelical churches have generally remained wary based on their concern for doctrinal purity, but charismatic elements have argued for the unifying power of the Holy Spirit.

42. An Age of Liberation

The international missions, bringing not only the gospel message but also Western values and viewpoints, were some of the forces behind liberation in many Christianized cultures. But many churches established by missionaries continued for years to have foreign leadership; indigenous clergy were typically not encouraged or trained. More recently, there has been a recognition of the need for partnering in missions, as a result of acknowledging that Christianity is not in fact a Western religion.

The eighteenth-century revival was a major factor in spurring the growth of Protestant missions around the world. Western imperialism also played an important role. Missionaries were often successful in bringing their message of freedom to traditional societies in which people were open to challenging old values.

The Christian populations of Asian countries like Japan and Korea increased markedly in the mid to late twentieth century. Missionaries had great success throughout many African nations beginning in the nineteenth century. Latin America, while dominated by the Catholic Church, saw a surge in growth by Protestant congregations in the latter years of the twentieth century.

The church has become a worldwide community, although missions still do not necessarily heed the call to partner with each other. Christians in developing nations have experienced colonialism and exploitation at the hands of their erstwhile Christian neighbors from the developed world. The wounds from years of such treatment do not heal easily, but there are serious efforts to increase understanding among Christians from powerful nations of the existing inequalities around the world and how they can work against them.

Additional Readings

1. From *The Quest of the Historical Jesus* (Fortress Press, 2001)

Albert Schweitzer explains the twofold challenge to writing a historically accurate biography of Jesus (7–8):

> The problem of the life of Jesus has no analogy in the field of history. No historical school has ever laid down canons for the investigation of this problem, no professional historian has ever lent his aid to theology in dealing with it. Every ordinary method of historical investigation proves inadequate to the complexity of the conditions. The standards of ordinary historical science are inadequate here, its methods not immediately applicable. The historical study of the life of Jesus has had to create its own methods for itself. . . . All that can be done is to experiment continuously, starting from specific presuppositions; and in this experimentation the guiding principle must ultimately rest upon historical intuition.

> The cause of this lies in the nature of the sources of the life of Jesus, and in the character of our knowledge of the contemporary religious world of thought.

> It is not that the sources are in themselves bad. Once we have made up our minds that we do not have the materials for a complete Life of Jesus, but only for a picture of his public ministry, it must be admitted that there are few characters of antiquity about whom we possess so much indubitably historical information, of whom we have so many authentic discourses. . . .

> But at this point a twofold difficulty arises. There is first the fact that what has just been said applies only to the first three Gospels, while the fourth, as regards its character, historical accounts, and discourse material, forms a world of its own. It is written from the Greek standpoint, while the first three are written from the Jewish. And even if one could get over this, and regard, as has often been done, the Synoptics and the Fourth Gospel as standing in something of the same relation to one another as Xenophon does to Plato as sources for the life of Socrates, the complete irreconcilability of the historical data would still compel the critical investigator to decide from the first in favour of one source or the other. Once more it proves that 'No man can serve two masters.'

> . . . The second difficulty regarding the sources is the lack of any connecting thread in the material which they offer us. While the Synoptics are only collections of anecdotes (in the best, historical sense of the word), the Fourth Gospel—as can be read in its closing words—professes to give only a selection of the events and discourses.

> From these materials we can get only a Life of Jesus with yawning gaps. How are these gaps to be filled? At worst with phrases, at best with historical fantasy. There is really no other means of arriving at the order and inner connection of the facts of the life of Jesus than the making and testing of hypotheses. If the tradition handed on by the Synoptists really includes all that happened during the time that Jesus was with his disciples, the attempt to discover the connection must succeed sooner or later. It becomes more and more clear that this presupposition is indispensable to the investigation. But if the evangelists have handed down to us merely a fortuitous series of episodes, we may give up the attempt to arrive at a critical reconstruction of the life of Jesus as hopeless.

Not only do the events lack historical connection; we have no indication of a connecting thread in the actions and discourses of Jesus, because the sources give no hint of the character of his self-consciousness. They confine themselves to outward facts. We only begin to understand these historically when we can mentally place them in an intelligible connection and conceive them as the acts of a clearly defined personality. All that we know of the development of Jesus and of his messianic self-consciousness has been arrived at by a series of working hypotheses. Our conclusions can only be considered valid so long as they are not completely ruled out by the facts that have been handed down.

QUESTIONS FOR DISCUSSION AND REFLECTION

What does Schweitzer identify as the two main aspects of the attempt to write a Life of Jesus? How would you describe Schweitzer's central concern regarding scholarship and Jesus?

2. From *Unitatis Redintegratio* (Decree on Ecumenism), *Documents of the II Vatican Council*, November 21, 1964

Today, in many parts of the world, under the inspiring grace of the Holy Spirit, many efforts are being made in prayer, word and action to attain that fullness of unity which Jesus Christ desires. The Sacred Council exhorts all the Catholic faithful to recognize the signs of the times and to take an active and intelligent part in the work of ecumenism.

The term "ecumenical movement" indicates the initiatives and activities planned and undertaken, according to the various needs of the Church and as opportunities offer, to promote Christian unity. These are: first, every effort to avoid expressions, judgments and actions which do not represent the condition of our separated brethren with truth and fairness and so make mutual relations with them more difficult; then, "dialogue" between competent experts from different Churches and Communities. At these meetings, which are organized in a religious spirit, each explains the teaching of his Communion in greater depth and brings out clearly its distinctive features. In such dialogue, everyone gains a truer knowledge and more just appreciation of the teaching and religious life of both Communions. In addition, the way is prepared for cooperation between them in the duties for the common good of humanity which are demanded by every Christian conscience; and, wherever this is allowed, there is prayer in common. Finally, all are led to examine their own faithfulness to Christ's will for the Church and accordingly to undertake with vigor the task of renewal and reform.

. . . Catholics, in their ecumenical work, must assuredly be concerned for their separated brethren, praying for them, keeping them informed about the Church, making the first approaches toward them. But their primary duty is to make a careful and honest appraisal of whatever needs to be done or renewed in the Catholic household itself, in order that its life may bear witness more clearly and faithfully to the teachings and institutions which have come to it from Christ through the Apostles.

. . . For although the Catholic Church has been endowed with all divinely revealed truth and with all means of grace, yet its members fail to live by them with all the fervor that they should, so that the radiance of the Church's image is less clear in the eyes of our separated brethren and of the world at large, and the growth of God's kingdom is delayed. All Catholics must therefore aim at Christian perfection and, each according to his station, play his part that the Church may daily be more purified and renewed. For the Church must bear in her own body the humility and dying of Jesus, against the day when Christ will present her to Himself in all her glory without spot or wrinkle.

All in the Church must preserve unity in essentials. But let all, according to the gifts they have received enjoy a proper freedom, in their various forms of spiritual life and discipline, in their different liturgical rites, and even in their theological elaborations of revealed truth. In all things let charity prevail. If they are true to this course of action, they will be giving ever better expression to the authentic catholicity and apostolicity of the Church.

On the other hand, Catholics must gladly acknowledge and esteem the truly Christian endowments from our common heritage which are to be found among our separated brethren. It is right and salutary to recognize the riches of Christ and virtuous works in the lives of others who are bearing witness to Christ, sometimes even to the shedding of their blood. For God is always wonderful in His works and worthy of all praise.

Nor should we forget that anything wrought by the grace of the Holy Spirit in the hearts of our separated brethren can be a help to our own edification. Whatever is truly Christian is never contrary to what genuinely belongs to the faith; indeed, it can always bring a deeper realization of the mystery of Christ and the Church.

Nevertheless, the divisions among Christians prevent the Church from attaining the fullness of catholicity proper to her, in those of her sons who, though attached to her by Baptism, are yet separated from full communion with her. Furthermore, the Church herself finds it more difficult to express in actual life her full catholicity in all her bearings.

This Sacred Council is gratified to note that the participation by the Catholic faithful in ecumenical work is growing daily. It commends this work to the bishops everywhere in the world to be vigorously stimulated by them and guided with prudence.

QUESTIONS FOR DISCUSSION AND REFLECTION

According to the Vatican Council, what is the purpose of ecumenical work? Why should Catholics be involved? How would you characterize the Vatican approach to ecumenism?

See also "Reading Historical Documents" (page 171 in this volume) for other questions to consider.

3. From *Bonhoeffer and King: Their Legacies and Import for Christian Social Thought* (Fortress Press, 2010)

In her essay "Bonhoeffer, King, and Feminism: Problems and Possibilities" Rachel Muers writes about "how the legacies of Bonhoeffer and King can be appropriated critically and fruitfully by feminist thinkers, without distorting or concealing the complexities of these legacies" (33). She begins with a discussion of their concept of "community" (36–39):

Both Bonhoeffer and King are known for the important role "community" played in their thought. For King, the eschatological promise of God to humanity, prefigured in the lives and actions of Christ's followers now, was existence in the "beloved community," the community in which the love of God for each is reflected in mutual love and service. Successive commentators on King's work have drawn attention to the deep roots of this vision in the life of the black church and in the African cultures that helped shape it. . . .

In Bonhoeffer's work, the church is, famously, "Christ existing as community"; the church-community is where Christ is present in and to the world. Community is where love is made real—where it becomes something other than a distant ideal or a fine feeling. Life in community confronts the Christian believer with the objective and unassimilable reality of the "brother for whom Christ died," the other person who is called and loved by God. . . .

So both Bonhoeffer and King are interested in the givenness of community and the particular practices that help to realize it in the midst of injustice and broken community. They do not idealize it, and in different ways their understandings of community are rooted in lived experiments—for Bonhoeffer in Finkenwalde and the Confessing Church, for King in the civil rights movement. It is this aspect of King's thought, in particular, that has attracted praise from womanist ethicists. Thus, [Katie G.] Cannon describes how King's pragmatism is allied with his vision of human solidarity, and discusses the role of black women as members of the beloved community in particular situations of oppression.

The very givenness of the communities with which Bonhoeffer and King sought to work, however, raises some questions for feminist readers. Their ways of thinking about and practicing community were responsive to what seemed to them, not without reason, to be the most pressing issues. As a result, for both of them women's work to sustain community, and the structuring of community such that certain forms of work (the home-maintainer, the pastor's wife) fell to women, could be—in effect—taken for granted. When the focus is on how the community relates to the world outside it, differences *within* the community are of (relatively) secondary concern. By contrast, differences within the community, in terms of how the community is experienced or how power within it is exercised, are of central concern to feminist thinkers.

For King, the urgent issue for much of his life was that of inclusion within community, the basic recognition of cohumanity. The denial of civil rights to black people forced him to ask: Who is affirmed as a human being? Who is allowed to be part of the networks of solidarity by which we claim that human life is constituted? Who, for example, is allowed to count as "American"? . . .

In [Bonhoeffer's] best-known community-focused work, *Life Together*, the particular characteristics and social location of the "brother"—that which might give rise to asymmetrical relationships or the possibility of domination—are played down in favor of the brother's objective givenness, as the individual in and through whom I encounter Christ. On the face of it, this sounds as if it should be promising from a feminist point of view. If the foundation of the community is the encounter with the particular other, mediated by Christ and not merely by a set of preconceived ideas about "proper" social relations, the Christian community might be able to become a space of social transformation, in gender relations as in other areas. But Bonhoeffer himself was, we must recognize, not going to realize this possibility. He saw a given set of relationships of subordination not as impediments to Christian community but as part of the reality of the world within which the Christian community has to operate. His thought about community requires further development and a more extended contextual analysis and critique in order to make good on its transformative, as well as its conservative, possibilities.

. . . If we look at actually-existing relationships of power—including the abuse of power—we cannot accept some of Bonhoeffer's general claims about the form of an *individual's* existence conformed to Christ. We may, however, be able to use his work as the starting point for thinking about how the *community* conformed to Christ can move beyond the abuse of power.

For both King and Bonhoeffer, then, *church*-community is particularly important for revealing the nature of human community as such; church-community is the place in which beloved community and the presence of Christ is practiced. Any given church-community is, however, among other things, a place of gendered power relations.

QUESTIONS FOR DISCUSSION AND REFLECTION

How does Muers differentiate among the different views of communities presented here—Bonhoeffer's, King's, and feminists'? What is she suggesting about the role of "extended contextual analysis and critique" in appropriating the legacies of important Christian thinkers like King and Bonhoeffer?

Selected Online Resources

▶ "Aimee Semple McPherson"—essays, photos, and links to related sites about the early-twentieth-century American evangelist
  http://xroads.virginia.edu/~ug00/robertson/asm/front.html

▶ "Walter Rauschenbusch: The Social Gospel, 1908" (Modern History Sourcebook)—an excerpt from Rauschenbusch's *Christianity and the Social Crisis*
  http://www.fordham.edu/halsall/mod/rausch-socialgospel.asp

▶ Center for Holocaust and Genocide Studies: "Video"—links to videos of Holocaust survivors, American concentration camp liberators, and others discussing aspects of the Holocaust, including Dr. Robert Ross discussing "The Churches and the Holocaust"
  http://chgs.umn.edu/educational/video.html

▶ Karl Barth International Website—a website dedicated to the life and work of Karl Barth, including video clips from a 1967 documentary (in German, with English subtitles)
  http://www.kbarth.org

▶ Dietrich Bonhoeffer Official—a website dedicated to the life and work of Dietrich Bonhoeffer, with biographical essay, images, quotes, and links to other resources including films
  http://www.dbonhoeffer.org

▶ "Dom Helder Camara: Poet, Mystic, Missionary"—illustrated essay by Father Tony Lalli from the Xaverian Mission newsletter (September 1, 1999)
  http://www.xaviermissionaries.org/M_Life/NL_Archives/99-N_Lett/BR_Helder_Camara.htm

Guide to Part 8: Epilogue

Key Terms

The number in parentheses refers to the page where the term is explained. Those terms marked with asterisks also appear in the Glossary.

Liberation Theology (587)*   Originating in Latin America, associates salvation with the political liberation of oppressed peoples. Its insights have been used by black Christians and feminists to challenge sexism and racism in traditional Christianity. Marked by a stress on the challenges to social action in the Bible, especially the prophetic books and the New Testament, and the reality of the Kingdom of God as a coming event.

uniate (583)   A Christian who adheres to some Greek/Eastern rite(s) while submitting to papal authority.

Vatican II (585)   The Second Vatican Council (1962–65) was a watershed in Roman Catholic history, marking an end to the years of Counter-Reformation exclusiveness from and the beginning of a new, more open, cooperative stance legitimized under Pope John XXIII's benign rule. After the council there was greater emphasis on the church as the whole body of all the baptized, lay and ordained. The liturgy was modernized and offered in the vernacular, and the Bible accorded a more significant place in Catholic life.

World Council of Churches (586)*   Body including many Protestant and Orthodox churches, first constituted at Amsterdam in 1948.

Chapter Summary

43. Present and Future

The Christian church exists within an increasingly globalized society with significant roles played by other major religions. It must acknowledge its historical role in colonialism just as it determines what part it will play in post-colonial communities.

After the fall of communist governments across Eastern Europe, churches there have experienced a resurgence. Meanwhile, what has been called the New Christendom has spread through the founding of new indigenous churches in developing nations.

Church leadership and laity have struggled with internal reform movements, such as those aimed at ordaining women and lesbian, gay, bisexual, and transgender people. Some would argue against any idea that threatens traditional authority, while ignoring the significant role reform and schism have played in Christian history.

In the United States conservative Christians have played important roles in political movements, promoting politicians who proclaim "family values" and stand against liberalism. Evangelicalism has grown since World War II and features a number of important, influential scholars.

Vatican II brought a new era of openness to the Catholic Church, modernizing the liturgy and promoting ecumenical efforts. Nonetheless, the scandal of child abuse has highlighted the need for a renewed focus on child welfare in congregations and true accountability on the part of church authorities.

The World Council of Churches played an important, though controversial, role in the fight against apartheid in South Africa. It attempts to play a prophetic role on a global scale while bringing together diverse church cultures.

Contemporary theologies—from liberation to *mujerista* to African—are as diverse as the Christians they speak of and to. They represent the clear need to connect Christian belief and tradition with individual identity and culture.

The World Council of Churches' 1990 convocation on Justice, Peace, and the Integrity of Creation is one example of a global effort to engage Christians in important social justice work.

Additional Readings

1. From *A Theology of Liberation: History, Politics, and Salvation* (Orbis Books, 1988)

In his landmark 1973 book the Peruvian theologian Gustavo Gutiérrez lays out his vision of a liberatory Christianity. In the chapter "Poverty: Solidarity and Protest" he explains his concept of the Christian witness of poverty (171–72):

> Material poverty is a scandalous condition. Spiritual poverty is an attitude of openness to God and spiritual childhood. Having clarified these two meanings of the term *poverty* [in the first part of the

chapter] we have cleared the path and can now move forward towards a better understanding of the Christian witness of poverty. We turn now to a third meaning of the term: poverty as a commitment of solidarity and protest.

Poverty is an act of love and liberation. It has a redemptive value. If the ultimate cause of human exploitation and alienation is selfishness, the deepest reason for voluntary poverty is love of neighbor. Christian poverty has meaning only as a commitment of solidarity with the poor, with those who suffer misery and injustice. The commitment is to witness to the evil which has resulted from sin and is a breach of communion. It is not a question of idealizing poverty, but rather of taking it on as it is—an evil—to protest against it and to struggle to abolish it. . . . Because of this solidarity—which must manifest itself in specific action, a style of life, a break with one's social class—one can also help the poor and exploitated to become aware of their exploitation and seek liberation from it. Christian poverty, an expression of love, is solidarity *with the poor* and is a protest *against poverty*. . . . It is a poverty lived not for its own sake, but rather as an authentic imitation of Christ; it is a poverty which means taking on the sinful human condition to liberate humankind from sin and all its consequences.

QUESTIONS FOR DISCUSSION AND REFLECTION

What distinctions does Gutiérrez draw between different kinds of poverty? Why is it important to him to make those distinctions? From his theological standpoint, what is Christian about poverty as "a commitment of solidarity and protest"?

2. From *Blow the Trumpet in Zion!: Global Vision and Action for the Twenty-First-Century Black Church* (Fortress Press, 2004)

In chapter 8, "Freeing the Captives: The Imperative of Womanist Theology," Jacquelyn Grant writes (86–90):

As we consider the call to sound the trumpet in Zion so the captives will be free, we must evaluate the role of patriarchy in the Black church, the effects the Black church has on women, and the role of sex, lies, and violence in the very institution that preaches against the same. We must ask ourselves: Is the Black church detrimental for Black women's physical and psychological health? . . .

The question, of course, assumes or suggests that there may be something about the church that is in fact unhealthy for Black women. Those who take seriously the call to set the captives free should ask some more critical and poignant questions, such as: What do women find when they enter the church? What are women taught about themselves? about others? What are women taught about men in the church? What options does the church provide for women? How much of what happens to women inside and outside of the church is related to what the church teaches about women?

. . . It is true that the church has been guilty of putting women in various kinds of prisons. In my work, I've talked about one prison called sexism. Women must be silent in the church—except if we need a choir or a soloist or someone to read the announcements and welcome the visitors. As a woman, your place is in the home—except when you're needed to take care of the chores to keep the church running. Women may not pastor—unless they are needed for those small and sometime rural churches that men do not care for. You may not minister because you bring too much baggage with you.

. . . Susan Thistlethwaite reminds us that women with a violent spouse have believed that the Bible actually says what they have been taught it says. They believe that women are inferior in status before husband and God and deserve a life of pain.

James Alsdurf conducted a study on the matter of domestic violence and how the church deals with it. . . . Seventy-one percent of the ministers said that they would never advise a battered wife to leave her husband or separate because of abuse, and 92 percent said they would never counsel her to seek divorce.

. . . As I conclude, based on the beliefs of many misguided clerics, being in the church can really be dangerous to the health of women. And in some instances it can even be life threatening. How do we reconcile all of these unhealthy activities in the church with the other side of the church's story— that story that we like to tell and tell over and over again? For it is in the church where we find Black women who are able to move from victim to vessel—to use the words of A. Elaine Crawford. We can celebrate the achievements of women who were able to find strength in spite of the oppressive structures of the church. We can celebrate the work of these women who were able to look beyond the sins of the church and to find salvation. We can celebrate the work of women who were able to redeem the church as they sought redemption for themselves. We can celebrate women like Jarena Lee, who was able to see Christ as a whole Savior instead of half of one, as many would have us believe. We indeed can celebrate that we can say with loud voices, as we are reminded by Cheryl Townsend Gilkes, in the vernacular of the people in spite of the sins of the church: "If it wasn't for the women . . ."—now, you finish the statement.

QUESTIONS FOR DISCUSSION AND REFLECTION

How does Grant portray the relationships between the Black church, Black women, the Bible, and Christian tradition? How would you describe a theology that supports Black women in the church, according to the themes and questions Grant raises?

3. From *Saving Jesus from Those Who Are Right: Rethinking What It Means to Be Christian* (Fortress Press, 1999)

The feminist theologian Carter Heyward challenges Christians to rethink their faith and reject "those who are right"—that is, those who advocate an authoritarian style of Christianity. Here she discusses trinitarian doctrine and argues for a more expansive idea of the Trinity (72–73):

Those who shaped the doctrine of the Trinity intuited that "something" of God was *in* Jesus; that this "something" had been always, from the beginning; and that this same "something" connected subsequent generations to Jesus and God. What was startling and new about the Trinity was that here were

Jews and Gentiles suggesting that this "something" of God—this ineffable divine mystery—was not only beyond human knowing and speaking but was also completely in our midst, fully human and fully divine and fully with us, able to be known and loved, in the flesh.

. . . The holy mystery that is our Sacred Power was in the beginning, it was in Jesus, and it is with us now. That is the trinitarian "structure" of God. It reflects the dynamic spiritual movement that *is* God.

In order to distinguish between these historical experiences of this power—the God of Israel to whom Jesus prayed; Jesus himself; and the way Jesus is connected to the rest of us—the early fathers, using relational terms that reflected their own experiences as men in the world, suggested that the One God of All is in "three persons"—Father, Son, and Spirit. (The Spirit is not "personal" in the sense that "Father" and "Son" are, but rather is a way of connecting them with the rest of us.)

Cast in this model of patriarchal social relation, trinitarian thinking in Christian history has functioned unquestionably to hold sexist power in place as ecclesiastical authority—"God is Father, so shall be His priests": "Only men can conform to the image of Christ"—and to contort our images and experiences of God such that they contribute to sacralizing men and boys and worshipping God in their image.

This interpretation dreadfully misrepresents God, Jesus, and the rest of us. Its consequences and causes continue to be the trivialization and too often the sacrifice of women and girls on the altars of male supremacy, "in the name of the Father, and of the Son, and of the Holy Spirit." This blasphemy against the God of love—God of mutuality and justice—is a violation of the Spirit that touches all persons who love God and their neighbors as themselves. It is not worthy of the name of Jesus, nor of your name, nor of mine.

As a theological image the Trinity, rightly understood, should *expand* our God images, not constrict them; it should *stretch* our capacities for wholeness and holiness, not shrink us; it should *sharpen* our religious imaginations, not dull our sensibilities. God as Trinity means that whatever is Sacred is *relational*, never self-absorbed; always moving beyond itself to meet the new, the other, the different, never set in its ways or stuck on itself as the only way.

A trinitarian faith rooted and grounded in the love of God would never require that people be Christian in order to be saved; that only males be priests; or that others be like us in order to be acceptable to God. A strong trinitarian faith, which most surely was the faith of Jesus—in God, in himself, and in others, all in relation to one another—is never acceptable to those who are right, those for whom God must be an authoritarian power.

QUESTION FOR DISCUSSION AND REFLECTION

In expounding on her view of the Trinity, how does Heyward simultaneously depend on Christian tradition and critique it?

Selected Online Resources

▶ "When the Catholic Church Met the Modern World: Photos from Vatican II"—a slideshow from *Life* magazine, with photos originally published in 1962
http://life.time.com/history/vatican-ii-when-the-catholic-church-met-the-modern-world-1962-1965/#1

▶ "20th Century Theology: Gustavo Gutierrez & Liberation Theology"—a bibliography of works by Latin American, feminist, and black liberation theologians
http://moses.creighton.edu/harmless/bibliographies_for_theology/vatican_ii_9.htm

▶ "Liberation Theology: 40 Years Later"—video (97:04) of the 2010 lecture by Gustavo Gutiérrez given at Vanderbilt University
http://news.vanderbilt.edu/2010/11/video-liberation-theology-40-years-later/

▶ "Black Liberation Theology, in Its Founder's Words" (NPR)—two brief articles with accompanying audio from 2008 interviews with black theologians
http://www.npr.org/templates/story/story.php?storyId=89236116

▶ "Religion and the Feminist Movement Conference: Panel I: Charlotte Bunch"—a video (21:20) of the human rights activist Charlotte Bunch speaking at the 2002 conference sponsored by Harvard Divinity School
http://www.hds.harvard.edu/multimedia/video/religion-and-the-feminist-movement-conference-panel-i-charlotte-bunch

SUPPLEMENTAL READINGS

From Birger A. Pearson, *Ancient Gnosticism: Traditions and Literature* (Fortress Press, 2007)

Here Birger Pearson describes the core concept of Gnosticism—a particular kind of knowledge and a dualistic philosophy (12–13):

> Knowledge (gnosis) is of central importance in Gnosticism; indeed, it is a prerequisite for salvation. But what kind of knowledge are we talking about? In Gnosticism saving gnosis comes by revelation from a transcendent realm, mediated by a revealer who has come from that realm in order to awaken people to a knowledge of God and a knowledge of the true nature of the human self. In Gnosticism knowledge of God and knowledge of the self are two sides of the same coin, for the true human self is of divine origin, and salvation ultimately involves a return to the divine world from which it came. As for the bearer of revelation, this differs from one Gnostic system to another. In Christian forms of Gnosticism, the revealer is Jesus Christ, but in other forms of Gnosticism other revealers are posited, often mythological beings (for example, Sophia, "Wisdom," in various manifestations), biblical characters (for example, Adam, Seth), or other noted figures from the past (for example, Zoroaster, Zostrianos).
>
> A characteristic feature of Gnosticism is a dualistic way of looking at God, humanity, and the world, involving a radical reinterpretation of earlier traditions. In terms of theology, the Gnostics split the transcendent God of the Bible into two: a super-transcendent supreme God who is utterly alien to the world, and a lower deity who is responsible for creating and governing the world in which we live. This theology is more or less elaborated in various Gnostic systems of thought, for a number of Gnostic systems posit various divine beings inhabiting the divine world, as well as lower demonic beings involved in the creation and governance of the cosmic order. Indeed, in most Gnostic systems the relationship between the higher and lower realms is expressed in terms of a tragic split in the divine world that results in the genesis of the lower beings responsible for the cosmos.

Human beings, too, are split personalities. The true human self is as alien to the world as is the transcendent God. The inner human self is regarded as an immaterial divine spark imprisoned in a material body. The human body and the lower emotive soul belong to this world, whereas the higher self (the mind or spirit) is consubstantial with the transcendent God from which it originated. Involved in this dualistic anthropology are creative reinterpretations of the creation stories in the book of Genesis.

In terms of cosmology, the spatiotemporal universe in which we live (the cosmos) is regarded by Gnostics as a prison in which the true human self is shackled. Created and governed by the lower creator and his minions, it is the realm of chaos and darkness in the view of most of the ancient Gnostics. However, it must be admitted that this radical dualism is somewhat mitigated in later Gnostic systems. Even so, the cosmos is regularly regarded as a product of creation, and not in any sense eternal.

Pearson discusses many examples of Gnostic writings, including the *Gospel of Thomas* (261–66):

Consisting of one hundred fourteen sayings attributed to Jesus, The *Gospel of Thomas* is by far the most studied and the most widely read of the tractates in the Nag Hammadi corpus. It is also the one about which there is the least amount of agreement among scholars on such issues as its relationship to the gospels of the canonical New Testament (dependent or independent?), its date (first century or mid-second century?), its original language (Greek or Syriac?), and its religious context (Gnostic or non-Gnostic?). . . .

Most of the sayings in the Gospel of Thomas are introduced with "Jesus says." The living Jesus is speaking now to the community. And right from the beginning the keynote is sounded: Jesus's words are life giving. They are also mysterious; so the effort must be made to "find the interpretation." In so doing, a person will not experience (literally "taste") death. We are reminded of a saying of Jesus in the Gospel of John, "If anyone keeps my word, he will never taste death" (8:52). But in John the emphasis is on "keeping," that is, "observing" Jesus's word, not on finding its meaning. There are a number of similarities between the *Gospel of Thomas* and the Gospel of John, but there are also profound differences as well. . . .

One of the mysteries of the *Gospel of Thomas* is that the sayings are strung together with no obvious coherence. Some of the sayings are repeated, but, more importantly, there are basic contradictions to be observed in the collection as a whole. The most plausible way of understanding these contradictions is to view the entire collection as an agglutinative work that reflects the development of a particular community, or group of communities. In other words, over time, sayings have been added to a core collection. The added sayings reflect stages in the religious development of the community. Most of the sayings in the core collection have parallels in the Synoptic Gospels of the New Testament (Matthew, Mark, and Luke). The added sayings lack parallels in the canonical New Testament. . . .

As is well-known, one can find within the New Testament a movement away from imminent end expectation and a settling down in the world of ongoing time. The profound differences that are observable between the Gospel of John and the Synoptic Gospels relate to this phenomenon. In John the emphasis is no longer on the near expectation of the end, but on believing in Jesus, who came from heaven and will return again to his Father in heaven, where he is preparing a place for his own. Those who believe already have life within them. Jesus himself is the resurrection and the life. "Whoever believes in me, though he die, yet shall he live, and whoever lives and believes in me shall never die" (John 11:25-26).

A somewhat similar phenomenon can be seen in the development of the Thomas community, as reflected in sayings in the *Gospel of Thomas* that were added over time to the core collection. For example, saying fifty-one reflects an emphasis similar to what we find in John. When the disciples ask Jesus when the "repose of the dead" will happen and when the "new world" will arrive, Jesus replies, "What you look forward to has already come, but you do not recognize it."

What is of special interest in the *Gospel of Thomas,* however, is that the horizontal end expectation typical of the earlier history of the community has been replaced by another facet of Jewish apocalyptic, that is, the vertical or mystical aspect. An example of this mystical aspect is saying eighty-three: "Jesus says, 'The images are manifest to man, but the light in them remains concealed in the image of the light of the Father. He will become manifest, but his image will remain concealed by his light.'" This saying reflects a background in Jewish mystical traditions involving a vision of God's "glory" (Hebrew *kabod*). God remains hidden in his light, but his light-image can be seen in a mystical vision by a person who is properly prepared. The oldest example of this in Jewish apocalyptic literature is the visionary experience of the seer Enoch in *1 Enoch 14* (probably third century BCE).

. . . self-knowledge is the beginning of salvation in Thomas Christianity. To know oneself is to know one's heavenly origin and destiny. As we have noted before, there are some interesting parallels between the Gospel of John and the *Gospel of Thomas*. But the latter's emphasis on self-knowledge underlines an important difference. In John, Jesus is the heavenly redeemer who descends to earth, dies on the cross for the salvation of the world, and returns to heaven again to prepare a place for those who believe in him. In the *Gospel of Thomas,* every elect soul originates in heaven and returns to heaven again. It is the role of Jesus to provide the message that leads a person to know oneself. In knowing oneself one also knows the living Jesus and is mystically united with him. But in the final analysis, one's salvation is grounded in oneself. "Jesus says, 'That which you have will save you if you bring it forth from yourselves. That which you do not have within you [will] kill you if you do not have it within you'" (saying 70).

Questions for Discussion and Reflection

1. What is the "radical dualism" at the core of Gnosticism? How is this different from orthodox Christian belief?

2. What aspects of the *Gospel of Thomas* mark it as a Gnostic work?

3. How would you characterize the comparison Pearson is making between the *Gospel of Thomas* and the canonical Gospel of John?

Heikki Räisänen, *The Rise of Christian Beliefs: The Thought-World of Early Christians* (Fortress Press, 2009)

In the following passage Heikki Räisänen describes the political and spiritual context of the time and culture in which Jesus lived (83–84):

The Maccabean uprising was successful. Yet paradise did not materialize nor did the martyrs wake up. The national heroes began to pursue very mundane power politics. A century later Rome arrived in Palestine, and the land was once more under the thumb of foreign overlords. In these circumstances the predictions of the great reversal stayed alive and were, time and again, reinterpreted. Calculations were revised, disappointments were overcome, and cognitive dissonance reduced by ever new contemporizations. A rich diversity of expectations was the rule.

Nonetheless, with due caution some main features, which must have been shared by a large number of people, can be singled out for the time of Jesus. A central hope (clearly visible in the Gospels) was still that of *collective national restoration,* fostered by reading scripture: God would maintain his covenant loyalty to Israel, or to the faithful among the people. The restoration would entail the deliverance of Israel from its foes, a general resurrection (though this was controversial), a judgment and destruction of the wicked, the reestablishment of the twelve tribes, the subjugation or conversion of Gentiles, possibly a renewed temple, and purity and righteousness in worship and morals. For some in the Diaspora, the notion of a dramatic reversal was replaced by the demythologized notion that the superiority of the Jewish religion would gradually win through universally, although the collective-national eschatology (found, for example, in *Sib. Or.* 3) was dominant even there.

The present was often assessed in pessimistic terms, so much so that a cosmic adversary of the true God—a fallen angel, variously called Mastema, Belial, or Satan—was thought to rule the earth with the aid of a host of demons. The perceived political and/or moral chaos could also be interpreted as divine punishment for the sins of the people. In many scenarios, the coming turn was to be preceded by tribulations, sometimes called "woes," the depiction of which was colored by horrible experiences from Maccabean times (the "desolating sacrilege" had become a stock figure of speech). A variety of eschatological mediator figures existed, too; yet the expectation of a Messiah was not the rule. But various historical events and persons could easily kindle the flames of hope of imminent fulfillment of the great predictions.

Different visions—earthly and transcendent—of the restoration lived side by side. Common to them is the conviction that there will be a point in history after which life will no longer continue its (hitherto) normal course on earth. There will be a great, dramatic reversal of fortunes. There will be a new start for one group of people and an enormous catastrophe for others. The reversal is conceived of in collective terms. One may conceive of the restoration as a fulfillment of paradisal-utopian hopes on this earth, on which a complete reversal will take place, a restructuring of the political and social order. The collective fulfillment can also take place on a new earth, or on the earth created anew, a vision that places less emphasis on historical continuity. Or again, the fulfillment may take place in a transcendent heavenly realm, but it will still have the form of communal life, lived in some continuity with previous communal life on earth.

It is of lesser importance just how soon the reversal is thought to take place—in any case it is expected to happen soon enough, surely in the lifetime of the generation in question. For the Essenes whose views are reflected in the Qumran texts, the crucial events had already begun; the consummation was anticipated in their worship, in which angels participated.

. . . The expectation of the great turn has its roots in experiences of political frustration or alienation (which need not, however, mean intolerable oppression) that are interpreted in the light of the traditions of God acting in history. "Eschatological hopes arise both to compensate for the powerlessness of Israel among the nations and to console groups that were alienated from the power structures within Jewish society." But once they have established themselves as part of a widespread worldview, they are capable of stirring the emotions and actions of people even apart from situations of deprivation (real or perceived). There is, of course, a moral side to the problem: the lack of justice in the world and, often enough, the perceived moral chaos in one's own community. The belief that God's justice will eventually be realized in Israel is based on the covenant relationship thought to exist between Yahweh and the people. The expectation thus also contains the answer to the problem of theodicy: right now few signs of God's loyalty may be visible, but without the slightest doubt the future will show that he *is* faithful to his promises.

Different roads to the great turn were conceived. Some people were guided by a militant view, others (probably the majority) by a more quietistic conviction. The militant tradition looked back to the stories about the conquest of Canaan, to Phinehas (Num. 25), to Gideon (Judg. 6–8), and to the more recent events of the Maccabean times. . . . The book of Daniel, however, does not. Many were indeed ready to die rather than transgress the law. This conviction, which relied on a direct intervention of God, independently of the doings of humans, could lean on the book of Isaiah and the bulk of apocalyptic literature. Intermediate expectations also existed: God would play the crucial part, but the faithful too would bear arms. Of course, there were those who, due to their social position and welfare (notably the aristocratic priests in Jerusalem), were more or less content with the status quo and did not wish for upheavals.

No doubt there were substantial socioeconomic factors that led to unrest, and finally to rebellion, in Roman Palestine. But the religious tradition itself contributed a great deal to that end. The memories of independence and the promises of a glorious future, both held alive through reading and interpretation of scripture, were themselves a reason for the disdain felt by many toward the Roman reign.

However, the expectation of a concrete, dramatic, collective reversal was never a central concern for all pious Jews. Individual hopes took more individualistic and personal forms. This holds true even for the apocalyptic literature, where we do find "hope for a glorious kingdom, but the hope of the individual even in many apocalyptic texts is for eternal glory with the angels." In a more Platonic vein, some authors in the Diaspora express a view of immortality that is largely disconnected from the historical orientation of the mainstream hopes and more attuned to the Greco-Roman world of thought. . . .

One may distinguish between two ideal types of future hope: a collective earthly expectation on one hand, and an individual transcendent expectation on the other. The former would involve an eternal kingdom of peace and prosperity on this earth into which the righteous dead would rise to share it with the righteous of the last generation. For the latter, events on this earth would be of little or no interest; the righteous would receive their reward, a spiritual eternal life in the transcendent heaven, immediately after death. But while one of these types generally predominates in a given source, features from the other type are more often than not present as well. The symbolic worlds reflected in the sources are a more colorful mixture than a simple logic of ideal types would dictate.

Not surprisingly, much of the diversity found in Jewish sources reappears in the thought world of nascent Christianity.

Questions for Discussion and Reflection

1. How would you characterize the climate or dominant mood of Mediterranean Jews in the time of Jesus, according to Räisänen's description?

2. What is the connection between historical events and Jewish eschatology of this period?

3. What distinction does Räisänen draw between the two kinds of future expectations found in the Jewish community of Jesus' time? What would influence an individual to be more likely to have one kind of expectation versus another?

Carolyn M. Schneider, *I Am a Christian: The Nun, the Devil, and Martin Luther* (Fortress Press, 2010)

Carolyn Schneider discusses the importance of a story about a nun in the writing and preaching of the great reformer Martin Luther (5, 15, 23–24):

> Over the course of twenty-four years, Luther often recounted the tale of a faithful woman who in the face of the demonic proclaimed her faith with the simple phrase "I am a Christian." The frequency with which this story appears in Luther's works indicates the theological importance he gave to her simple confession. He referred to the story in a variety of genres, including theological treatises, class lectures, sermons, and table talks. . . .
>
> In June 1538 the focus of Luther's sermon series on John's Gospel was the very familiar verse John 3:16: "For God so loved the world that he gave his only Son, so that everyone who believes in him may not perish but may have eternal life." Luther understood eternal life to be a clinging to Christ, by which one entered trouble, death, and even hell with Christ, but also broke through in victory to life. Luther laced the nun's story throughout the sermon as an example.
>
>> Thus one reads a fine example of a nun (our Lord God has had quite a few in all positions who have been preserved and blessed). She had high anxiety over death and sins, as all who have not been stomach-servants have felt God's wrath and judgment, because of which one sought refuge from them in the saints. Meanwhile, then, the little nun, too, feared God's wrath and wanted to be blessed. So when the devil plagued her with his temptations to anxiety, she got

into the habit of saying to the devil, "Leave me in peace, I am a Christian." So the devil had to leave her in peace. This really seems like an easy thing and quickly learned. But make sure that one also speaks out of faith, as this little nun has done, because the devil did not greatly fear this word: I am a Christian, but rather her faith, on which she relied firmly and said, "I am baptized in Christ and I trust in him alone because he is my life, salvation, and wisdom."

. . . For Luther the story of the woman vanquishing the devil with her confession contained the essence of Christian faithfulness in a nutshell. "This Word has everything in it," he told Johann Feldkirch in 1534. . . .

From all of this it is clear that when Luther told and retold the story of the nun and the devil, his primary interest was not the identity of the person who said, "I am a Christian," in times of desperation. Rather, he was interested in the theology tucked into the phrase and its use in situations of despair. In 1542 a significant theological move in Luther's application of the story occurred when Luther began to use the story as a way out of the anguish caused by thoughts about predestination.

In a later chapter Schneider shows how Luther used this story to emphasize certain theological principles (96–98):

Jesus calls people to leave everything and follow him. This includes leaving the "old" person that was one's self behind. The author says that the new person "is Christ and obedience. When one speaks of dying and destroying and things like that, one means that the old man should come to nought. And when and where that happens in a true divine light, the new man is born again."

This is the theology that Luther applied to baptism. He connected it over and over again with "Mechthild's" response to the devil in the story he tells about her resistance to despair. When she says, "I am a Christian," Luther understands that to mean "'I am dead, but Christ lives; I am a sinner, but Christ is righteous, because I believe in Jesus Christ and was baptized in His name.'" For Luther's "little nun," to be "baptized in Christ" means that "he is my life, salvation, and wisdom." In telling her story, Luther was always urging people not to remain with themselves but instead to "oppose the devil and his attacks in Christ alone."

Iserloh notes that "Luther's negative theology," as opposed to Pseudo-Dionysius's negative theology, "is a theology of the cross." . . . Human experience includes sin, suffering, and death. These are the things that bring one to nothing and cause the *Anfechtung* against which the heroine of Luther's story fights. In this becoming nothing Luther saw two temptations. One was the temptation to make one's humiliation into a virtue in an attempt to gain God's favor. The other was the temptation to despair of God's love altogether. This second temptation was the one that inflicted so many medieval Mechthilds as they came face to face with (or back to back with) the hidden God, God in God's opposite. This was what Luther meant when he spoke of sharing the cross of Christ and the temptation that Christ felt on it. The cross cuts a sharp and very thin line between God's judgment and God's mercy, damnation and salvation, hell and heaven. For Luther, the judgment of God against sinners on the cross of Christ would lead to hell where they would remain unless the Holy Spirit drew a person through faith into the life of Christ so that a new person could be born out of the death of the old. This was why, nearly every time he told the story of Mechthild staving off despair with the assertion, "I am a Christian," Luther called people back to their baptisms, where they were put to death and raised with Christ. This act of salvation is fearful; it requires one to "press on against God to God."

> In the bridal embrace of Christ, the soul grasps the cross, that is, death and hell, and thereby receives life. "For as Christ, by his union with the immortal divinity, overcame death by dying, so the Christian, through his union with the immortal Christ, arising through faith in Him, also overcomes death by dying. And thus God destroys the devil himself, and carries out his own work by means of his alien work."

Historian Steven Ozment has argued that even where Luther is profiting from "the *resignatio* motif of [Johannes] Tauler" (the theme of resigning oneself to hell), he uses it to say something different from Tauler. He argues that in Tauler, to become nothing is to clear the clutter out of one's soul so that the only thing left is the ground of one's being, which is the link between the soul and God. Thus, for Tauler, when one resigns oneself to hell, the highest part of the soul is exposed. The similarity between this apex or foundation of the soul and God is ultimately the basis for one's union with God. For Luther, in contrast, to become nothing is to acknowledge not only that what one is and wills is different from God but that it is opposed to God and thus stands sinful and under God's righteous condemnation. Thus there is no basis for union with God in oneself, but only in Jesus, who bears the damned with their judgment in himself on the cross.

If this is an accurate analysis, it is yet another example of how Luther used his sources in his own way, whether or not Luther himself realized that he was reworking Tauler's ideas. Even when Luther was using the story of the martyrs confessing, "I am a Christian," he altered it to suit his purposes. He did not repristinate the theology of the early Christian martyrs. Rather, he seized on their confession because so much of his own theology could be expressed through it. His goal was never simply to copy the theological system of someone else, but to use what he liked in that system to develop his own theology in light of his own context and experiences. When he named the heroine of his story, it was "Mechthild," not "Blandina." As we saw with the way Luther transformed the story about the early martyrs of the church into a story about a medieval nun suffering and overcoming demonic temptation to despair, Luther was attuned to the needs of his own time as he plumbed the theology of the past for images, phrases, and ideas with which to express the gospel.

Questions for Discussion and Reflection

1. What does his use of a story about a nun confronting the devil tell you about Luther as a preacher and Christian teacher?

2. What is the importance of baptism according to Luther?

3. What does "becoming nothing" mean in Tauler's theological view, according to Steven Ozment? What does it mean in Luther's, according to Carolyn Schneider? Based on this analysis, how would you characterize Luther's outlook on the relationship between the believer and God?

Samuel Torvend, *Luther and the Hungry Poor: Gathered Fragments* (Fortress Press, 2008)

Samuel Torvend discusses how Luther's upbringing and scholarly training influenced his views of a core Christian belief (40–42):

Luther and his reforming colleagues at the University of Wittenberg would never depart from the primacy of the teaching on justification by grace. They considered it the "article of faith" on which everything stood firm or collapsed; there could be no vital and faithful Christianity without this biblical and theological principle as its foundation. It should come as no surprise that Luther's focus on the metaphor of justification responded to his own spiritual anxiety. The discovery of the meaning of the "righteousness of God" as it related to the "justification of the sinner by grace alone" spoke to him existentially, to the depths of his anxiety: "I felt that I was altogether born again and had entered paradise itself through open gates."

We should note the manner in which Luther arrived at this primary insight. First, he was influenced by his own upbringing in a home where his father, Hans Luther, had worked diligently to move his family upward from their peasant origins to the enviable status of mine owners. Luther's father expected his son to become a lawyer, an achievement that would place him among the wealthy who could afford legal counsel. Luther was raised in an emerging economic system that made it possible for people without land or noble lineage to prosper financially through sheer labor and smart business practices. It was evident from the life of his father that hard work yielded results and rewards. Second, having ended his progress toward a legal profession, Luther entered one of the most rigorous of religious communities where strenuous ascetic discipline demonstrated one's love of God and growth in holiness. In this regard the young Luther was influenced by the spiritual-economic world of late medieval Christianity, a world that offered a plethora of means for earnest Christians who sought to secure their salvation. Third, Luther was a student and a biblical scholar, a professor of theology. It was through his meticulous study of the Bible in preparation for his lectures, in particular his sometimes tortured examination of Paul's letters, that his personal anxiety was dispelled and he felt himself to be "born again," released from his anxious quest.

From his gradual recognition of the implications of the powerful symbol of "justification by grace," he began to question the foundations of the theological world he had inherited and inhabited. For Luther and the university colleagues who gravitated to his emerging theology, the Pauline metaphor of justification was not only the key to rethinking the existential, hermeneutical, theological, soteriological, sacramental, and ecclesial dimensions of Christianity, it also became the key through which they responded to the communities and individuals who, having accepted Luther's teachings, were engaged in the pressing economic, political, and social issues of their time. If "justification by grace" was the key, the foundation, the center of the reform project, then *it was the key to everything*, not only God's relationship with humanity but also one's relationship with others in the world. And since life in this world is lived within the economic, political, and social fabrics of a particular culture, the "article" upon which everything stood or collapsed would possess economic, political, and social implications, or it would prove utterly irrelevant and, thus, useless.

Luther rejected the late medieval search for salvation and the spiritual-economic system that was intended to support Christians in that search. No work, no behavior, no purchase, no claim to spiritual privilege based on gender, class, education, or religious standing could secure one's eternal destiny. While the teaching on justification set forth the assertion that God justifies humanity apart from any and every kind of work, it also encoded a radical egalitarianism: all were caught in the centripetal field of sin and all could be liberated from that field by the word and action of Another. Perhaps it was release from the anxiety that attended such a quest and its inherent competitiveness that elicited criticism from those who supervised and benefited from the sale of spiritual "goods" and approval from those who accepted the notion that the accumulation of capital no longer mattered.

At the same time Luther's theology of grace as God's unmerited regard for humanity effectively criticized the notion that some persons—the hungry poor and the destitute—could be "used," even "charitably," for those who sought to advance their spiritual if not social standing with donations. Luther's sharp criticism of Christians who act as "masters and gods" in their treatment of the weak underscored a relational dynamic alive in German urban centers but also expressed the social utility of the teaching on justification, one that could subvert the tendency to value persons of another socioeconomic class only to the degree that they "received" goods (the hungry poor) or "offered" goods (the wealthy). If the needy were not to be used for spiritual gain, they were to be encountered as real persons with real needs. . . .

Torvend also discusses Luther's interpretation of the scriptural command to feed the hungry (69–70):

As a young biblical student and monk, Luther had followed a scrupulously ascetic regimen, one that included fasting, physical mortification, and disdain for the ordinary needs and pleasures of life. Without asserting a causal relationship, it would seem, nonetheless, that his early interpretation of Scripture corresponded in some ways with his ascetic dedication. For instance, in his commentary on Psalm 104, part of his early lectures on the Psalms (1513–15), Luther admitted of God's providence in providing creatures with physical nourishment (the plain sense of the text). Yet he quickly elaborated on the spiritual significance of the text, suggesting that the verse "When you open your hand, they are filled with good things" (v. 28) should be interpreted as God "feeding" the creation with and through the preaching and teaching of the Word: "Wisdom plays this whole game mystically in the church, for He feeds all the creatures of God without the work of men, and when He gives and opens His hand they gather and are filled with good, which is the Word of the Gospel. For who but Christ has opened the Gospel? And so, behold, he expresses the same thing by means of many symbols."

Luther would not depart from interpreting Scripture in a spiritual sense, yet his appreciation for the plain or historical sense would continue to grow throughout the early 1520s and beyond as he responded to requests for advice concerning the economic, political, and social concerns of his day. Indeed, one ought not to exclude the influence of his biography on his theology. His departure from and published criticism of monastic life, his entrance into marriage and the subsequent birth of children, and his encounter with the hungry poor at his door or on the streets of Wittenberg helped him participate in the Reformation's "wide recovery of the earthy humanity of Scripture." As a biblical scholar whose imagination was shaped by the study of Scripture and as a theologian engaged in the pressing crises of the early sixteenth century, Luther allowed the biblical text to interpret the questions and controversies of his day.

On the one hand, Luther was acutely sensitive to the powerful role of self-preservation in human thought and action, an aggressive self-centered focus that could obscure too readily the neighbor's need and one's dependence on the Creator. At the same time, he also grew in his "appreciation for the goodness of God's creation" and the appropriate use of God's natural gifts in the social order. "Luther's discovery of the world as a given, promised domain extricates him from a monastic denial of life and corresponding flight from the world. As a reformer living entirely out of joy in creation, he discovers worldliness as a theological category." This "appreciation" of creation in its plain or earthy or "worldly" sense became clearer in his explanations of the first article of the Apostles' Creed ("I believe in God, the Father Almighty, Creator of heaven and earth") and the fourth petition of the Lord's Prayer ("Give us today our daily bread"), first preached in a series of catechetical sermons in the summer of 1528 and then revised for publication as the German Catechism or Large Catechism in the fall of 1528. There one can recognize the theological implication embedded in the teaching on justification by grace: the movement of God toward, into, and through this creation: "You see, God wishes to show us how he cares for us in all our needs and faithfully provides for our daily sustenance. Although he gives and provides these blessings bountifully, even to the godless and rogues, yet he wishes us to ask for them so that we may realize that we have received them from his hand and may recognize in them his fatherly goodness toward us."

Questions for Discussion and Reflection

1. How did Luther's evolving understanding of justification by grace affect his view of his own social standing and his role in the world?

2. What was the theological viewpoint behind Luther's critique of maltreatment of poor people?

3. How did Luther interpret God's providence both literally (historically) and spiritually? How did these different interpretations fit into his larger theological view?

Kyle Jantzen, *Faith and Fatherland: Parish Politics in Hitler's Germany* (Fortress Press, 2008)

Kyle Jantzen discusses the relationship between German Lutherans and the Third Reich in a study focusing on three large towns, Nauen, outside of Berlin; Pirna, outside of Dresden, and Ravensburg. Here he discusses the specific question of whether clergy in these towns were concerned about the Nazi treatment of Jews (93–94):

There is no evidence from the correspondence, publications, or actions of Protestant clergy in Nauen, Pirna, and Ravensburg to suggest that they were significantly affected by or preoccupied with the euthanasia crisis or the "Jewish question." As Wolfgang Gerlach found in his probing study of the relationship between the Confessing Church and the persecution of the Jews, pastors and church leaders were either too conflicted, too preoccupied, or too afraid to defend persecuted Jews. They were too conflicted because so many of them had so earnestly welcomed Hitler and National Socialism as a providential salvation for Germany and for their own Protestant churches. They believed in Hitler's mission to reform and revitalize German society and actively supported that mission by participating in public events that contributed to Nazi rule. Even when many clergy frowned on the violent or intolerant facets of Nazism, they still affirmed other aspects of the Third Reich, such as the new emphasis on order or Hitler's tough foreign policy. During the Second World War, loyalty to the Fatherland overrode any thoughts of criticizing the Nazi regime.

Protestant pastors were also too preoccupied to defend German Jews. Theological battles against aggressive German Christians put the Confessing Church on the defensive for much of the Third Reich, reasserting the authority of the traditional confessions of faith and struggling to free their churches from state or party influence. Too often they debated the content of theological statements, skirting the very real needs of the physically or mentally handicapped Germans or the German Jews who were suffering all around them.

Finally, pastors were too afraid to defend Jews or other enemies of the Third Reich. Even Julius von Jan, the Wurttemberg pastor whose sermon condemning the Kristallnacht Pogrom earned him a severe beating, home invasion, arrest, and imprisonment remarked, "We were afraid to touch this sensitive spot of the regime."

As we have already seen, pastors in Nauen, Pirna, and Ravensburg were enthusiastic supporters of the "national renewal" of 1933. They believed the National Socialist revitalization of Germany would also usher in a profound moral renewal that would reawaken Protestant spiritual life. Furthermore, they believed Hitler was calling them to assist him in his mission to Germany, and they praised the Nazi leader for his successful defeat of godless Communism. As a result, clergy in the three districts were obsessed with the relationship between their churches and their faith, on the one hand, and the German nation and National Socialist movement, on the other. And all this was founded theologically on the conviction that the nation, race, family, state, and soil were sacred orders of life created by God and worthy of special status on earth. Indeed, many theologians and pastors regarded racial purity as a divine mandate. All of this led Protestant clergy quite naturally into a positive stance toward National Socialism and meant that, at best, they were too conflicted to be anything but ambivalent about the fate of the Jews. . . .

Caught up in the nationalism of the Third Reich, some pastors ventured beyond the general excitement over the rebirth of Germany and the desire to forge a strong relationship between church and nation. They began to encourage the pursuit of German blood purity as a religious mission, using language that mirrored the propaganda of the NSDAP. In November of 1934, Pastor Ernst Ranft of Helmsdorf addressed his colleagues in the Pirna district with a message titled "The Importance of Race Research for Religion and Christianity." Significantly, the starting point for Ranft's talk was neither theological nor scriptural but rather ideological—he began by explaining the fundamental importance of race in the National Socialist worldview. When Ranft eventually turned to the connection between race and religion, it was only so that he could affirm his conviction that religions were racially specific in nature and that there were definite limits to the universality of any religion. Ranft *did* state that the revelation of Christ was God's answer for all humanity and added that the demand to tailor Christian preaching to specific racial preferences could not be allowed to reduce the content of the gospel. Indeed, Ranft explained how Christian preaching for a particular race must be "a loving entrance into the special certainties of the life of a nation and a race, not least into the failures and peculiarities attached to it." The Christian sermon must always be a call to repentance, though the outworking of preaching in the practices of faith and piety "should and ought to be thoroughly racially specific." According to Ranft, the life application of the preaching of the Word of God demanded the serious efforts of German Protestant clergy in order that it might produce a renewed Christian-German community. What Ranft *failed* to mention was that most of the new racially specific preaching that he and other Lutheran pastors were engaged in neglected to point out any of the failures of the German nation. Rather, their sermons exalted Germany and its Lutheran legacy, conflating Protestant piety and German patriotism.

Jantzen goes on to give examples of how individual pastors handled the question of the Jewish roots of Christianity (96–97):

Curate Immanuel Spellenberg of Friedrichshafen, near Ravensburg, sent conflicting messages about the Jews. Spellenberg's background seemed solid enough—as an SA man, he had conducted a propaganda tour of Romania in 1936, and earlier still, as a student, he had conducted research on the life of the nineteenth-century nationalist Ernst Moritz Arndt. Still, in January 1939, for reasons that are not clear, Spellenberg felt compelled to issue a written clarification about his views on Jews and the Old Testament. On the one hand, Spellenberg affirmed how, as a National Socialist and old SA leader, he had always taught children about the destructive influence of godless Judaism and about the judgments of the Old Testament prophets against the Jews. In the same way, he declared his determination to continue teaching the Old Testament so that "the moral sensitivities of the German race are not hindered." On the other hand, Spellenberg tempered his condemnation of Jewish influence in Germany by arguing that because of his belief in the New Testament, he could not completely reject the Old Testament. Since Jesus Christ had taught from the Old Testament and had proclaimed the fulfillment and not abolition of the Old Testament law, Spellenberg refused to part completely with the Hebrew Scriptures. His statement cut to the core of the predicament faced by Christians in National Socialist Germany. As much as they might agree with the anti-Semitic ideology of the NSDAP, they could never escape the charges of party extremists that Christianity was a Jewish religion. To do so would amount to the abandonment of the historical foundation of the Christian faith and the denial of the essential Jewishness of Jesus.

If pastors like Priester and Spellenberg were unwilling to deny the essential connection between Judaism and Christianity, several of the most radical German Christian pastors in Nauen, Pirna, and

Ravensburg were willing to cross that theological threshold in their attempt to expunge Jews and Judaism from German Protestantism. In Nauen, Pastor Friedrich Siems inveighed against "Judaism and its fearfully destructive influence," attacking them both as communists and capitalists. He denied any substantial connection between Judaism and Christianity, even doubting that Jesus was Jewish: "As German Christians, we have discerned that the founder of Christianity had nothing, really nothing at all to do with the Jewish people, rather they were always his sharpest opponents. . . . The personality of Christ is too great and too holy for us to bring it into connection with [Jews, who have] become a curse for the whole world." In fact, because Siems believed German blood purity was a divine order of creation, the presence of Jews posed not only a risk to the German racial community but also an obstacle to the fulfillment of God's law. In other words, it was an act of faith to eliminate both Judaism from Christianity and Jews from Germany.

In Pirna, Pastor Paul Teichgräber of Eschdorf denigrated Jews and Judaism in the course of a 1934 report about the activities of the local Seventh-day Adventist sect. Above all else, Teichgräber judged the Adventists harshly for their political subversion and their Jewish practices. He claimed that the sect followed "Jewish teaching and tendencies" even more closely than the outlawed Jehovah's Witnesses and supported his contention with examples of "Sabbath-keeping, tithing, a materialistic view of salvation and law-keeping, and the *exaltation of the Jewish people as the people of God.*" Teichgräber denied the idea that the Jews were the means God used to bring the message of salvation to earth, or that the experiences of Old Testament Israel foreshadowed either Christ or Christianity. He rejected the assertion that Old Testament sacrifices were similar to Jesus' death, or that the Passover feast and Christian sacrament of communion were essentially comparable.

Questions for Discussion and Reflection

1. What made Protestant pastors in Nauen, Pirna, and Ravensburg enthusiastic about supporting National Socialism? How did Ranft's talk on "race research" illustrate the connection Lutheran pastors were making between nationalism and religion?

2. From the examples Jantzen gives, how would you describe the range of viewpoints among German Protestant clergy about the relationship between Judaism and Christianity?

3. What general conclusions would you draw so far about the role of Protestant clergy under the Third Reich? What other questions would you raise if you pursued this topic for a research paper?

READING HISTORICAL DOCUMENTS

You'll notice that throughout *Introduction to the History of Christianity* are excerpts from historical documents, including theological treatises, journal entries, letters, and church doctrinal statements. These kinds of primary sources are rich material for increasing your understanding of a historical subject. You'll need to develop skills to read these texts closely and critically analyze their content and significance.

When you first encounter a historical document, it's best to make sure you know some basic facts about it before plunging in. For example, find the answers to these questions:

▶ What is the date? If not known, can you find an estimate or approximation?
▶ Who is the author?
▶ What kind of document is it, or what is the genre? (For example, a constitution, a letter, a poem)
▶ What is the national and/or cultural context of the document?

After you've read the document at least once, consider these questions:

▶ Who is the intended audience?
▶ What are the document's main themes or its core message?
▶ What underlying assumptions does the author have about the topic and/or the audience?
▶ What makes this document significant historically? culturally? religiously?

You may not be able to answer these questions on your own even after reading the document several times. You may need to do research, starting with the source of the document (such as the book or website where you first encountered it) and then expanding from there. You'll want to keep in mind these further questions:

▶ What have previous scholars concluded about this document?
▶ What, if any, controversies or arguments have arisen about it?
▶ Has there been a scholarly consensus about any controversial questions? Has that consensus changed over time?

Finally, to spur your critical thinking, ask questions like these:

- ▶ What do I think is important about this document?
- ▶ Do I agree or disagree with any scholarly conclusions I've read about?
- ▶ How would I argue for or against a particular thesis about this document?

Let's take an example. Below is a "Letter Concerning a Pious Woman" published in *A Reformation Reader: Primary Texts with Introductions*, ed. Denis R. Janz (Fortress Press, 1999), 218–219:

At issue is a request from a pious woman who, because of her desire to follow the truth and pure religion, has been treated badly by her husband and subjected to cruel and harsh servitude. Thus she wishes to know if it is permissible to leave her husband and to come here or withdraw to another church where she might rest her conscience in peace. Accordingly, we offer the following advice.

First of all, with respect to her perplexity and agony, we are filled with pity and compassion for her and are drawn to pray that it will please God to give her such a sense of relief that she will be able to find the wherewithal to rejoice in him. Nevertheless, since she has asked for our counsel regarding what is permissible, our duty is to respond, purely and simply, on the basis of what God reveals to us in his Word, closing our eyes to all else. For this reason, we beg her not to take offense if our advice does not correspond with her hope. For it is necessary that she and we follow what the Master has ordained, without mingling our desires with it.

Now, with regard to the bond of marriage, one must remember that a believing party cannot, of his or her free will, divorce the unbeliever, as St. Paul makes clear in 1 Cor. 7:13. Without a doubt, St. Paul emphasizes this, fully knowing the suffering each party may be experiencing. For at that time the pagans and the Jews were no less poisoned against the Christian religion than the papists are today. But St. Paul commands the believing partner, who continues to persevere in the truth of God, not to leave the partner who resists God.

In brief, we ought so to prefer God and Jesus Christ to the whole world that fathers, children, husbands, and wives cease to constitute something we value. So much is this so, that if we cannot adhere to him and renounce all else, we ought to make ourselves do so. This does not mean that Christianity ought to abrogate the order of nature. Where the two parties consent, it is especially fitting for the Christian wife to double her efforts to be submissive to her husband—here regarded as an enemy of the truth—in order to win him if at all possible, as St. Peter advises in 1 Pet. 3:1.

Nevertheless, as matters stand today in the papal church, a believing wife ought not to relinquish her hope without striving and trying to direct her husband toward the road of salvation. No matter how great his obstinacy might be, she must not let herself be diverted from the faith; rather she must affirm it with constancy and steadfastness—whatever the dangers might be.

However, if the above party should be persecuted to the extent that she is in danger of denying her hope, then she is justified in fleeing. When a wife (or husband, as the case may be) has made her confession of faith and demonstrated how necessary it is not to consent to the abominations of the papacy, and if persecution arises against her for having done so and she is in grave peril, she may justly flee when God grants her an occasion to escape. For that does not constitute a willful divorce but occurs because of persecution.

Hence it is appropriate that the good lady who has sought our counsel endure until the above occurs. For according to her letters, she currently only holds her peace and quietly goes along; being required to taint herself before idols, she bows before them in condescension. For this reason she may not justify leaving her husband until she has amply declared her faith and resisted greater pressures than presently encountered. Therefore she needs to pray for God to strengthen her, then she needs to fight more valiantly than she has, drawing upon the power of the Holy Spirit, to show her husband her faith, doing so in gentleness and humility, explaining to him that she must not offend God for the sake of pleasing him.

We have also taken into consideration her husband's rudeness and cruelty, of which she has advised us. But that ought not to prevent her from taking heart to commend the matter to God. For whenever we are so preoccupied with fear that we are afraid to do what we ought, then we are guilty of infidelity. That is the foundation on which we should build.

If, after having attempted what we have advised, she should come into imminent peril, or her husband should persecute her to the point of death, then she is free to exercise that liberty which our Lord grants to all his own, i.e., to flee ravenous wolves.

Now let's attempt to ask and answer some questions about the document:

1. What is the date?

The Reformation Reader provides a date of July 22, 1552.

2. Who is the author?

Again, the *Reader* tells us that it is John Calvin.

3. What kind of document is it?

It's a letter Calvin addressed to a laywoman, who in this case is anonymous, who wrote him—probably multiple times, since he refers to "her letters."

4. What is the national and/or cultural context of the document?

Calvin was based in Geneva and was a leader of the Reformation. He would have been seen as a theological authority and looked to for advice. He would have dealt with many upheavals caused by conflicts between Catholics and Protestants, including domestic conflicts such as the one that led to this letter.

5. Who is the intended audience?

Clearly, the primary audience is the woman who wrote asking for advice. But we can assume, too, that Calvin was thinking of all Protestant laypeople in marriages with Catholics. We could also theorize that he wished to state principles he felt other Protestant leaders should support when they dealt with similar situations in their congregations and communities.

6. What are the document's main themes or its core message?

Calvin was clearly concerned with the situation of couples in which one partner was Catholic and the other was Protestant: he saw an opportunity for conversion ("believing wife ought not to relinquish . . . trying to direct her husband toward the road of salvation") as well as a danger for the Protestant partner of returning to their original faith or giving up on converting their partner ("she must not let herself be diverted from the faith"). He urges the woman to try harder to show her husband the error of his ways: "she needs to fight more valiantly than she has," although she must do so "in gentleness and humility"—Calvin here emphasizes her traditional female role. He also asserts that divorce is out of the question, quoting Scripture to reinforce his argument, and yet he gives the woman an out: if she is "in grave peril," she may leave her husband. He does not specify what would constitute "grave peril."

7. What underlying assumptions does the author have about the topic and/or the audience?

John Calvin reiterates his opposition to Catholic beliefs and institutions; he states that Catholics have been "poisoned against the Christian religion." He assumes his audience—the laywoman who wrote him and anyone else who reads this letter—wishes to follow the strictest Protestant interpretation of Scripture and expectations for Christian behavior. He uses biblical references to support his arguments, and he clearly believes in his own religious authority over others.

8. What makes this document significant historically? culturally? religiously?

This letter gives us insight into John Calvin's theological principles as well as his views on marriage. We get a taste of how Protestant women were expected to comport themselves, and what it might have been like to be in a "mixed" marriage of a Protestant and a Catholic during the Reformation. This brief letter is clearly not a significant church document, like a creed or treatise, but it does provide important information about how Protestant beliefs were brought to bear on ordinary domestic life.

If you were to use this letter in a research paper, you would need to find out what other scholars have said about the document itself as well as about John Calvin's role as authority and advice giver. You might look for other letters Calvin wrote and compare them. Finally, you might consider using any one or more of several critical lenses to analyze this letter and the themes it raises, such as a feminist critique (e.g., Calvin's attitude toward women and marriage), a literary analysis (keeping in mind that this version of the letter is a translation), a theological interpretation (e.g., the role of Scripture within the advice Calvin gives), and a historical review (e.g., the letter in the context of events and developments in Geneva in 1552).

Additional Resources

"How to Read a Document": http://www.clas.ufl.edu/users/sterk/junsem/reading.html
"How to Read Primary Sources": http://www.wisconsinhistory.org/turningpoints/primarysources.asp
"Historical Documents: How to Read Them": http://libguides.tru.ca/historicaldocuments
"How to Read a Primary Source": http://www.bowdoin.edu/writing-guides/primaries.htm

A SHORT GUIDE TO WRITING RESEARCH PAPERS ON THE HISTORY OF CHRISTIANITY

This guide is meant to help you organize and compose a traditional academic research paper on the history of Christianity. You may also find the basic sequence and resources helpful in other disciplines.

Short or long, your research paper can be crafted in five steps: (1) choose a topic, (2) research your topic, (3) outline your argument, (4) write the first draft, and (5) refine the final paper.

1. Choose a Topic

If your topic is not chosen for you, you should aim to choose one that is (1) interesting to you, (2) manageable (with readily available sources) and malleable (so you can narrow in on an especially interesting or important aspect), and (3) arguable. Your research paper will essentially be an *argument* based on the available primary and secondary sources and authorities.

A good place to start is the chapters of *Introduction to the History of Christianity*. Perhaps there was a topic in one of the chapters (such as mysticism or the Great Awakening) that caught your interest. Also, look over this study guide. Did one of the additional readings intrigue you? Check out the Selected Online Resources; perhaps a website will lead you to a good research topic. Here are some additional suggestions:

Methodological Topics

How has the field of archeology contributed to the study of the Bible and its historical context?
How did Paul Tillich integrate existentialism and depth psychology into his systematic theology?
What scientific theories and perspectives have challenged the church and its traditional teachings?

Historical Topics

What roles did monastic women play in the life of the medieval church?
What was worship like in the first African American churches?
Who among the early patriarchs had the most significant impact on the Eastern Orthodox church?

Interpretive or Comparative Topics

How did the encounter between Christian missionaries and indigenous peoples affect both indigenous religions and the church?

What are the similarities and differences in the roles played by John Calvin and Martin Luther in the development of their respective Protestant church movements?

What were the opportunities for Quaker and Methodist women to be preachers and leaders in the early American colonial period?

Resources for Writing Research Papers

Bombaro, Christine. *Finding History: Research Methods and Resources for Students and Scholars*. Lanham, MD: Scarecrow, 2012.

Booth, Wayne C., Gregory G. Colomb, and Joseph M. Williams. *The Craft of Research*. 3rd ed. Chicago: University of Chicago Press, 2008.

Mann, Thomas. *The Oxford Guide to Library Research*. 3rd ed. New York: Oxford University Press, 2005.

Vyhmeister, Nancy Jean. *Quality Research Papers: For Students of Religion and Theology*. Grand Rapids, MI: Zondervan, 2001.

2. Research Your Topic

Material about your topic may reside in a single text or an array of historical texts by one or many authors or in the conflicting opinions of contemporary scholars. In most cases, you can build your research by moving from general to specific treatments of your topic.

One caution: In your research, take care not to allow your expanding knowledge of what others think about your topic to drown your own curiosities, sensibilities, and insights. Instead, as your initial questions expand and then diminish with increased knowledge from your research, your own deeper concerns, insights, and point of view should emerge and grow.

Encyclopedia articles, scholarly books, dictionaries of church history, journal articles, and other standard reference tools contain a wealth of material and helpful bibliographies to orient you to your topic and its historical context. Look for the most authoritative and up-to-date sources. Checking cross-references will deepen your knowledge.

General Reference Works

The Blackwell Encyclopedia of Modern Christian Thought. Alister McGrath, ed. Oxford: Blackwell, 1993.

Encyclopedia of Early Christianity. Ed. Everett Ferguson. 2nd ed. New York: Garland, 1999.

Encyclopedia of Religious Rites, Rituals, and Festivals. Ed. Frank A. Salamone. New York: Routledge, 2004.

MacHaffie, Barbara J. *Her Story: Women in Christian Tradition*. 2nd ed. Minneapolis: Fortress, 2006.

McGuckin, John Anthony. *The Orthodox Church: An Introduction to Its History, Doctrine, and Spiritual Culture*. Malden, MA: Wiley-Blackwell, 2011.

New Catholic Encyclopedia. 15 vols. 2nd ed. Detroit: Thomson Gale, 2002.

The Oxford Companion to Christian Thought. Adrian Hastings, Alistair Mason, and Hugh Pyper, eds. With Ingrid Lawrie and Cecily Bennett. Oxford: Oxford University Press, 2000.

Oxford Dictionary of the Christian Church. F. L. Cross and E. A. Livingstone, eds. 3rd ed. New York: Oxford University Press, 1997.

Online Resources

Note: Although not all Internet sources meet scholarly standards, some very good reference tools do appear online. Some of them are listed here.

▶ "Internet Guide to Religion"—an annotated guide to online resources in religion from the Wabash Center for Teaching and Learning in Theology and Religion

  http://www.wabashcenter.wabash.edu/resources/guide-headings.aspx

▶ Internet Sacred Text Archive: "Christianity"—links to several Bible versions, plus apocrypha and Gnostic texts

  http://www.sacred-texts.com/chr/index.htm

▶ Christian Classics Ethereal Library—web pages and downloadable files of primary sources, including the works of the early church fathers

  http://www.ccel.org

▶ "Virtual Religion Index"—lists of primarily academic links related to all world religions, plus biblical studies

  http://virtualreligion.net/vri

▶ The World Religions & Spirituality Page—academic research site based at Virginia Commonwealth University primarily on new religious movements (Christian and non-Christian) with extensive listing of religions and information on origins, history, principle beliefs and practices, and additional bibliographies

  http://www.has.vcu.edu/wrs/

It's wise to start listing the sources you've consulted right away in standard bibliographical format (see section 5, below, for examples of usual formats). You'll want to assign a number or code to each one so you'll be able to reference them easily when you're writing the paper.

Periodical Literature

Even if you are writing on a single text (e.g., the Gospel of Mark, a papal bull, Augustine's *City of God*), you'll be able to place your interpretation in contemporary context only by referring to what other scholars today are saying. Their work is largely published in academic journals and periodicals. In consulting the chief articles dealing with your topic, you'll learn where agreements, disagreements, and open questions stand; how older treatments have fared; and the latest relevant tools and insights. Since you cannot consult them all, work back from the latest, looking for the best and most directly relevant articles from the last five, ten, or twenty years, as ambition and time allow.

A good place to start is the ATLA Religion Database (www.atla.com), which indexes articles, essays, book reviews, dissertations, theses, and even essays in collections. You can search by keywords, subjects, persons, or scripture references. Below are other standard indexes to periodical literature. Check with your institution's library to learn which ones it subscribes to.

Guide to Social Science and Religion in Periodical Literature (http://www.nplguide.com)

Readers' Guide to Periodical Literature

Dissertation Abstracts International

ATLA Catholic Periodical and Literature Index

Humanities International Index

Research the Most Important Primary and Secondary Sources

By now you can identify the most important sources for your topic, both primary and secondary. Primary sources are actual historical documents or artifacts that provide data for interpretation. These include sacred writings (such as the Bible, prayers, sermons, hymns); church documents (e.g., papal encyclical, *Book of Concord*, the Rule of Benedict); interviews; and memoirs. Secondary sources are all the articles or books that analyze or interpret primary sources.

Your research topic might be in a single primary source—for example, the idea of original sin in Augustine's *Confessions*—with many secondary commentaries, analyses, or interpretations. Or your primary resources may be large—the polled opinions of thousands of people, mystical writings from the Middle Ages, or all papal bulls issued in the eighteenth century—and may or may not have many associated secondary sources.

Apart from books and journal articles you've identified, you can find the chief works on any topic readily listed in your college or seminary library's catalog, the Library of Congress subject index (http://catalog2.loc.gov), and other online library catalog sites. Many theological libraries and archives are linked at the "Religious Studies Web Guide": http://www.ucalgary.ca/~lipton/catalogues.html.

The eventual quality of your research paper rests entirely on the quality or critical character of your sources. The best research uses academically sound treatments by recognized authorities arguing rigorously from primary sources.

Take Notes

Now review each source, noting down its most important or relevant facts, observations, or opinions. Be sure to keep your notes organized consistently; you may choose to create a separate document for the notes on each source you consult, for example. As you take notes, you should identify the subtopic, the source information (including page numbers), and the main idea or direct quotation.

While most of the notes you take will simply summarize points made in primary or secondary sources, direct quotes are used for (1) word-for-word transcriptions, (2) key words or phrases coined by the author, or (3) especially clear or summary formulations of an author's point of view. Remember, re-presenting another's insight or formulation without attribution is plagiarism. You should also be sure to keep separate notes about your own ideas or insights into the topic as they evolve.

When Can I Stop?

As you research your topic in books, articles, or reference works, you will find it coalescing into a unified body of knowledge or at least into a set of interrelated questions. Your topic will become more and more focused, partly because that is where the open question or key insight or most illuminating instance resides and partly for sheer manageability. The vast range of scholarly methods and opinions and sharply differing points of view about most religious topics (especially in the contemporary period) may force you to narrow your topic further. While the sources may never dry up, your increased knowledge will gradually give you confidence that you have the most informed, authoritative, and critical sources covered in your notes.

3. Outline Your Argument

On the basis of your research findings, in this crucial step you refine or reformulate your general topic and question into a specific question answered by a defensible thesis. You then arrange or rework your supporting materials into a clear outline that will coherently and convincingly present your thesis to your reader.

First, review your research notes carefully. Some of what you initially read may now seem obvious or irrelevant, or perhaps the whole topic is simply too massive. As your reading and note taking progressed, however, you might also have found a piece of your topic, from which a key question or problem has emerged and around which your research has gelled. Ask yourself:

▶ What is the subtopic or subquestion that is most interesting, enlightening, and manageable?

▶ What have been the most clarifying and illuminating insights I have found into the topic?

▶ In what ways have my findings contradicted my initial expectations? Can this serve as a clue to a new and different approach to my question?

▶ Can I frame my question in a clear way, and, in light of my research, do I have something new to say and defend—my thesis—that will answer my question and clarify my materials?

In this way you will advance from topic and initial question to specific question and thesis. For example, as you research primary and secondary sources on mysticism in the Renaissance period, you might find that women mystics were important figures in promoting a personal experience of God for laypeople. You might then advance a thesis that mystics such as Teresa of Avila were able to subvert their typically marginalized role in society by expressing direct spiritual experiences unmediated by male church leaders. So you have:

Topic: Women mystics in the Renaissance period

Specific topic: The role of mysticism in liberating some women from their restricted societal roles

Specific question: How did mysticism liberate some women from Renaissance society's margins and promote spiritual autonomy?

Thesis: The overwhelming and ecstatic power of mystical experience gave women like Teresa of Avila a measure of spiritual autonomy and a model of direct experience of the divine unmediated by male church leaders.

You can then outline a presentation of your thesis that organizes your research materials into an orderly and convincing argument. Functionally your outline might look like this:

Introduction: Raise the key question and announce your thesis.

Background: Present the necessary literary or historical or theological context of the question. Note the "state of the question" or the main agreements and disagreements about it.

Development: Present your own insight in a clear and logical way. Present evidence to support your thesis, and develop it further by:

> offering examples from your primary sources
> citing or discussing authorities to bolster your argument
> contrasting your thesis with other treatments, either historical or contemporary
> confirming it by showing how it makes good sense of the data, answers related questions, or solves previous puzzles.

Conclusion: Restate the thesis in a way that recapitulates your argument and its consequences for the field or the contemporary religious horizon.

The more detailed your outline, the easier your writing will be. Go through your notes, reorganizing them according to your outline. Fill in the outline with the specifics from your research, right down to the topic sentences of your paragraphs. Don't hesitate to set aside any materials that now seem off-point, extraneous, or superfluous to the development of your argument.

4. Write the First Draft

You are now ready to draft your paper, essentially by putting your outline into sentence form while incorporating specifics from your research notes.

Your main task, initially, is just to set your ideas down in as straightforward a way as possible. Assume your reader is intelligent but knows little or nothing about your particular topic. You can follow your outline closely, but you may find that logical presentation of your argument requires making some adjustments to the outline. As you write, weave in quotes judiciously from primary or secondary literature to clarify or punch your points. Add brief, strong headings at major junctures. Add footnotes to acknowledge ideas, attribute quotations, reinforce your key points through authorities, or refer the reader to further discussion or resources. Your draft footnotes will refer to your sources as abbreviated in your notes, and be sure to include page numbers. You can add full publishing data once your text is firm.

5. Refine the Final Paper

Your first draft puts you within sight of your goal, but your project's real strength emerges from reworking your initial text in a series of revisions and refinements.

In this final phase, make frequent use of one of the many excellent style manuals available for help with grammar, punctuation, footnote form, abbreviations, and so forth:

Alexander, Patrick H., et al., eds. *The SBL Handbook of Style: For Ancient Near Eastern, Biblical, and Early Christian Studies*. Peabody, Mass.: Hendrickson, 1999.

The Chicago Manual of Style. 16th ed. Chicago: University of Chicago Press, 2010.

MLA Handbook for Writers of Research Papers. 7th ed. New York: Modern Language Association, 2009.

Turabian, Kate L. *A Manual for Writers of Term Papers, Theses, and Dissertations*. 7th ed. Rev. by Wayne C. Booth, Gregory G. Colomb, Joseph M. Williams, and the University of Chicago Press Editorial Staff. Chicago: University of Chicago Press, 2007.

Online, see the searchable website Guide to Grammar and Writing: http://grammar.ccc.commnet.edu/grammar/

Polishing the Prose

To check spelling and meaning of words or to help vary your prose, try Merriam-Webster Online, which contains both the Collegiate Dictionary and the Thesaurus: http://www.m-w.com.

Closely examine your work several times, paying attention to:

▶ Structure and Argument. Ask yourself, Do I state my question and thesis accurately? Does my paper do what my introduction promised? (If not, adjust one or the other.) Do I argue my thesis well? Do the headings clearly guide the reader through my outline and argument? Does this sequence of topics orchestrate the insights my reader needs to understand my thesis?

▶ Style. "Style" here refers to writing patterns that enliven prose and engage the reader. Three simple ways to strengthen your academic prose are:

—Topic sentences: Be sure each paragraph clearly states its main assertion.

—Active verbs: As much as possible, avoid using the linking verb "to be," and instead rephrase using active verbs.

—Sentence flow: Above all, look for awkward sentences in your draft. Disentangle and rework them into smooth, clear sequences. To avoid boring the reader, vary the length and form of your sentences. Check to see if your paragraphs unfold with questions and simple declarative sentences, in addition to longer descriptive phrases.

Likewise, tackle some barbarisms that frequently invade academic prose:

▶ Repetition: Unless you need the word count, this can go.

▶ Unnecessary words: Such filler phrases as "The fact that" and "in order to" and "There is/are" numb your reader. Similarly, such qualifiers as "somewhat," "fairly," and "very" should be avoided unless they are part of a clearly defined comparison.

▶ Jargon. Avoid technical terms when possible. Explain all technical terms that you do use. Avoid or translate foreign-language terms.

▶ Overly complex sentences. Short sentences are best. Beware of run-on sentences. Avoid "etc."

Along with typographical errors, look for stealth errors—the common but overlooked grammatical gaffes: subject-verb disagreement, dangling participles, mixed verb tenses, overuse and underuse of commas, misuse of semicolons, and inconsistency in capitalization, hyphenation, italicization, and treatment of numbers.

Footnotes

Your footnotes credit your sources for every direct quotation and for other people's ideas you have used. Below are samples of typical citation formats in Modern Language Association style. (For more information on citing online sources, see Robert Harris's "Citing Web Sources MLA Style": http://www.virtualsalt.com/mla.htm.)

- Basic order
  Author's full name, *Book Title,* ed., trans., series, edition, vol. number (Place: Publisher, year), pages.
- Book
  Dennis E. Smith, *From Symposium to Eucharist: The Banquet in the Early Christian World* (Minneapolis: Fortress, 2003), 89.
- Book in a series
  Marcus J. Borg, *Conflict, Holiness, and Politics in the Teaching of Jesus*, Studies in the Bible and Early Christianity 5 (Toronto: Edwin Mellen, 1984), 1–2.
- Essay or chapter in an edited book
  Karen E. Mosby-Avery, "Black Theology and the Black Church" in *Living Stones in the Household of God: The Legacy and Future of Black Theology*, ed. Linda E. Thomas (Minneapolis: Fortress, 2004), 33–36.
- Multivolume work
  Karl Rahner, "On the Theology of Hope," *Theological Investigations*, vol. 10 (New York: Herder and Herder, 1973), 250.
- Journal article
  Joan B. Burton, "Women's Commensality in the Ancient Greek World," *Greece and Rome* 45, no. 2 (October 1998): 144.
- Encyclopedia article
  Hans-Josef Klauck, "Lord's Supper," *The Anchor Bible Dictionary,* ed. David Noel Freedman, vol. 2 (New York: Doubleday, 1992), 275.
- Online journal article
  Pamela Sue Anderson, "The Case for a Feminist Philosophy of Religion: Transforming Philosophy's Imagery and Myths," *Ars Disputandi* 1 (2000/2001); http://www.arsdisputandi.org.
- Bible
  Cite in your text (not in your footnotes) by book, chapter, and verse: Gen. 1:1-2; Exod. 7:13; Rom. 5:1-8. In your Bibliography list the version of the Bible you have used.

If a footnote cites the immediately preceding source, use "Ibid." (from the Latin *ibidem*, meaning "there"). For example: 61. Ibid., 39.

Sources cited earlier can be referred to by author or editor's last name(s), a shorter title, and page number. For example: Burton, "Women's Commensality," 145.

Bibliography

Your bibliography can be any of several types:

▶ Works Cited: just the works—books, articles, etc.—that appear in your footnotes;

▶ Works Consulted: all the works you checked in your research, whether they were cited or not in the final draft; or

▶ Select Bibliography: primary and secondary works that, in your judgment, are the most important source materials on this topic, whether cited or not in your footnotes.

Some teachers might ask for your bibliographic entries to be annotated, that is, with a comment from you on the content, import, approach, and helpfulness of each work.

Bibliographic style differs somewhat from footnote style. Here are samples of typical bibliographic formats in MLA style:

▶ Basic order

Author's last name, first name and initial. *Book Title*. Ed. Trans. Series. Edition. Vol. Place: Publisher, Year.

▶ Book

Smith, Dennis E. *From Symposium to Eucharist: The Banquet in the Early Christian World*. Minneapolis: Fortress, 2003.

▶ Book in a series

Borg, Marcus J. *Conflict, Holiness, and Politics in the Teaching of Jesus*. Studies in the Bible and Early Christianity 5. Toronto: Edwin Mellen, 1984.

▶ Edited book

Thomas, Linda E., ed. *Living Stones in the Household of God: The Legacy and Future of Black Theology*. Minneapolis: Fortress, 2004.

▶ Essay or chapter in an edited book

Mosby-Avery, Karen E. "Black Theology and the Black Church." In *Living Stones in the Household of God: The Legacy and Future of Black Theology*, 33–36. Ed. Linda E. Thomas. Minneapolis: Fortress, 2004.

▶ Multivolume work

Rahner, Karl. "On the Theology of Hope." In *Theological Investigations,* vol. 10. New York: Herder and Herder, 1973.

▶ Journal article

Burton, Joan B. "Women's Commensality in the Ancient Greek World." *Greece and Rome* 45, no. 2 (October 1998): 143–65.

▶ Encyclopedia article

Klauck, Hans-Josef. "Lord's Supper." *The Anchor Bible Dictionary*. Ed. David Noel Freedman. Vol. 2. New York: Doubleday, 1992.

▶ Online journal article

Anderson, Pamela Sue. "The Case for a Feminist Philosophy of Religion: Transforming Philosophy's Imagery and Myths." *Ars Disputandi* 1 (2000/2001); http://www.arsdisputandi.org.

▶ Bible

   The Holy Bible: Revised Standard Version. New York: Oxford University Press, 1973.

Final Steps

After incorporating the revisions and refinements into your paper, print out a fresh copy, proofread it carefully, make your last corrections to the electronic file, format it to your teacher's or school's specifications, and print your final paper.